IMAGES
of Modern America

BELL COUNTY

On the Front Cover: Clockwise from top left:
Bell County Expo Center (Courtesy of the Bell County Expo; see page, 18), Mikeska's Bar-B-Que in 2012 parade (Courtesy of the Belton Chamber of Commerce; see page 23), 1st Cavalry Fort Hood in 2012 parade (Authors' collection; see page 22), Alexander house on South Main Street in Belton (Authors' collection; see page 12), Virginia Graff (Authors' collection; see page 85)

On the Back Cover: From left to right:
Summer fun in Belton (Authors' collection; see page 16), Badge and friends (Courtesy of Cheryl Grote; see page 20), Dr. Long's wagon train in 2012 parade (Authors' collection; see page 9)

IMAGES
of Modern America

BELL COUNTY

Michael and Nancy Kelsey

ARCADIA
PUBLISHING

ISBN 978-1-4671-3467-5

Published by Arcadia Publishing
Charleston, South Carolina

Printed in the United States of America

Library of Congress Control Number: 2015948002

For all general information, please contact Arcadia Publishing:
Telephone 843-853-2070
Fax 843-853-0044
E-mail sales@arcadiapublishing.com
For customer service and orders:
Toll-Free 1-888-313-2665

Visit us on the Internet at www.arcadiapublishing.com

Contents

ACKNOWLEDGMENTS

Our intent with this book is to familiarize readers with the people and places of modern Bell County. We chose photographs of a variety of subjects from organizations including the Belton Chamber of Commerce, Belton Senior Center, City of Belton, Killeen Area Heritage Association, Robertson Plantation, Central Texas Area Museum, City of Temple Parks and Recreation, and Temple Public Library. Jerri Gauntt, Cheryl Grote, Ara McGregor, Tiffany Schreiner, and Jerry Taylor provided photographs from their personal collections. We also used photographs our own collection. Thank you to all for making your photographs available to us. Thank you also to our daughter Ginny Guinn Parsons for her research assistance.

INTRODUCTION

When the Texas Legislature created Bell County in 1850, the area was on the fringe of the frontier. In the ensuing 100 years, the people of Bell County derived much of their livelihood from the soil. This changed following the Great Depression and World War II. Rapid advancements in the mechanization of agriculture and the modernization and expansion of the transportation system brought many changes to the area. Improved technologies in agriculture reduced the need for both animal and human farm labor to plant, harvest, and process crops. Employment in agriculture decreased. Improved roads made it possible for people living in small towns and rural communities to work and shop in larger cities that offered a greater variety of commodities and higher wages. These changes altered the people's living, working, driving, and purchasing patterns.

The shift from a predominately rural society to a more urban one brought with it unexpected consequences. Although Bell County's population increased from 73,824 in 1950 to 124,483 in 1970, small towns and farming communities, including Rogers, Bartlett, and Holland, experienced a decrease in population.

Post–World War II construction of the federal Interstate Highway System from 1956 through the 1960s gave Central Texas and Bell County a modern transportation network. Bell County cities located along the Interstate Highway 35 corridor have benefited from continued economic growth associated with its construction. Expansion and improvements to the Interstate Highway 35 corridor ongoing since 2000 will accommodate increased traffic, projected population growth, and anticipated economic growth.

Bell County's industrial base includes both national and international corporations representing the agribusiness, computer, communication, distribution, energy, school-furniture manufacturing, plastics, and transportation sectors. Facilities reserved and restricted to promoting manufacturing are located in the major cities of Bell County. The Temple Industrial Park, formed in the early 1970s in north Temple, occupies over 3,000 acres and serves more than 70 companies. The Killeen Business Park, established in 1990, provides 361 acres for industrial development.

Fort Hood, the largest military post in the United States, is located near Killeen and covers 214,000 acres, extending west into Coryell County. Among the many units stationed at Fort Hood are III Armored Corps, 1st Cavalry Division, and Carl R. Darnall Army Medical Center. Named in honor of Confederate general John Bell Hood, the post has played an important role in every military conflict since World War II. In recent years, Department of Defense funding cuts, troop withdrawals, reassignments, and deployments have negatively affected the local economy. However, the post continues to provide economic advantages to the area. Currently, there are 8,900 civilians employed by Fort Hood.

Killeen–Fort Hood Regional Airport is centrally located in the heart of Texas on the site of Robert Gray Airfield at Fort Hood. Killeen signed an agreement with the Army in 2000 providing for joint use of the airfield. The airport, built in 2004 at a cost exceeding $80 million, provides the Killeen, Belton, and Temple centroplex with commercial airline service directly to and from Atlanta, Dallas–Fort Worth, and Houston.

In the early 20th century, Temple emerged as a major hospital center in the Southwest. The healthcare industry throughout Bell County grew and today provides premier health care in a wide range of specialties. Area hospitals and associated fields of nursing, medical research and development, nursing homes, retirement centers, and medical-supply services are a major source of employment. In 2013, Baylor Medical Center merged with Scott & White to become Baylor Scott & White, the largest not-for-profit healthcare system in Texas. Recent developments include the newly formed hospital district in Temple, which encompasses a broad working alliance with Texas A&M University, Olin E. Teague Veterans Medical Center, Baylor Scott & White, regional educational institutions, and the City of Temple.

Educational opportunities abound in Bell County. Local postsecondary schools in the area are University of Mary Hardin–Baylor, Central Texas College, and Texas A&M University–Central Texas. It appears that the presence of University of Mary Hardin–Baylor in Belton is so important to the area that the City of Belton favors all things for and in the interest of the school.

The relocation of Scott & White Hospital to south Temple and the opening of Temple's first mall, Town and Country Mall, in the 1960s set in motion a chain of events that redirected the city's urban and commercial growth. Upon construction of a second, larger mall south of Scott & White Hospital in the mid-1970s, three major retail stores, Sears, Roebuck & Company, JC Penney, and Montgomery Ward & Company, abandoned Temple's central business district and moved to or near the new mall complex. Other retail stores followed, and the central business district collapsed, leaving behind empty buildings that decayed over time. The cities of Killeen and Belton experienced similar fates, resulting in buildings being occupied by pawnshops, bail bondsmen, and adult-entertainment businesses. Many historic buildings throughout Bell County deteriorated, and some were lost due to abandonment, demolition, or fire.

Following decades of neglect, revitalization efforts on the part of city officials in Killeen, Temple, and Belton to reclaim the business areas in their respective cities began to materialize. The old business areas were designated historic districts and placed in the National Register of Historic Places. City planners implemented preservation guidelines to protect historic structures, provided grants to property owners in designated districts, and introduced extensive beautification and landscaping projects. A portion of this publication highlights the successful efforts made by those dedicated individuals who laid the framework for preservation in Bell County. Efforts to preserve historic buildings and sites are an indication of an appreciation for the importance of preserving the past for current and future residents of Bell County.

The two large reservoirs in Bell County created by the US Army Corps of Engineers are Belton Lake, built in the early 1950s, and Stillhouse Hollow Lake, built in the 1960s. The reservoirs serve as sources of water and recreation in Central Texas. Communities north of Austin receive water from Bell County reservoirs.

Bell County has become a preferred place of retirement for both civilian and military personnel. The county offers numerous inducements that encourage and attract retirees to the area, among them sustained economic growth, affordable housing, numerous diversions in the entertainment field, parks and recreation, convention facilities, museums, arts, hospitals, and close proximity and easy access to larger metropolitan cities.

Availability of land and water attracted early settlers to Bell County, and while many things have changed in the 165 years since the county formed, land and water, combined with advances in transportation, a significant military presence, and the existence of large and small businesses and medical and educational facilities continue to attract current and prospective residents.

One

Belton

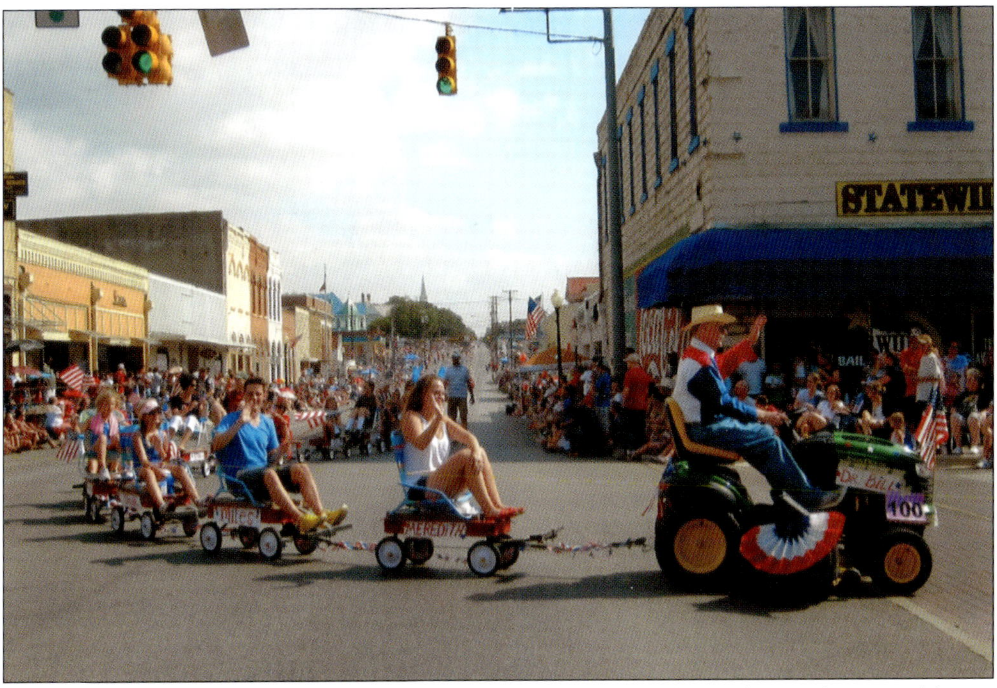

Each year, the Belton Chamber of Commerce sponsors the 4th of July Parade, viewed by an estimated 30,000 spectators. Decorated floats, bands, marching units, horses, businesses, and local government vehicles and antique automobiles participate in the parade. Dr. William Long leads the Long family train of wagons in the 2012 parade, carrying on the annual tradition started by his father, Dr. Bill Long. (Authors' collection.)

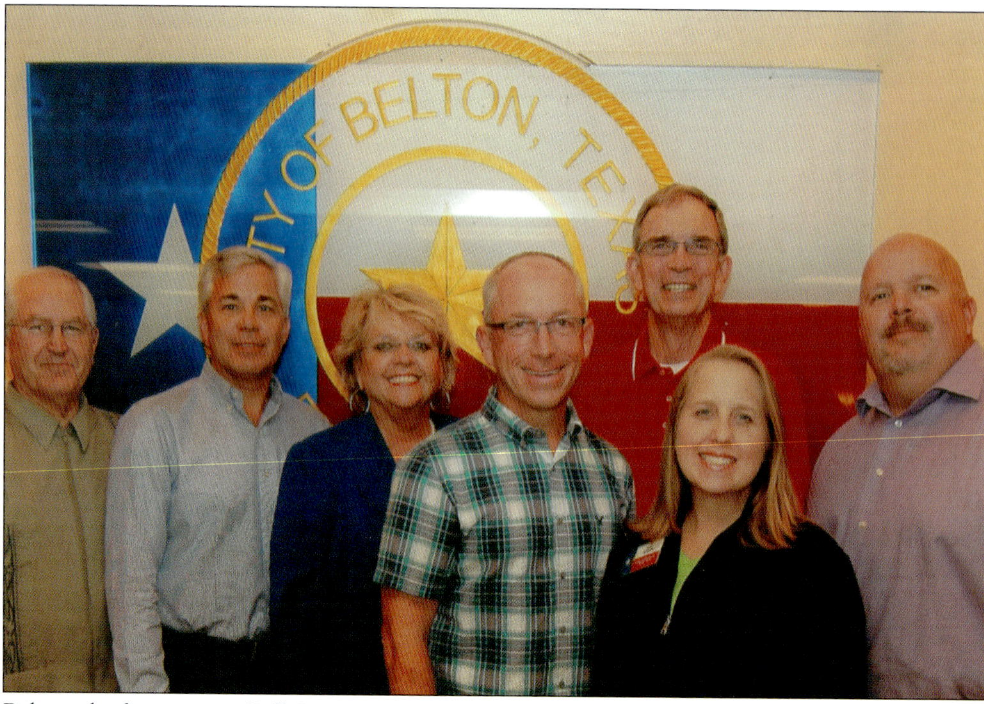

Belton, the first town in Bell County, was established in 1850. Belton's population is approximately 20,000. The governing body is a city council composed of a mayor and six council members. The council and mayor are elected for two-year terms. Pictured here are the 2014 city council members, from left to right: Dan Kirkley, Paul Sanderford, Marion Grayson, David K. Leigh, Craig Pearson, Jerri Gauntt, and Guy O'Banion. (Courtesy of the City of Belton.)

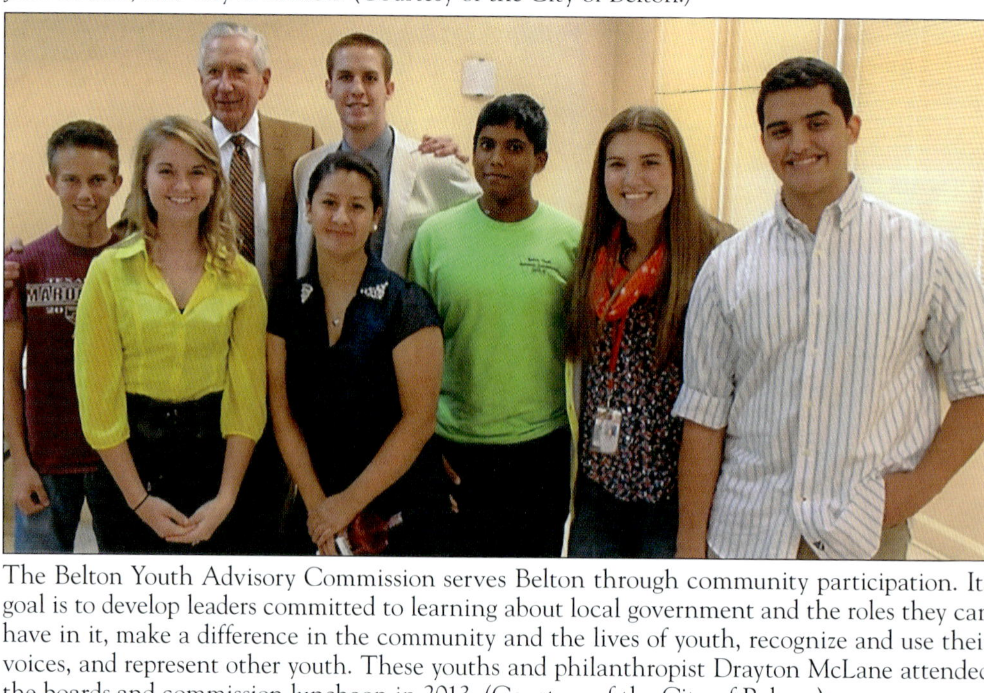

The Belton Youth Advisory Commission serves Belton through community participation. Its goal is to develop leaders committed to learning about local government and the roles they can have in it, make a difference in the community and the lives of youth, recognize and use their voices, and represent other youth. These youths and philanthropist Drayton McLane attended the boards and commission luncheon in 2013. (Courtesy of the City of Belton.)

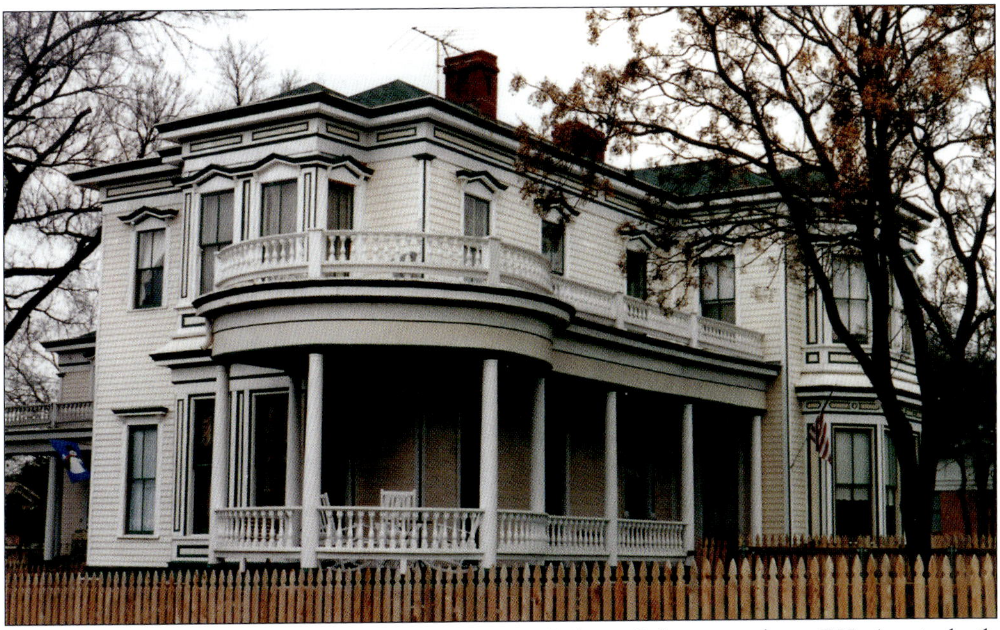

A few of the old landmarks and houses remain in Belton. Belton merchant F.K. Austin built his spacious two-story frame house, above, about 1885. His adventurous father, Norman Austin, arrived in Texas in 1835 and became entangled in the Texas Revolution. Norman Austin served in Horton's Company, a part of Col. James Fannin's ill-fated regiment, which the Mexican army massacred at Goliad. He moved to Belton, where his family operated a successful grocery. Below, across the street from the Austin house, is the home of Orville T. Tyler (1810–1886). His marriage to Caroline Childers in 1850 marked the first recorded marriage in Bell County. Before moving to Belton, Tyler was a Salado College trustee, the first mayor of Salado, and a charter member of the Salado Grange. (Both, authors' collection.)

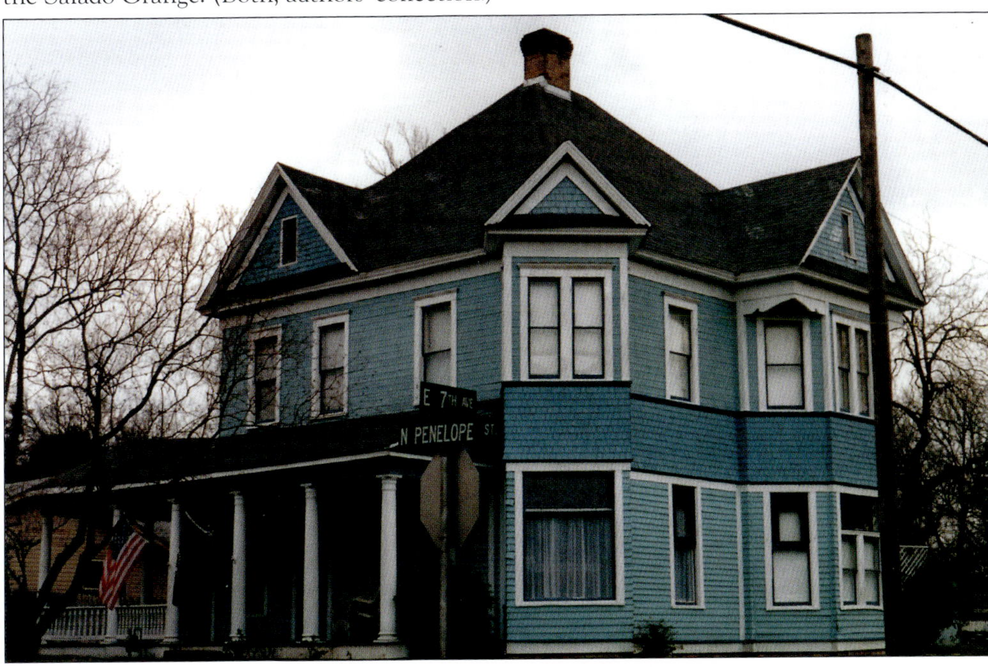

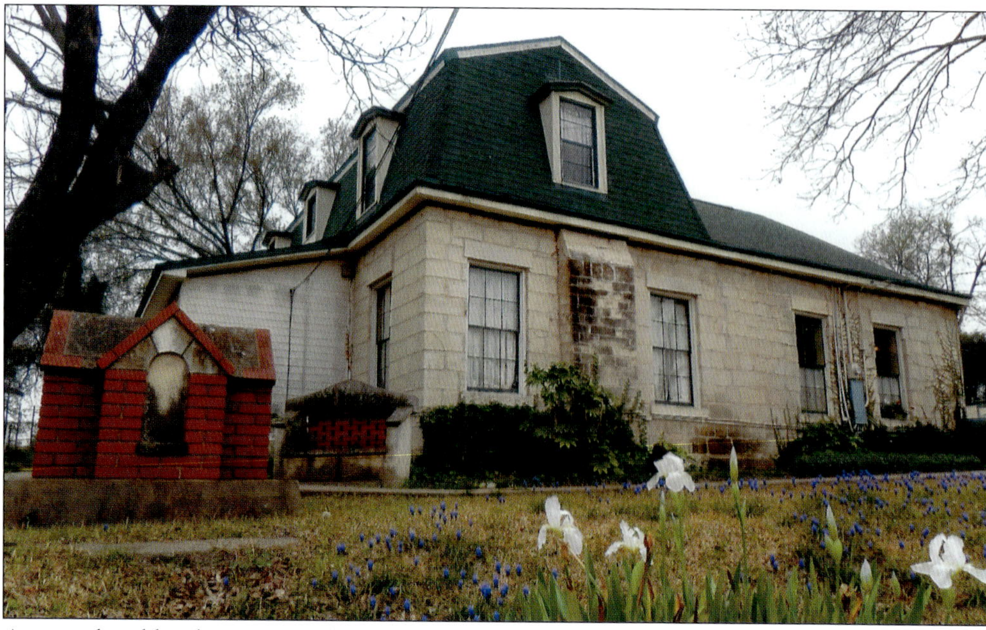

Among the oldest houses in Belton is this native-stone house on Main Street, built about 1868 by merchant and developer J.T. Alexander. Alterations include the addition of the mansard roof in 1908. At the rear of the main house is a rock building constructed in 1931 from the rubble of Luther Hall after it burned. The redbrick ornamental structure on the lawn is a squirrel house. (Authors' collection.)

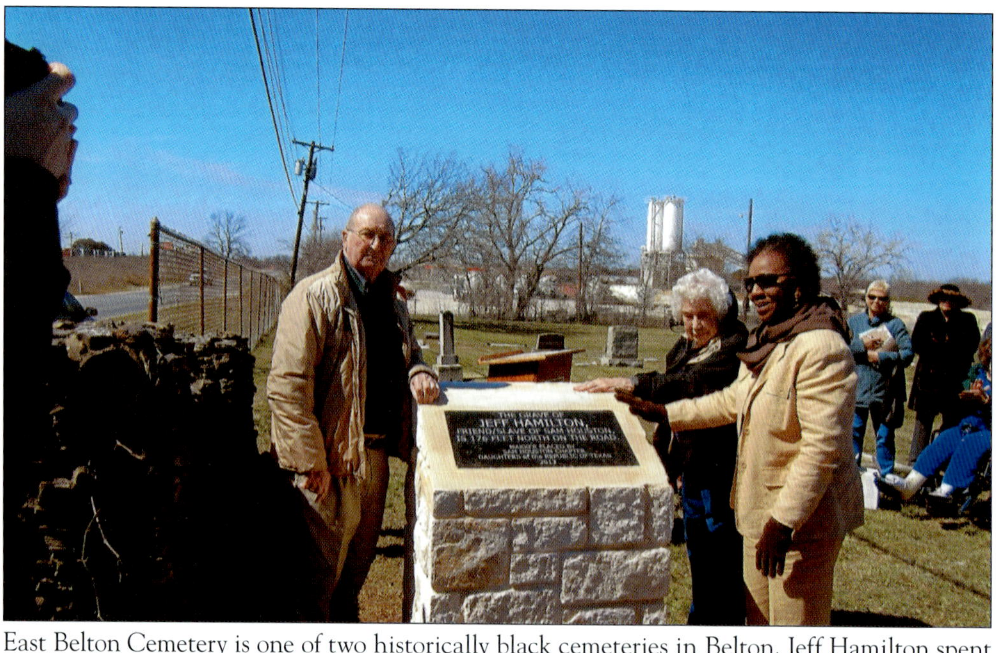

East Belton Cemetery is one of two historically black cemeteries in Belton. Jeff Hamilton spent his boyhood and early manhood as a slave of Sam Houston. He was at the bedside of Houston when he died. Two of Houston's grandsons spoke at Hamilton's funeral in 1941. In 2013, the Sam Houston Chapter Daughters of the Republic of Texas placed a directional marker to Hamilton's gravesite. (Authors' collection.)

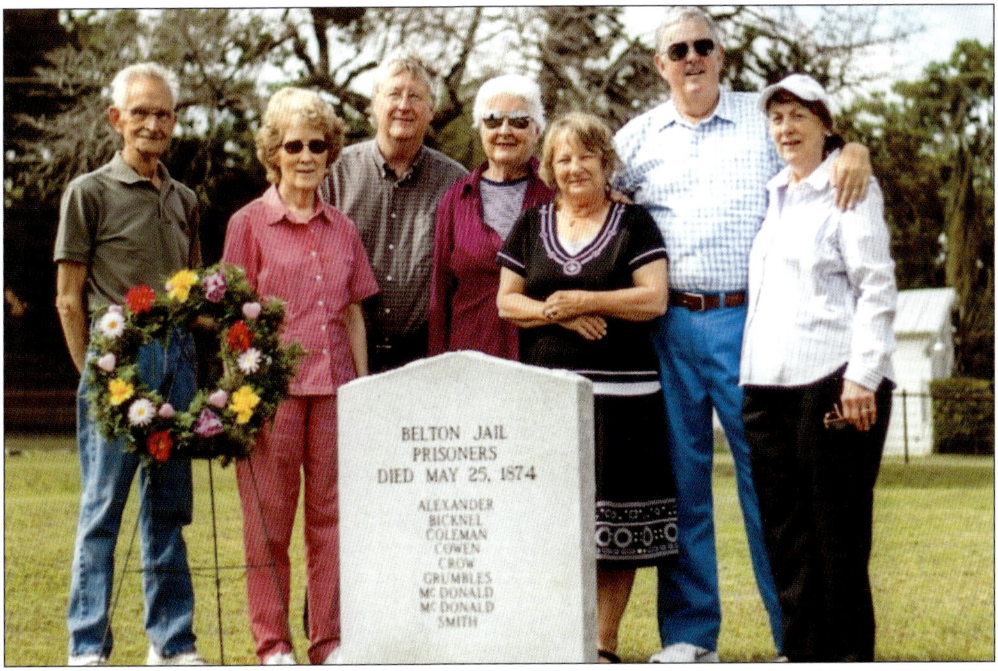

Established 1851, South Belton Cemetery is Belton's oldest cemetery and one of the oldest in Bell County. In an effort to preserve and promote Bell County's history, members of the community placed a marker at the cemetery that commemorates the murder of nine jailed prisoners by vigilantes in 1874. An anonymous person regularly places flowers at the marker. (Authors' collection.)

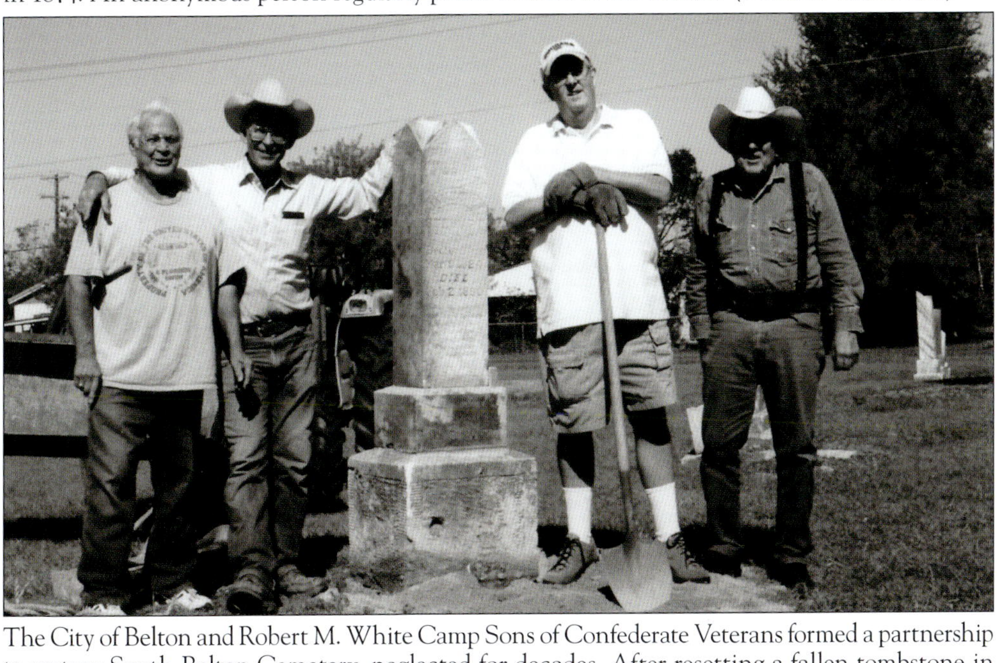

The City of Belton and Robert M. White Camp Sons of Confederate Veterans formed a partnership to restore South Belton Cemetery, neglected for decades. After resetting a fallen tombstone in 2009, from left to right, Frank Irions, Rocky Sprott, Tom Hughes, and George Johnson posed for this photograph. Buried at the cemetery is the camp's namesake, Robert M. White, who lost his life in the Civil War. (Authors' collection.)

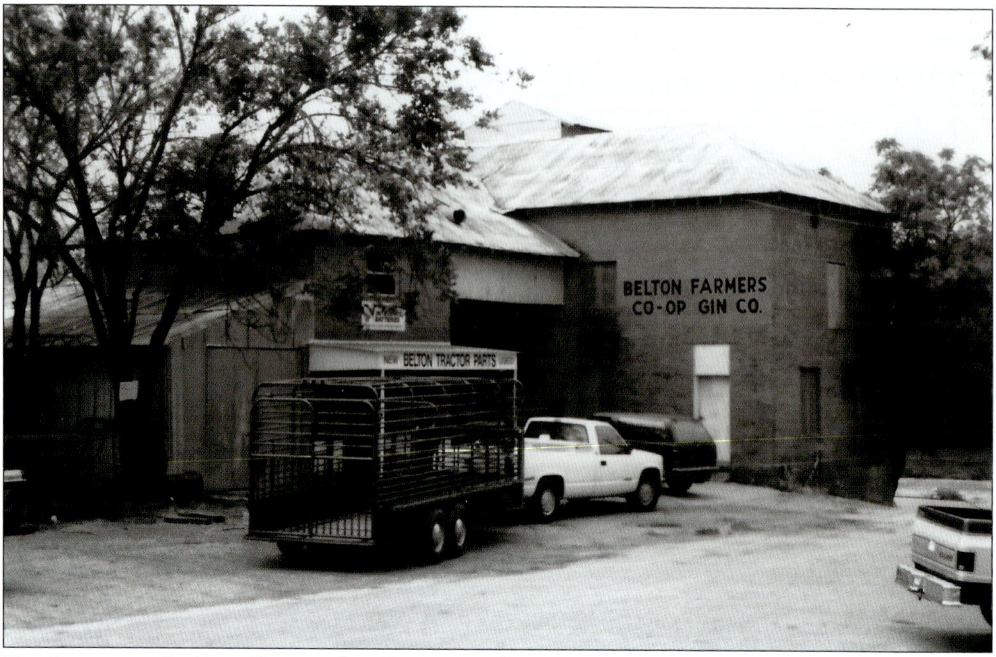

First known as the Farm Bureau Gin Company, the Belton Farmers Co-Op Gin was built in 1927 on the former site of the Belton Planning Mills. Constructed of red brick, the building represents a unique architectural feature among gins. The building, shown in 1986, is listed in the National Registry of Historic Places. (Authors' collection.)

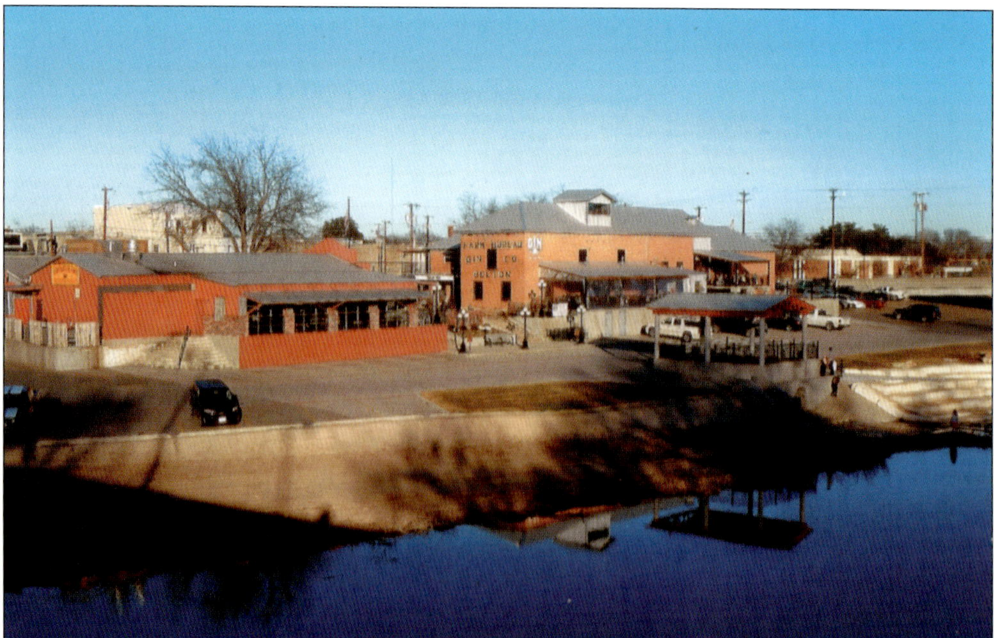

Nolan Creek Gin Partnership purchased the Belton Farmers Co-Op Gin property and in 2005 began a multimillion-dollar project to develop the site for retail shops and restaurants. The old Belton Farmers Co-Op Gin building, pictured here in 2015, represents one of Belton's finest examples of successful adaptive reuse of an historic structure for commercial use. (Authors' collection.)

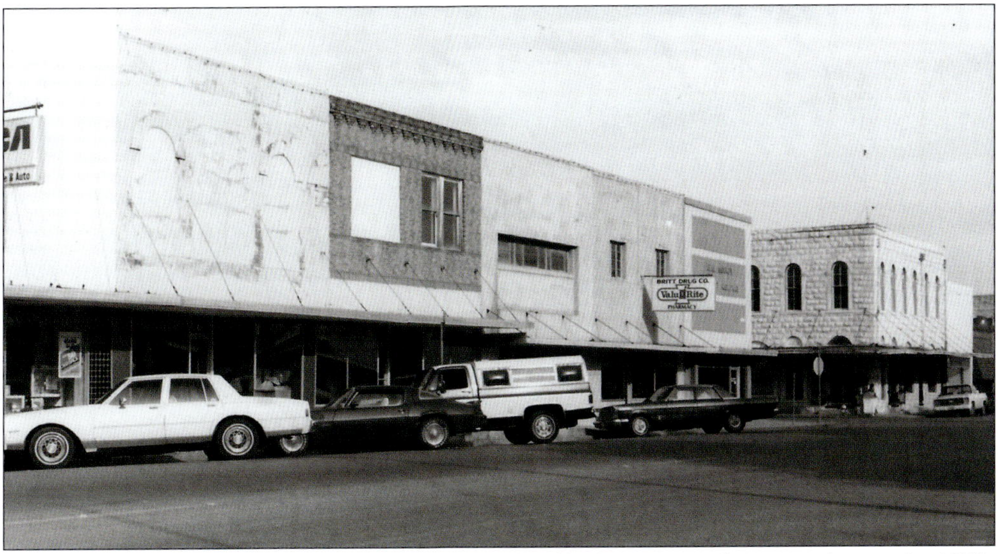

Several of the buildings in the central section of this block on Central Avenue date to the 1850s and are the oldest standing commercial structures in Bell County. On January 5, 1861, Sam Houston gave a fiery speech against secession from a stand made of boxes about the middle of this block. Public awareness of community heritage led to revitalization by property owners to restore many of the buildings in the Commercial Historic District. The City of Belton provided generous facade grants. Revitalization on Central Avenue included iron balconies, sidewalks, landscaping, and new pole lighting. Tammy Wilson, owner and operator of Sarsaparilla Saloon Café, was the first, in 2010, to install a balcony. Above is Central Avenue before revitalization, as it appeared in 1986. The photograph below displays Central Avenue in 2015. (Above, courtesy of the Temple Public Library; below, authors' collection.)

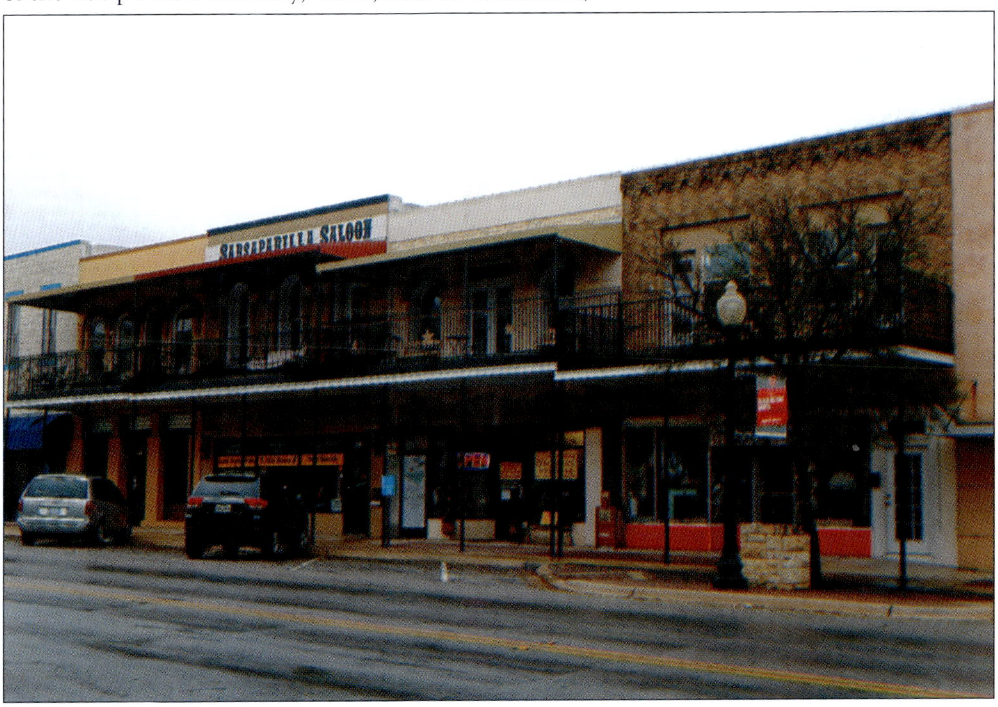

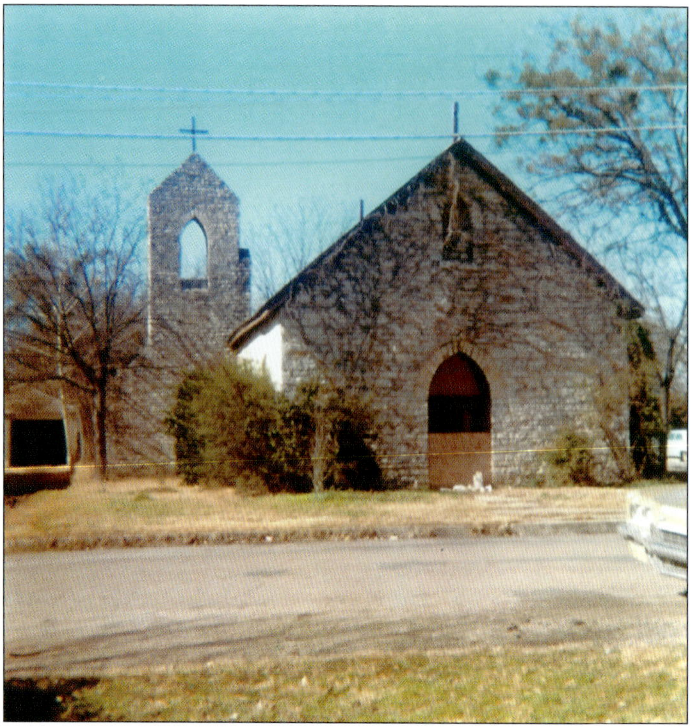

St. Luke Episcopal Church, erected in 1874, is pictured here when the building was 100 years old. After condemnation in 2007, the 1874 Church Restoration Committee formed to stabilize, preserve, restore, and protect the 30-by-40-foot building of limestone rubble masonry by making it available for compatible new use. As of 2015, the building remains uninhabitable. (Courtesy of the Lena Armstrong Public Library.)

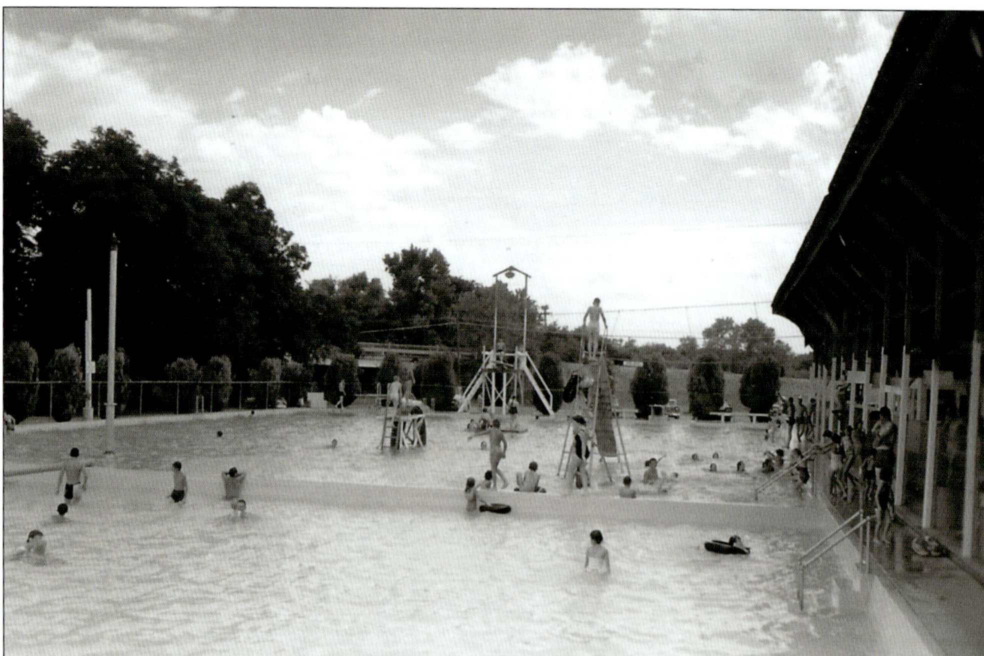

In 1920, W.C. Knight and a group of 25 Temple investors organized Riverside Swimming Pool Company. The facility opened in 1921 on a seven-acre tract on Leon River and featured an 86-by-185-foot pool filled with pure artesian water. At the time of the pool's construction, it was among the largest in the state. Today, Riverside Swimming Pool is known as Summer Fun. (Authors' collection.)

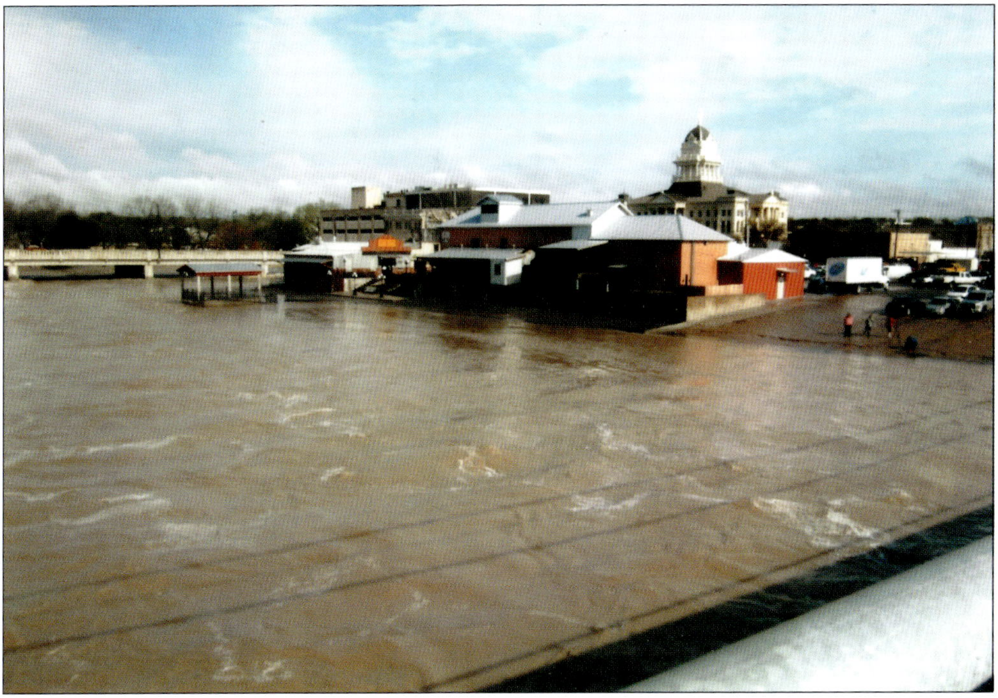

The first recorded flood of Nolan Creek occurred in 1852. Flooding continues to today. The photograph above of the 2011 flood taken from the Penelope Street Bridge depicts the extent of flooding at the Gin Restaurant. Below, floodwaters in Yettie Polk Park at the Mount Zion United Methodist Church caused widespread damage to Yettie Polk Park and Confederate Park. (Both, authors' collection.)

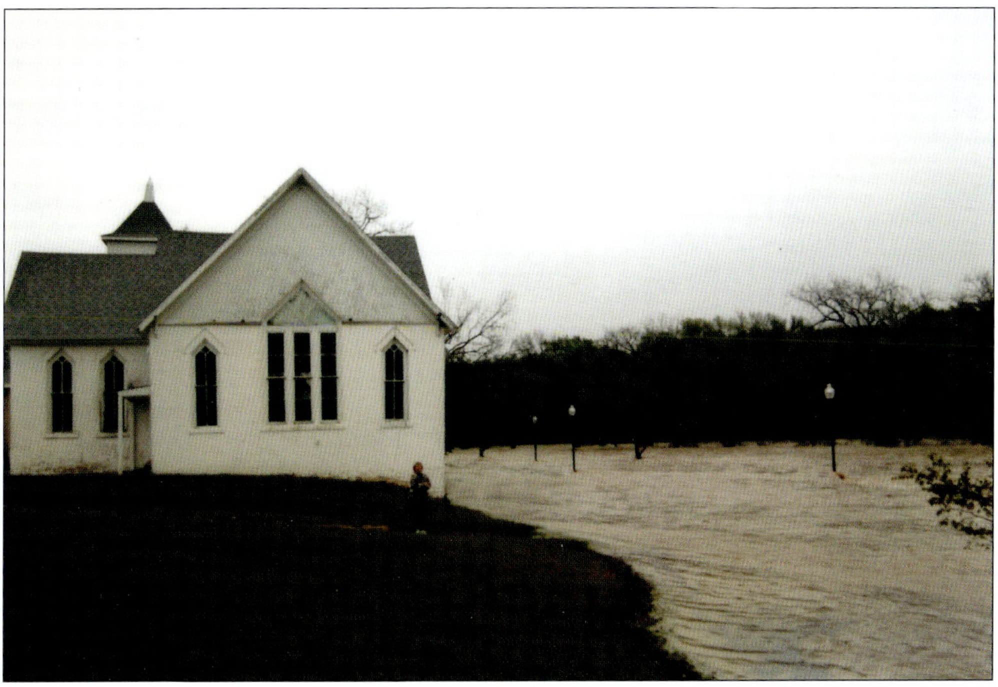

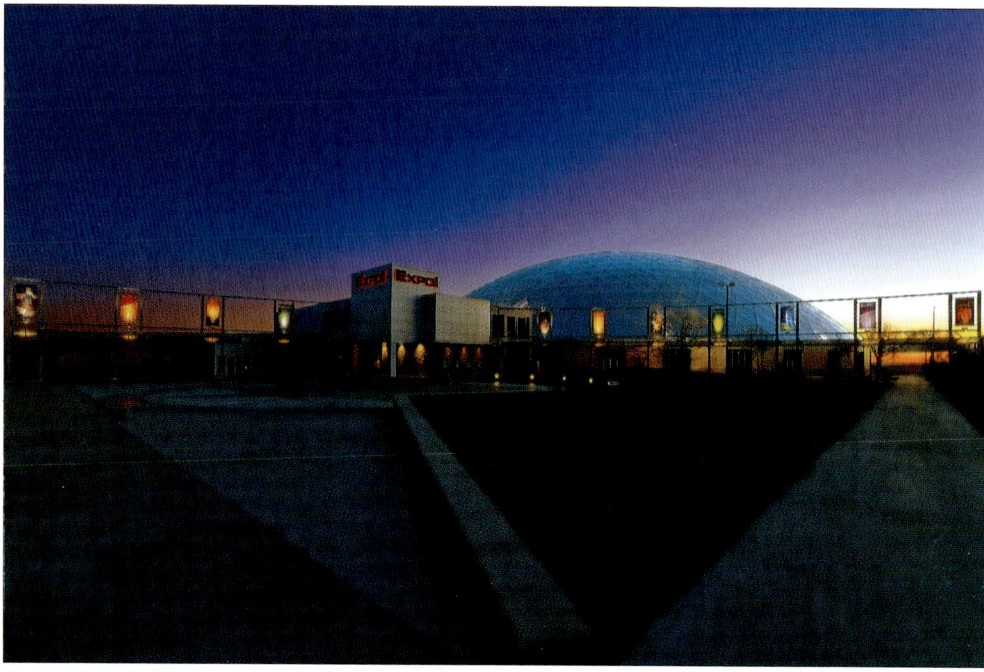

Opened in 1987 and renovated in 2007, the Bell County Expo Center on Interstate Highway 35 south of Belton is the site for conventions, concerts, sports, livestock, and consumer shows. The Professional Rodeo Cowboys Association (PRCA) holds a rodeo at the center each July in conjunction with the Belton 4th of July Celebration. George Strait, Garth Brooks, and Bruce Springsteen are among the many performers that have played here. Below is one of the Southwest Texas Cutting Horse Association events held at the Expo Center. (Both, courtesy of the Bell County Expo Center.)

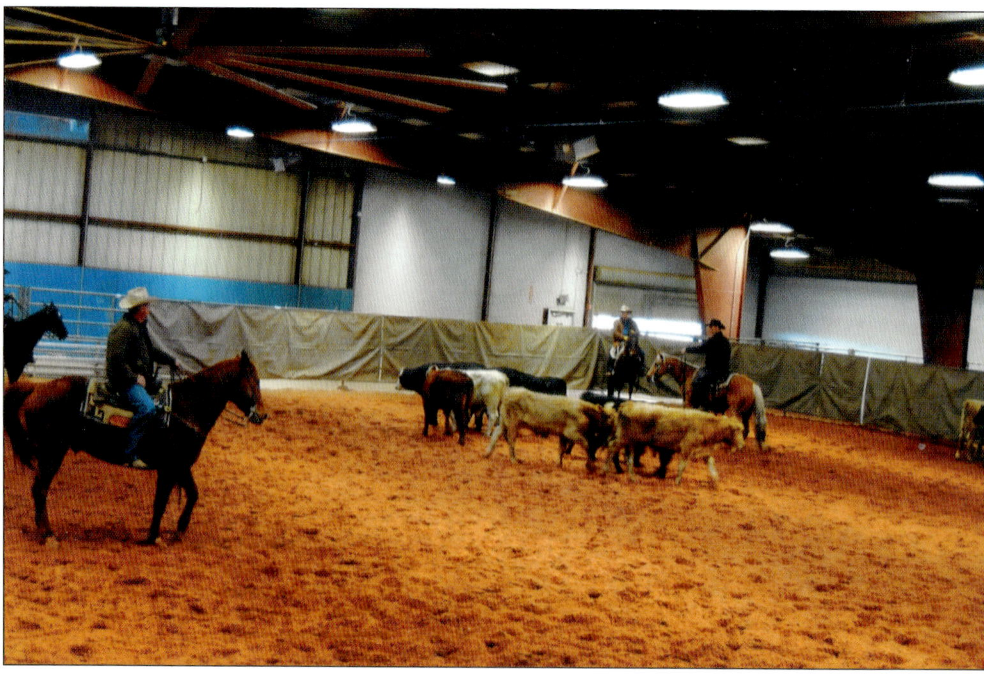

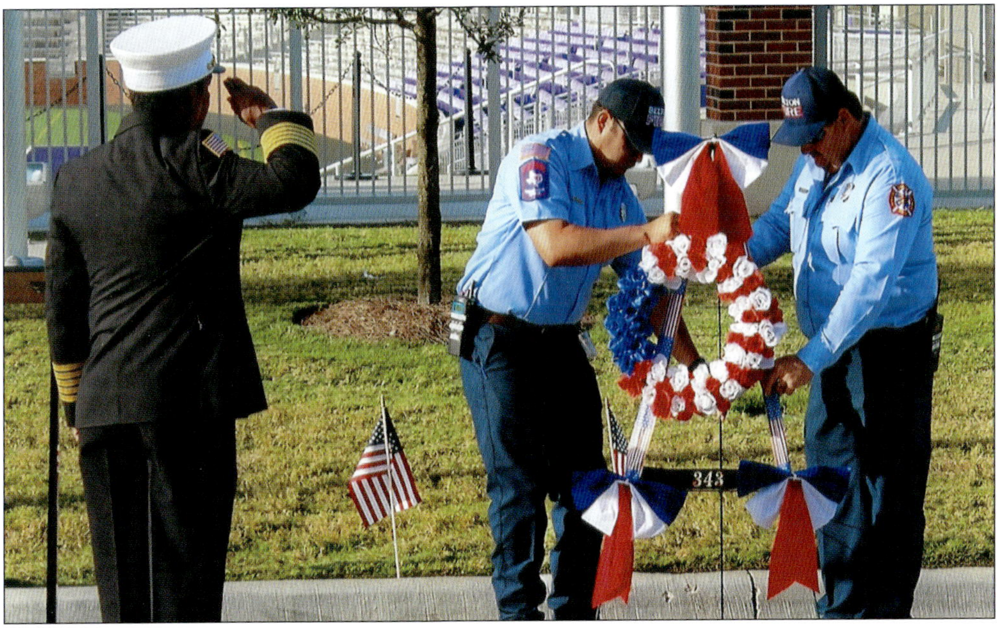

The Belton Fire Department has come a long way since it purchased its first horse-drawn hose cart in 1891. Before the horse-drawn cart, firemen pulled the hose cart. A brass bell mounted on a wooden tower at a little fire station sounded at the notice of a fire. Today there are two fire stations, and the department covers a broad area for emergency medical service and fire protection. Volunteer firefighters supplement the department's regular firefighters and paramedics. The top photograph, taken in 2014, shows Belton firefighters as they place a wreath to commemorate the 13th anniversary of the September 11, 2001, terrorist attack. Belton Fire Department trains and prepares for emergency service, including water rescue techniques practiced in Leon River, as seen in the lower photograph. (Both, courtesy of the City of Belton.)

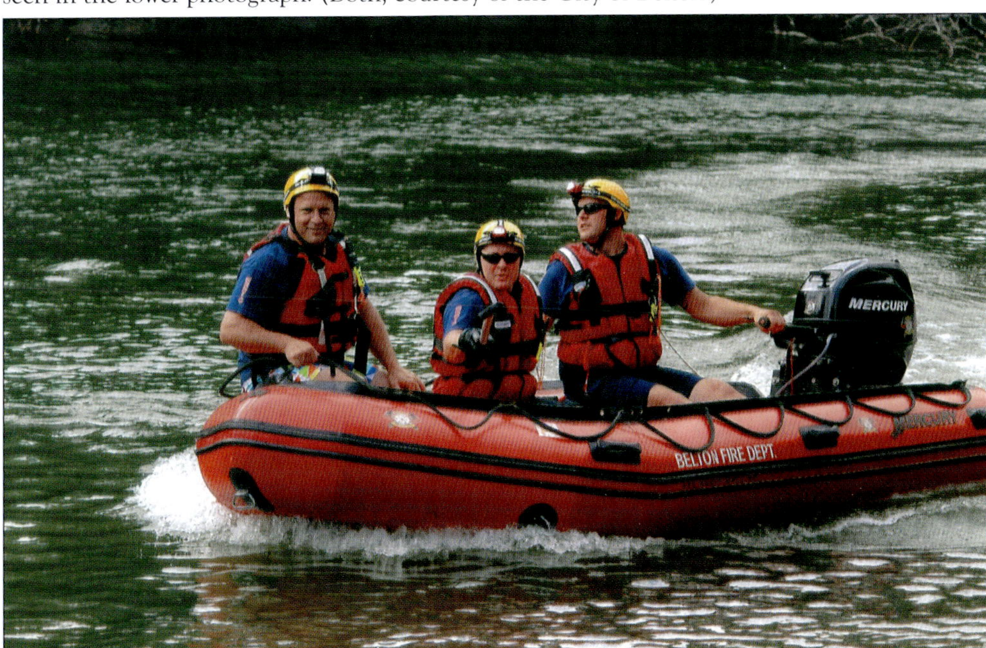

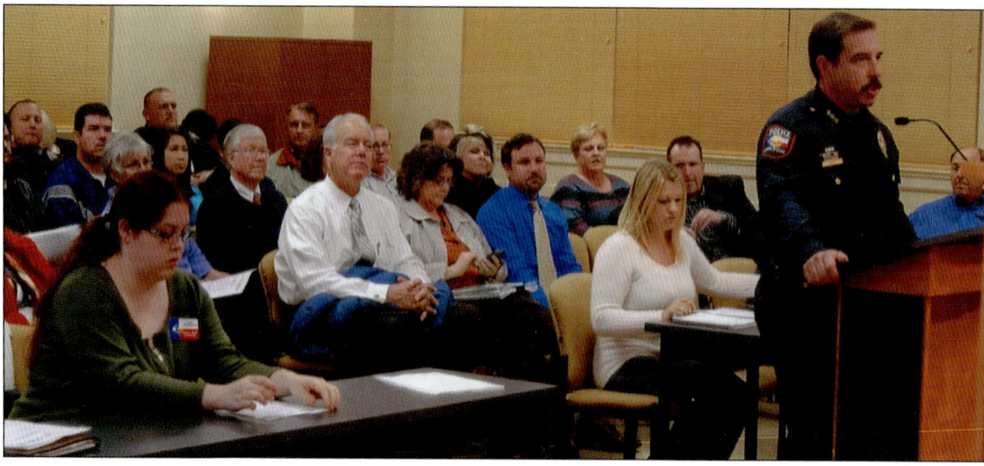

Chief of police Gene Ellis, of Pasadena, Texas, came to Belton in 2009. Since then, he has been instrumental in building a bridge between the police department and the community. He is pictured here making a presentation to the Belton City Council. Badge joined the police force in 2010 and serves as mascot. Jerry and Cheryl Grote took the idea of Badge the police dog to Chief Ellis. In a naming contest, the second grade class at Pirtle Elementary School came up with the name. Badge visits community events, schools, and police department functions. He encourages children to avoid drugs and tobacco and promotes anti-bullying, Internet safety, and stranger danger. Badge strikes a pose with his friends Officer Barnett (center) and Citizens Helping in Police Service member Jerry Grote at the Sparta Fire Department. (Above, courtesy of the City of Belton; below, courtesy of Cheryl Grote.)

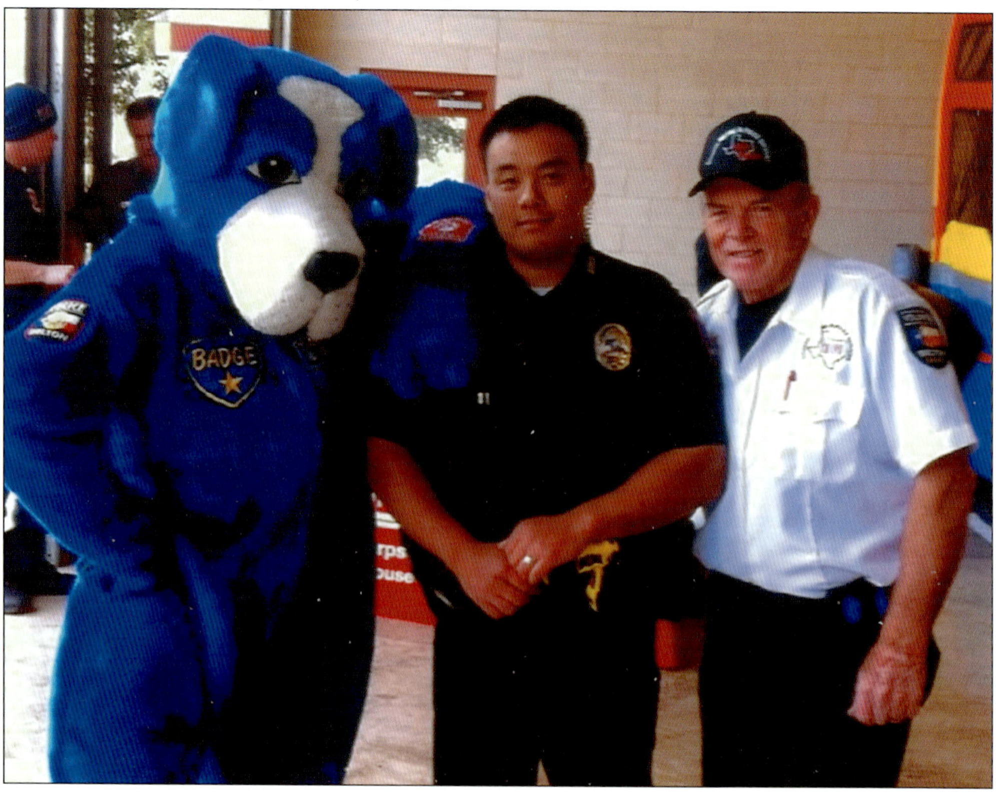

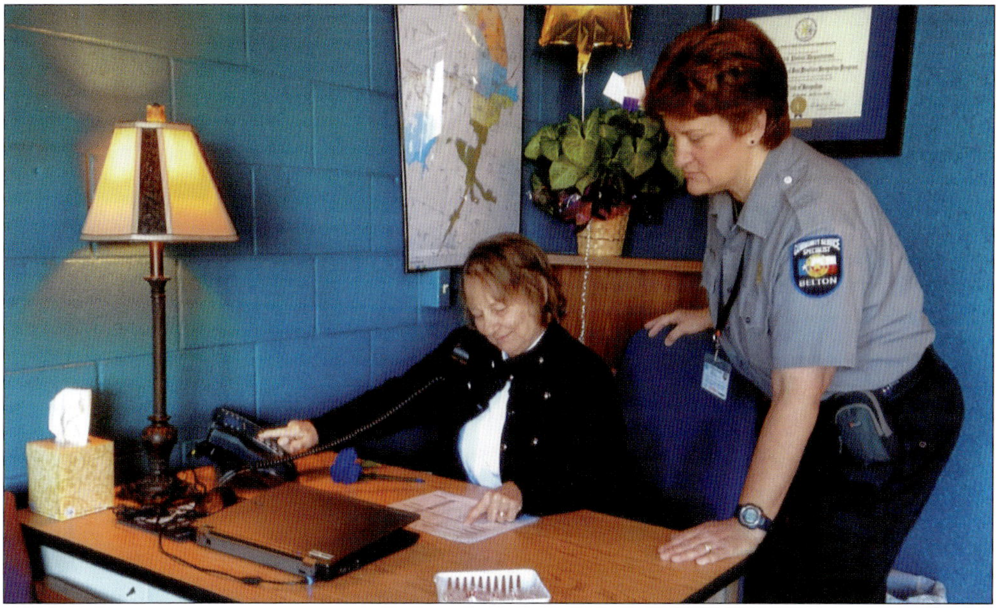

With a focus on involving the community in day-to-day operations of the Belton Police Department, Chief Ellis established Citizens Helping in Police Service (CHIPS) in 2011 as well as the RU OK? Senior Program in 2013. The CHIPS program expands police resources through citizen volunteers. CHIPS volunteers serve the department and community as extra eyes and ears patrolling parks, shopping centers, and other areas where large groups may gather. The RU OK? Senior Program involves welfare calls to senior citizens signed up for the free service. Volunteers call program participants and request dispatch of a police officer if needed for a safety check. In early 2015, the police department established a substation at a local HEB grocery store where CHIPS volunteers make calls, above. Officer Joseph Thomas, his family, and volunteers are pictured below in the 4th of July Parade in 2012. (Both, authors' collection.)

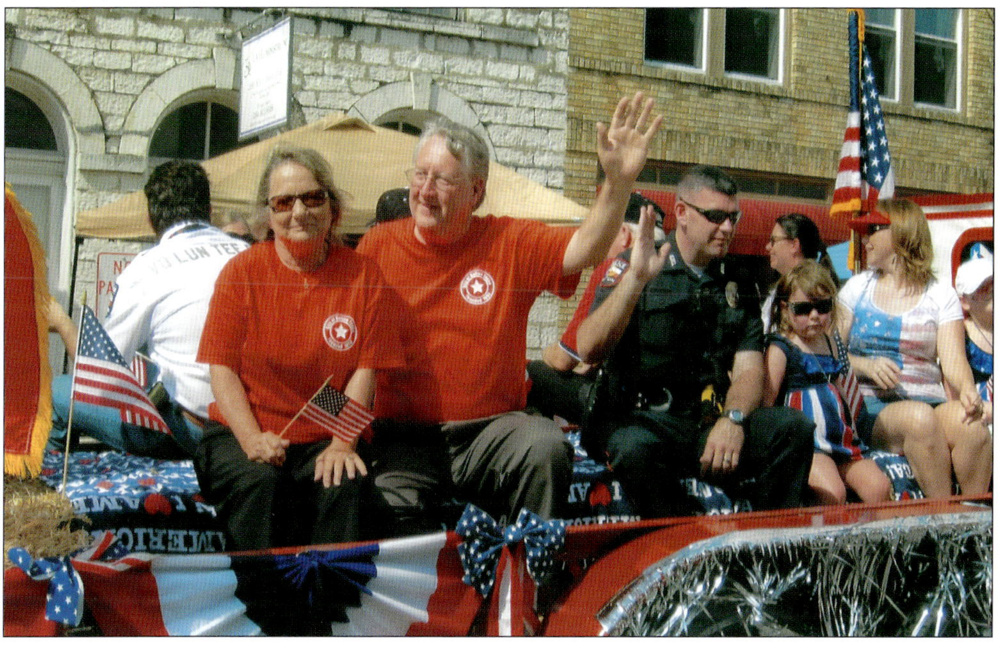

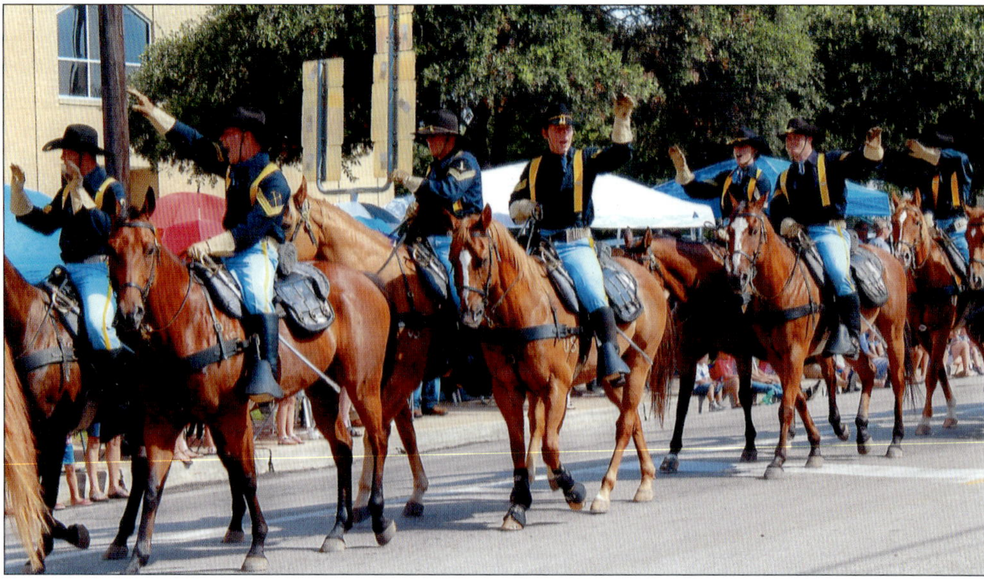

A carnival, Festival on Nolan Creek, Bar-B-Q Kick Off, parade, and rodeo highlight the Belton 4th of July Celebration. The members of the US armed forces stationed at nearby Fort Hood play an integral part in each of the Independence Day celebrations. Since 1972, 1st Cavalry Division Horse Cavalry Detachment, Fort Hood, has brought to life the spirit of the cavalry by its transformation into a unit from the proud heritage of the cavalry. Capt. Elizabeth Rascon, the first woman to lead the group, assumed command in June 2014. The cavalry detachment is pictured here at the 4th of July Parade in 2014. Festival on Nolan Creek is held in Yettie Polk Park. The free event includes vendors, shopping, food, live music, and entertainment. Below are dancers at the event in 2013. (Both, courtesy of the Belton Chamber of Commerce.)

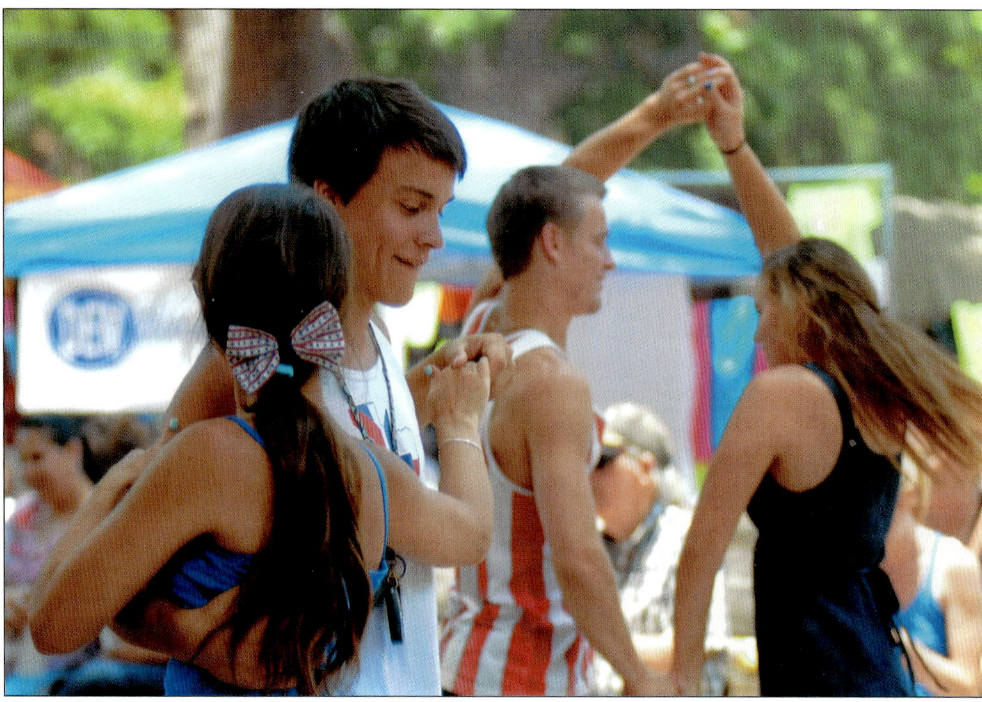

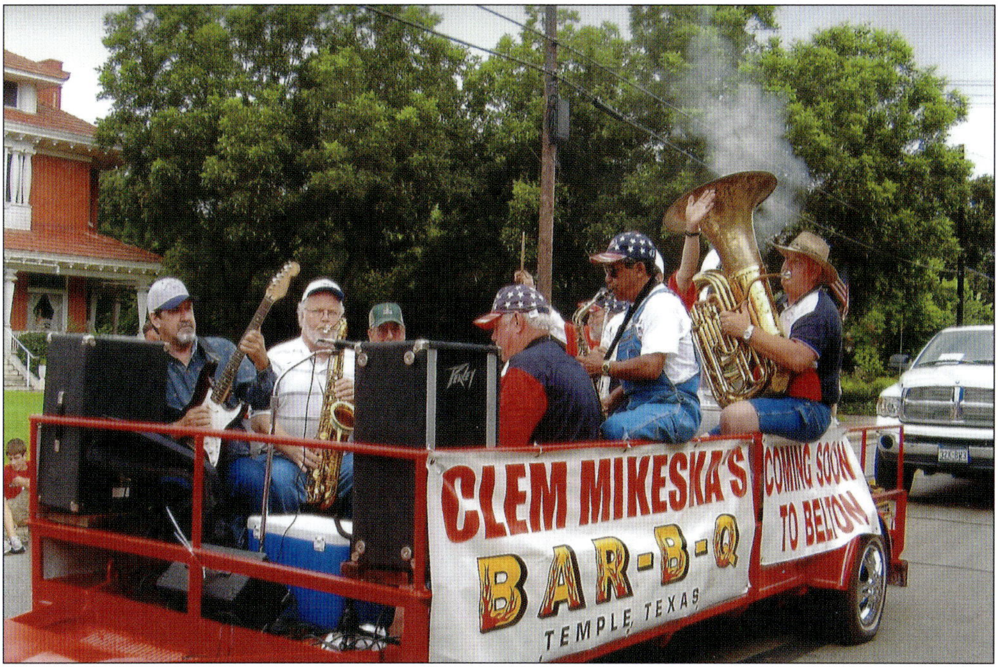

The 4th of July Parade begins on North Main Street and proceeds along a 1.5-mile route that takes the parade past the historic 1884 Bell County Courthouse. Clem Mikeska, a descendant of Czech immigrants, started Clem Mikeska's Bar-B-Q in 1965 in Temple. The Clem Mikeska band performs polka music every year in the parade. Led by Jesse Ybarbo since 1980, the band entertains the crowd with lively tunes, including audience favorite "The Chicken Dance." The colorful dancers below, from the 4th of July Parade in 2010, represent Central Texas's diverse ethnic heritage. (Both, courtesy of the Belton Chamber of Commerce.)

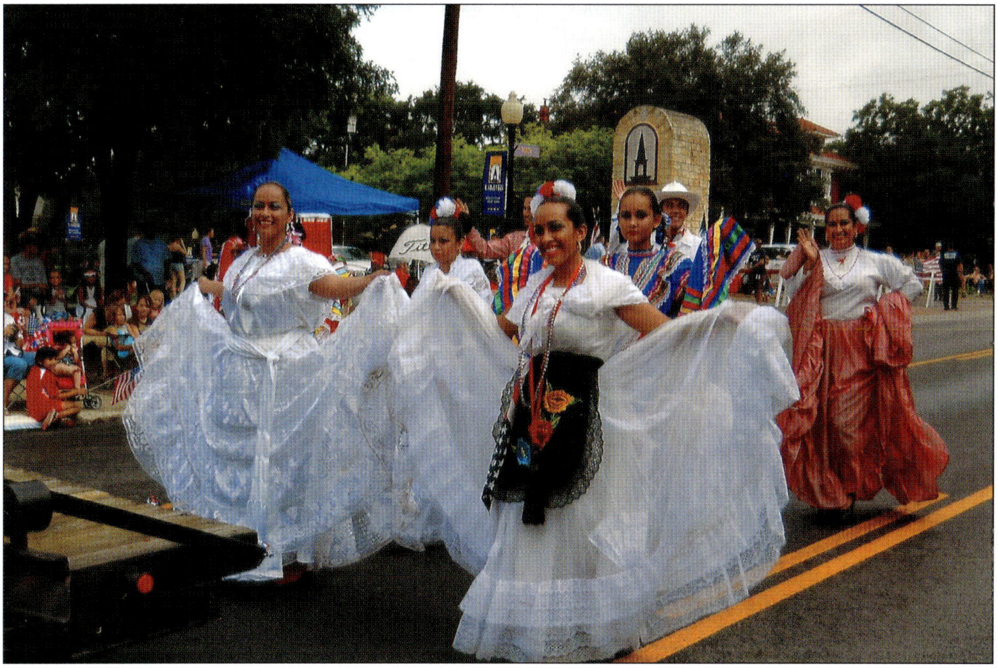

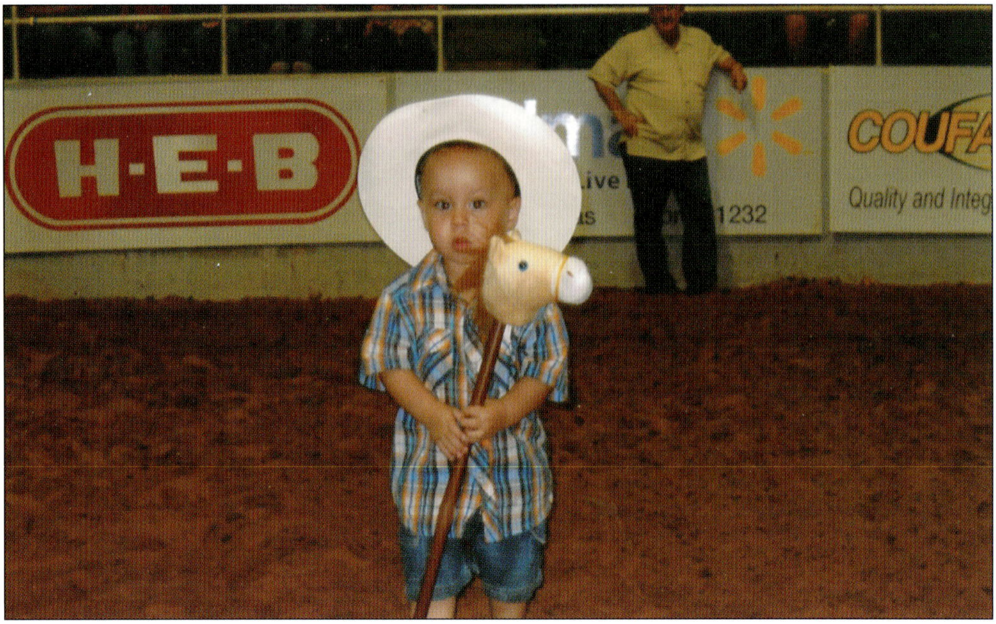

During the 4th of July Celebration, children ages eight and under compete for the title of Stick Horse Cowgirl and Stick Horse Cowboy. Children parade their decorated stick horses around the rodeo arena at Family Celebration Night, with prizes given for the 10 best-decorated stick horses and crowns for Stick Horse Cowgirl and Stick Horse Cowboy. (Courtesy of the Belton Chamber of Commerce.)

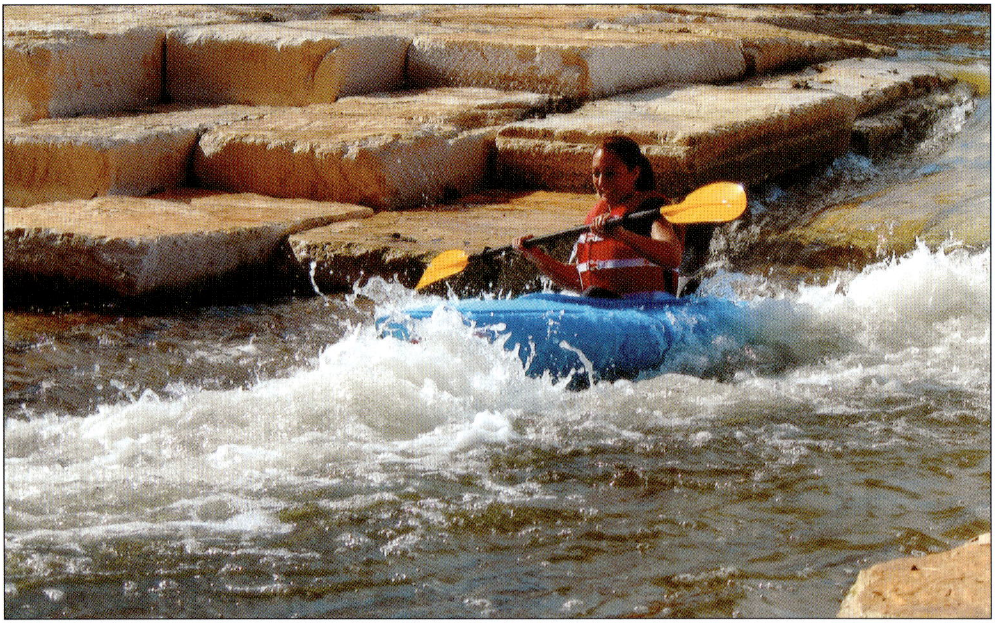

A dam erected on Nolan Creek at the Main Street Bridge formed Lake Bassel in the 1930s. The dam was later demolished. In 2014, revitalization of Nolan Creek began east of the Main Street Bridge. Large limestone blocks were used to landscape the area, raise the creek's water level, and control the flow. Megan Jackson is pictured here kayaking in the newly revitalized Nolan Creek. (Courtesy of the City of Belton.)

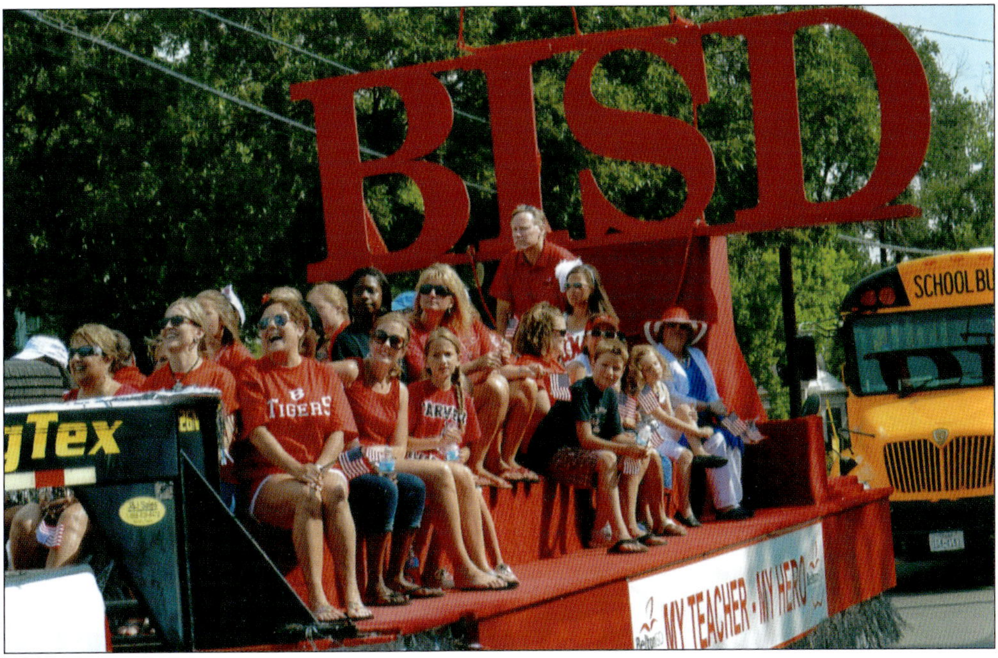

Belton Independent School District encompasses approximately 200 square miles in Belton and Temple. The district's enrollment is 10,300. The 2,500-student Belton High School is ranked as the 100th-largest public high school in Texas. School district representatives are pictured here during the 4th of July Parade in 2012. (Authors' collection.)

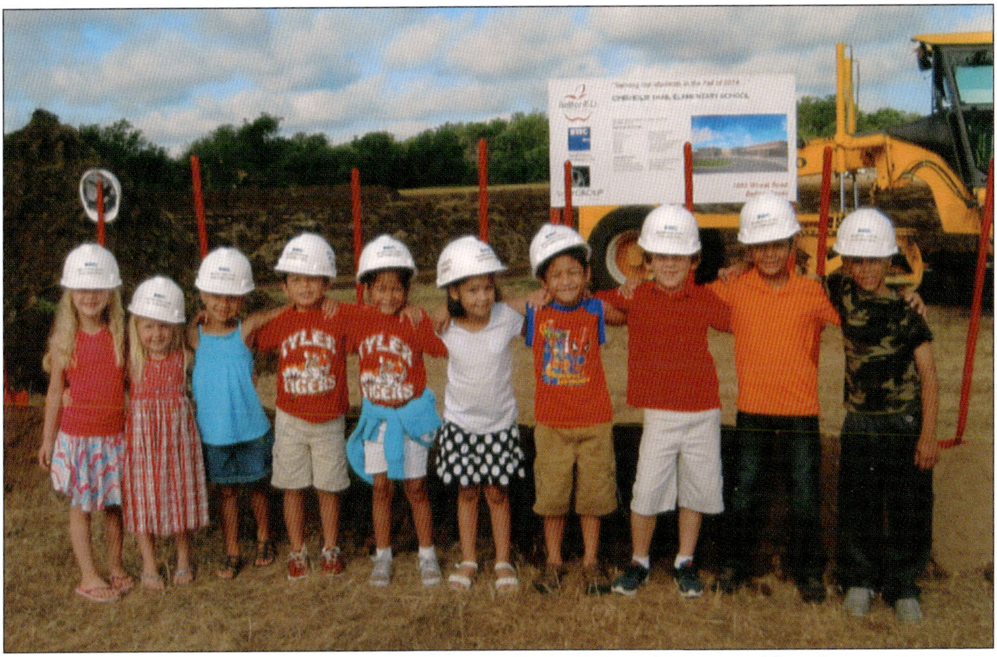

In 2013, Tyler Elementary School children participated in the ground-breaking ceremonies for Chisholm Trail Elementary School on Wheat Road in west Belton. The school opened in September 2014. Students at the school attend first through fifth grade. Belton Rotary donated the flagpole at the school. (Courtesy of Jerri Gauntt.)

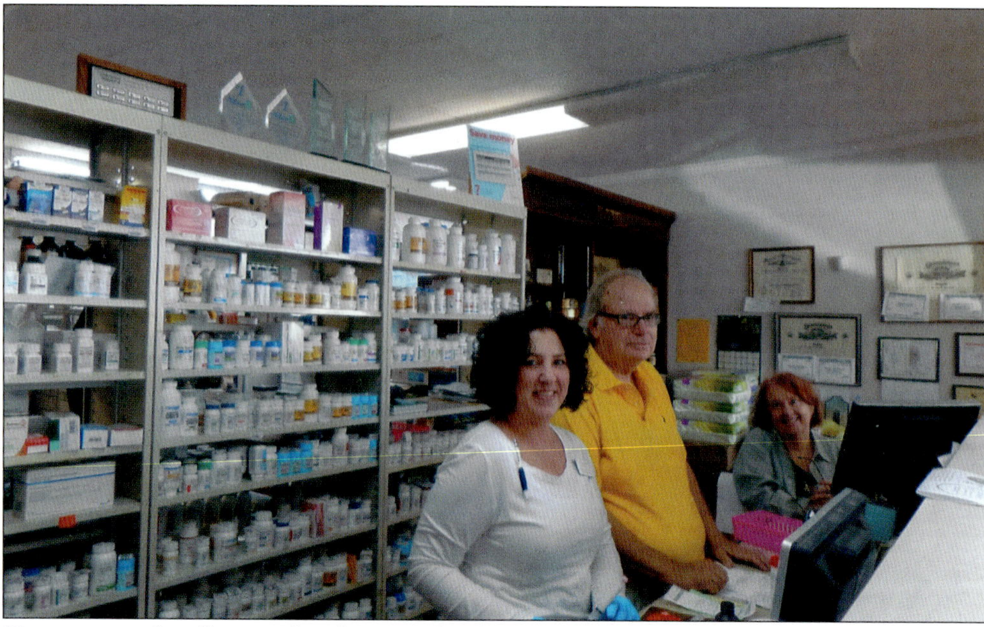

Shopping at a locally owned and operated Belton business is still possible. Toby Young opened Medicine Shoppe Pharmacy in the former Dairy Queen building on Central Avenue in 1984. When he purchased the building 10 years after Dairy Queen closed, food from the Dairy Queen was still in the cabinets and freezer. Pharmacists Young and Harriett Monsell own and operate the drugstore. As owners and operators of the last of the drugstores in downtown Belton, they know their customers by name. Pictured above are, from left to right, Kady Grant (pharmacy technician), Toby Young, and Harriett Monsell. Always a favorite for a hamburger, Crow's Hamburgers is on Old Waco Road. There is no inside service; however, outside there are shade-covered tables and benches. (Both, authors' collection.)

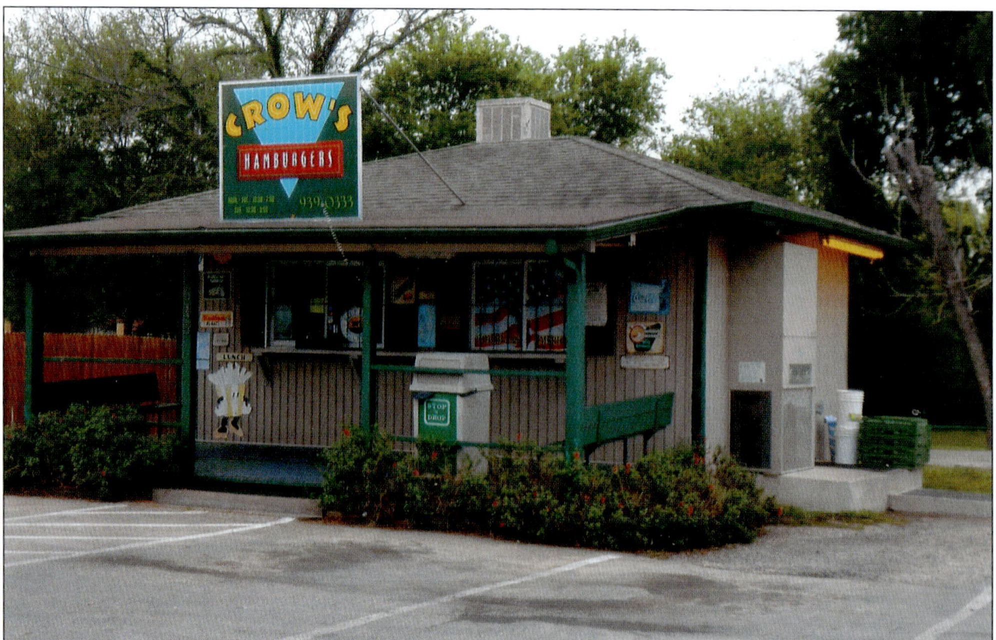

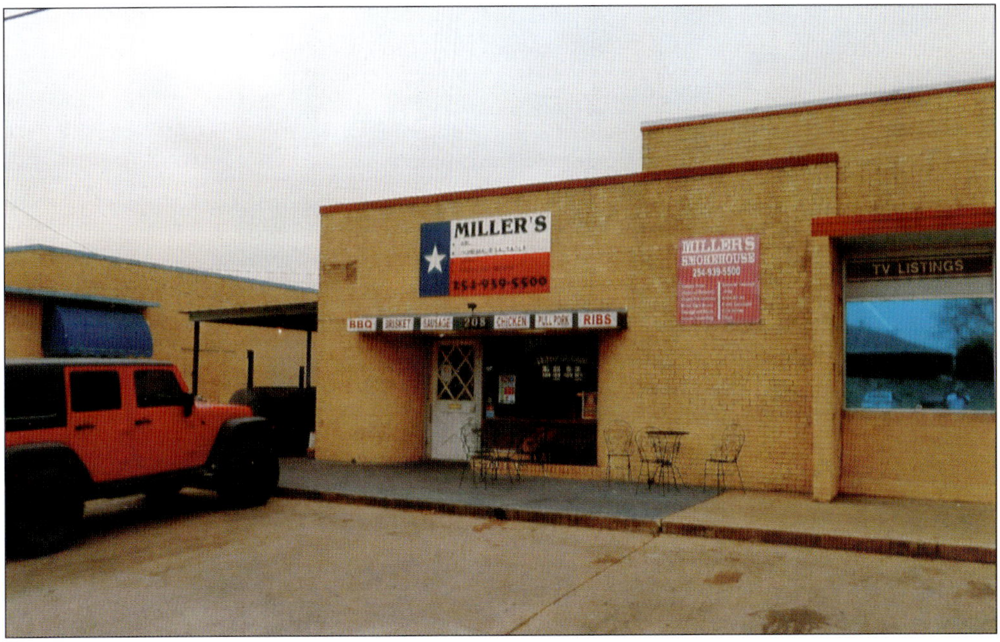

Miller's Smokehouse, locally owned and operated by five members of the Miller family, has become an iconic institution to Central Texas barbecue enthusiasts since it opened in 2008. Miller's received honors for its exclusively oak slow-cooked brisket, ribs, and sausage and ranks among the top 50 barbecue joints in Texas. Dylon Miller runs the deer-processing and taxidermy shop on South Main Street. The yellow brick building, shown above, is located on North Penelope Street. A second building is used for banquets. Below are pit masters Dirk Miller (front) and Dusty Miller, posing in front of the pits. (Both, authors' collection.)

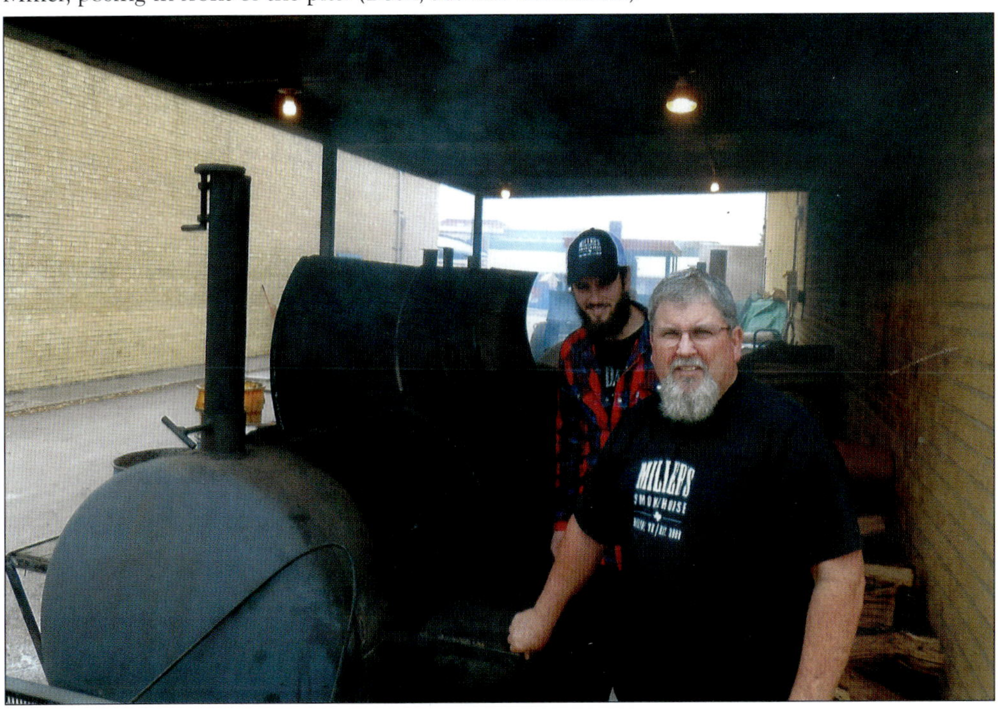

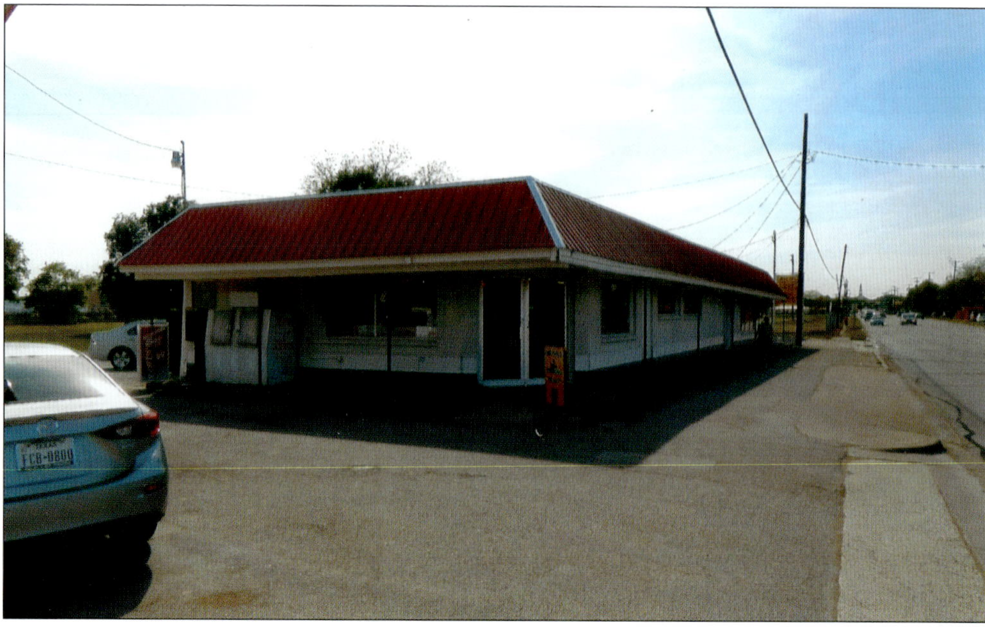

The Smith family has been connected with the grocery business in Belton since 1951. At one time, the Smiths owned three grocery stores. They have operated the convenience store with a car wash and washeteria on Sixth Street since 1969, one of the oldest family-owned businesses remaining in Belton. They built the Red and White Grocery on South Main Street in 1971 and sold it in 2001. (Authors' collection.)

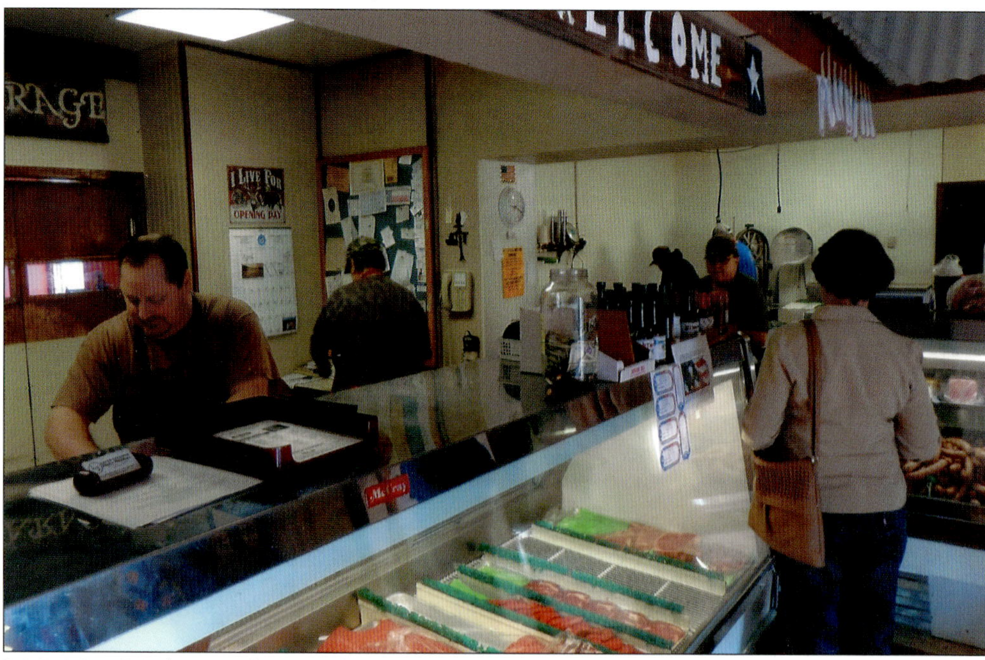

L&R Meat Market, in the same location for 26 years, specializes in old-fashioned quality meat and sausages. To assure quality, L&R purchases meat from local suppliers. In addition to selling traditional cuts of meat, it offers four types of sausage, summer sausage, and beef jerky. Some 500 pounds of sausage are processed daily. (Authors' collection.)

A descendant of Charles Schoepf, citizen of the Republic of Texas and a Texas Revolution veteran, Ronnie Schoepf owns and operates Schoepf's Bar-B-Q. He purchased the business from his father in 2007 and hosts the Texas Music Series there. Barbecue is prepared using five coal-filled pits. Schoepf is pictured here with the coal fire pit, where coals are made to use for cooking. (Authors' collection.)

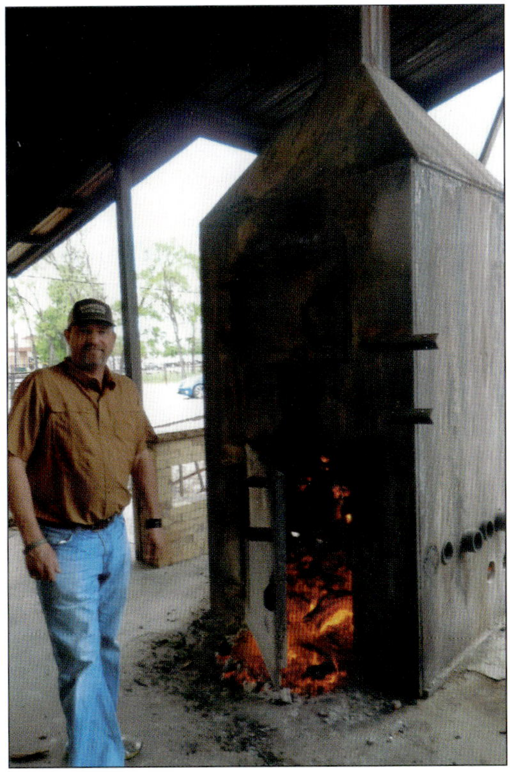

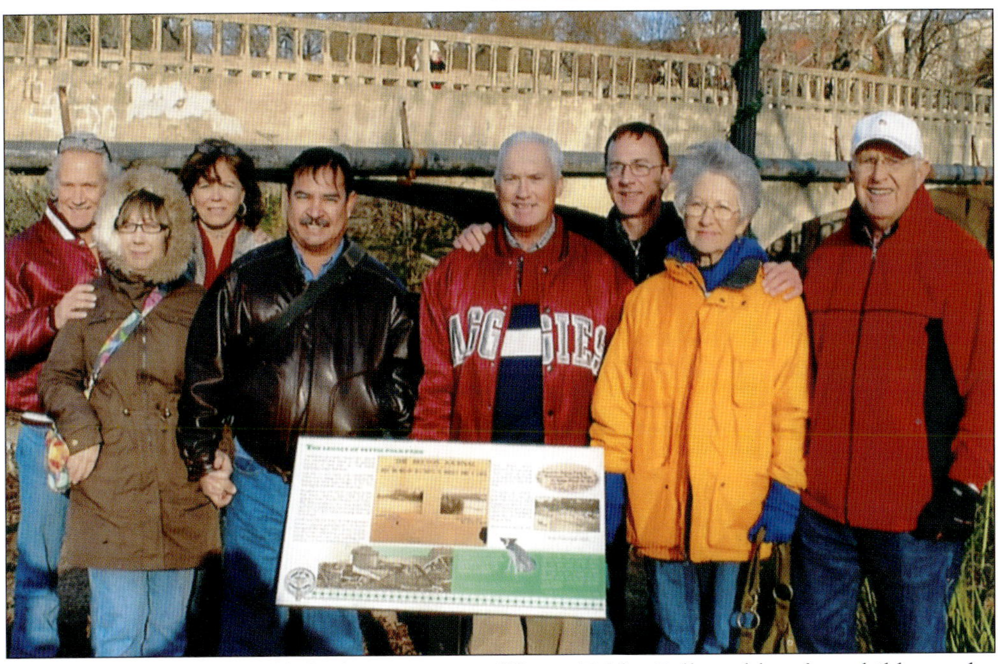

Yettie Polk Park was established in memory of Yettie Tobler Polk and her four children, who drowned in the 1913 Nolan Creek flood. Descendants of Yettie Polk attended the dedication ceremony for an interpretive sign depicting the tragedy. The sign is located in Yettie Polk Park, near the old one-lane Jail Bridge. (Courtesy of the City of Belton.)

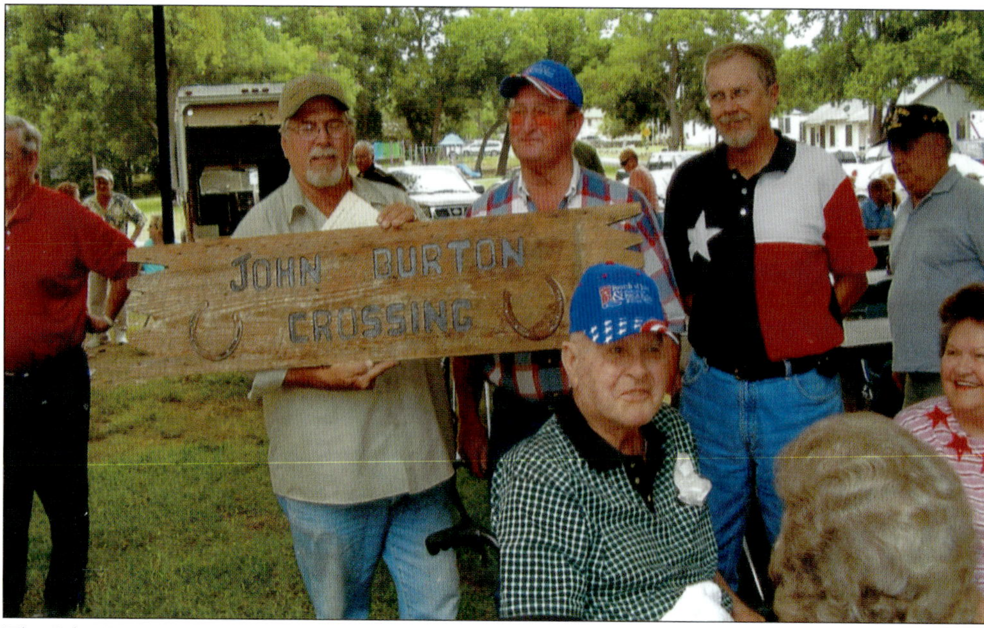

The John Burton Crossing sign placed at the crossing of the hike and bike trail on Nolan Creek in 2006 honored John Burton, who worked for the City of Belton for many years. Burton (seated in front) attended the ceremonial placement of the sign, which washed away in the 2011 flood. The city did not replace the sign and demolished the crossing in 2014. (Courtesy of the Belton Chamber of Commerce.)

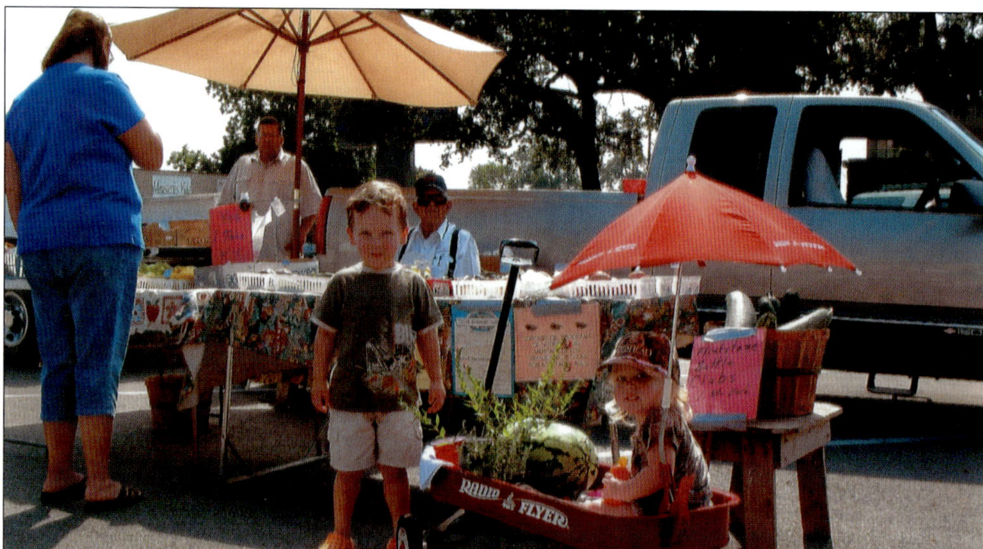

Soon after the establishment of Belton in 1850, men from across the county started bringing produce, livestock, horses, hides, and wood to town to sell and trade. In 2008, the customs of yesteryear were revived somewhat with Belton Market Days and Farmers Market. John and Jane Gauntt carry on the tradition of their Bell County ancestors by shopping at the Belton Farmers Market. (Courtesy of Jerri Gauntt.)

Two

Fort Hood and Killeen

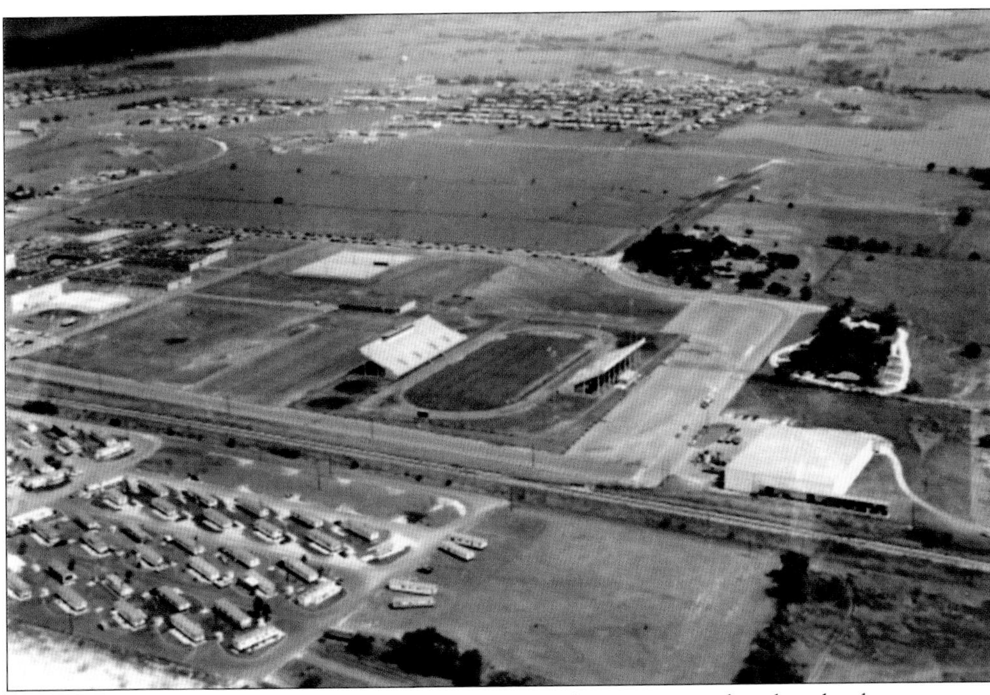

One hundred years ago, Killeen had three gins, five physicians, two hotels, a lumber company, general stores, two banks, and four churches. When Camp Hood, now known as Fort Hood, was established in 1942, Killeen's population was approximately 1,000. The post steadily increased in size and population, as did Killeen. Today, Killeen is much larger and more densely populated than this 1980s aerial view displays. (Courtesy of the Killeen Area Heritage Association.)

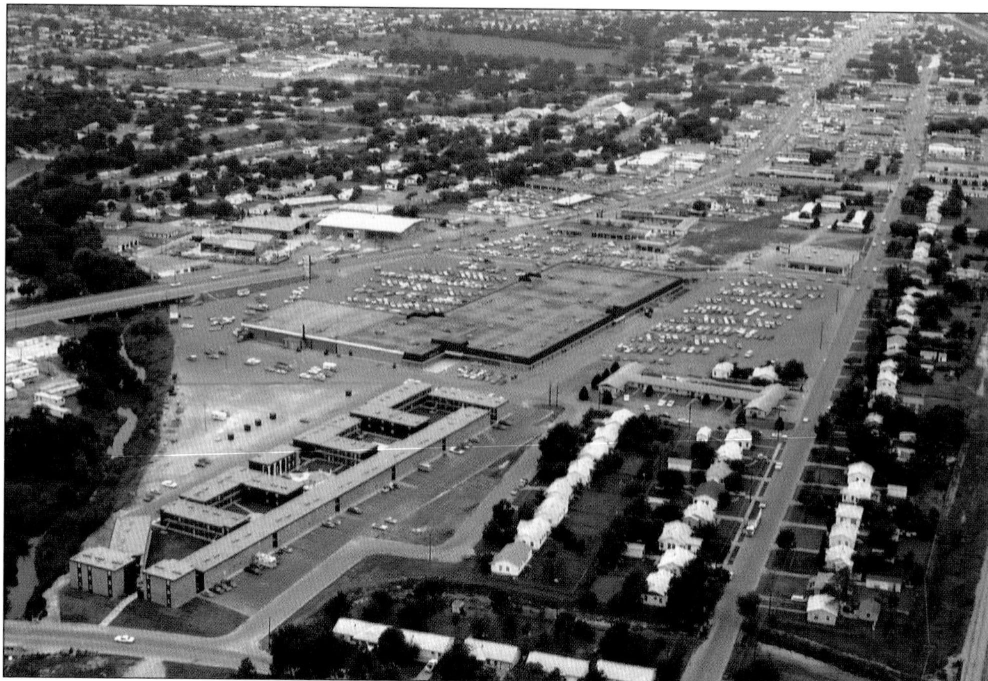

The large building in the above photograph, with cars parked on either side, is the Mid-Town Mall, Killeen's first air-conditioned shopping mall, which opened in 1970. On the left is Nolan Creek with the Veterans Memorial Boulevard Bridge spanning it. At the bottom left is an apartment complex, and the small, white houses are probably on Avenue G. Anchor stores at the mall were Woolworth, HEB, and Bealls. (Courtesy of the Killeen Area Heritage Association.)

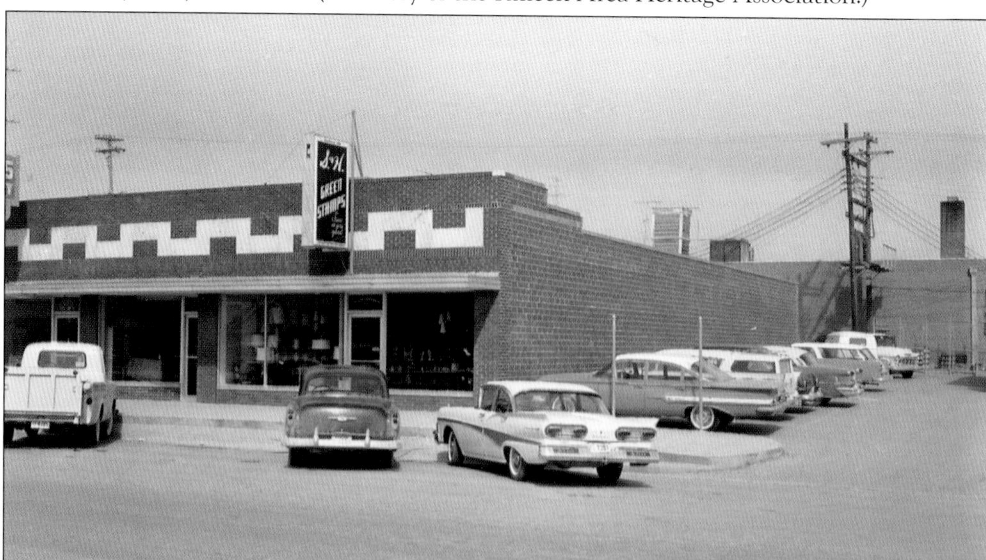

Stamps programs were popular until the 1970s. S&H Green Stamps, probably the most popular of the stamp companies, sold stamps to retail organizations that in turn gave the stamps to their customers as a bonus with each purchase—the more purchased, the more stamps received. Stamps were redeemed for various merchandise at this store in Killeen. (Courtesy of the Killeen Area Heritage Association.)

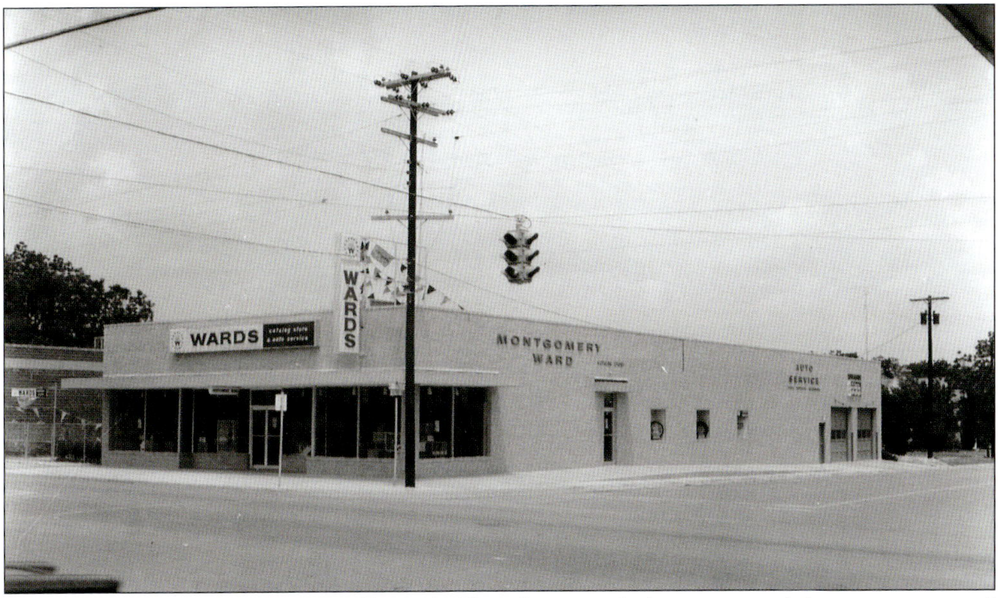

Montgomery Ward sold a range of household appliances, clothing, automobile accessories, and electronics. Full automobile service included brake adjustments and front-end alignments. The store offered weekly newspaper specials that included coupons to take to the store for discounts on merchandise. In the 1970s, Ward's occupied three downtown buildings in Killeen. The store closed in 1985, and Love Car Care & Appliances opened in the building. (Courtesy of the Killeen Area Heritage Association.)

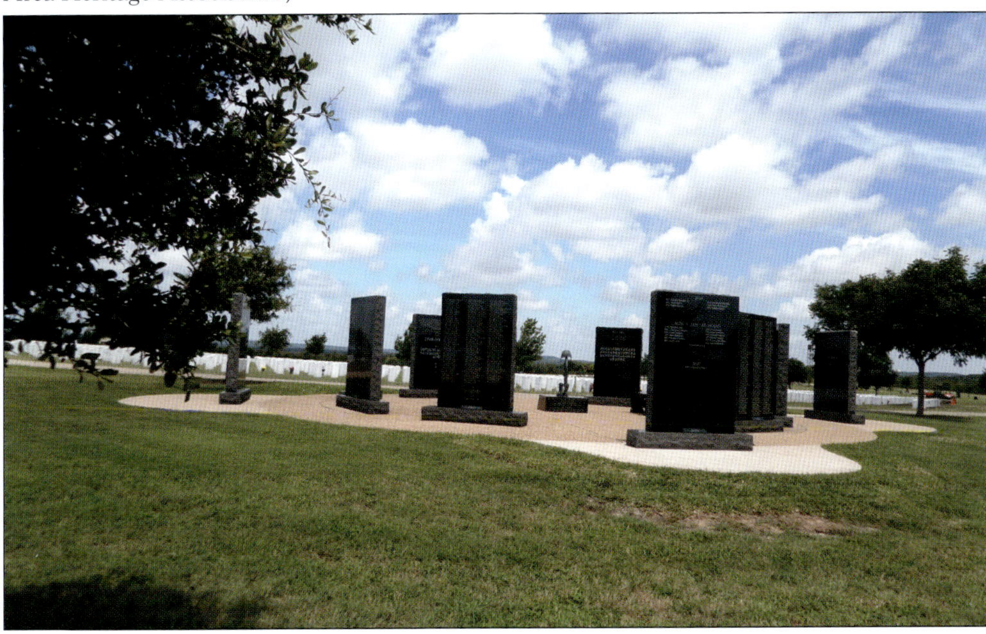

More than 60 years after World War II ended, the 174-acre Central Texas State Veterans Cemetery opened in 2006 on land formerly part of Fort Hood. The cemetery was the first of four Texas veterans' cemeteries. By mid-2015, there were more than 6,000 burials. The 11 black granite monuments honor the fallen heroes of the Iraq and Afghanistan conflicts and victims of the 2009 Fort Hood shooting. (Authors' collection.)

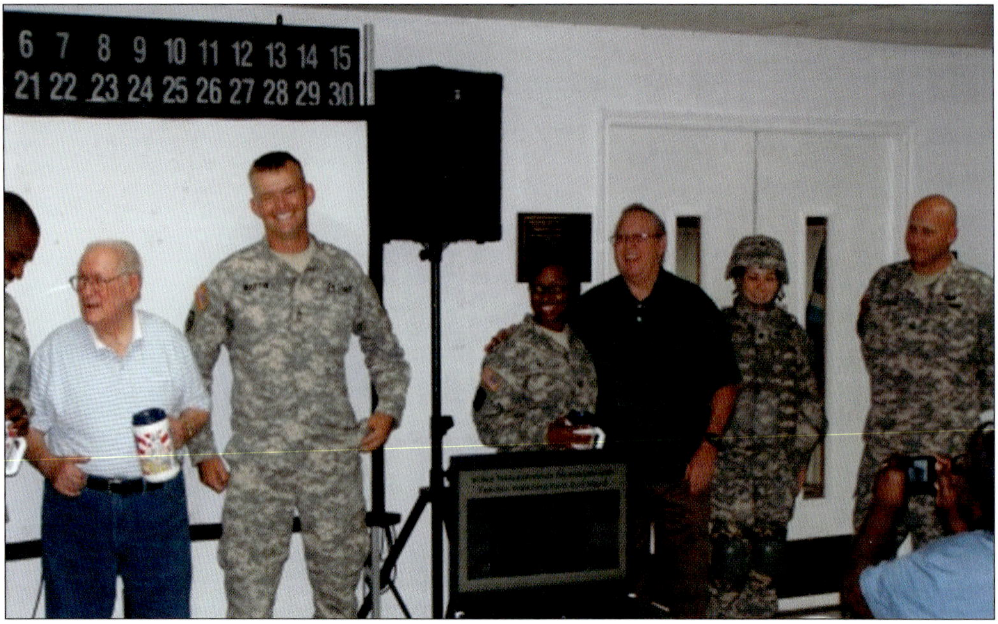

The Army encourages soldiers to volunteer their time and energy for on- and off-post causes. Soldiers of the 3rd Battalion, 395th Armor Regiment maintain Dulaney Cemetery, and Fort Hood soldiers sponsor schools throughout the county. Soldiers are pictured here visiting Belton Senior Center, where they presented a program and let seniors sit in a Humvee. At the center, soldiers recognized World War II veteran Ernest Swinden. (Courtesy of the Belton Senior Center.)

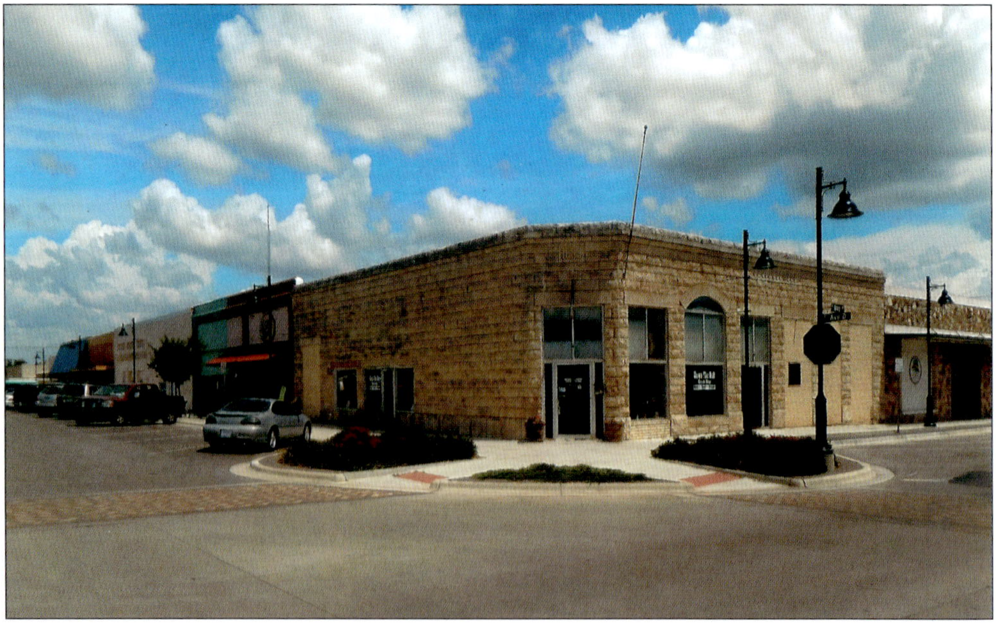

This 2015 photograph illustrates a typical street view of restored buildings in the downtown Killeen Historic District. Many of the brick and limestone structures that dominate the district retain their original facades. At the time these buildings were erected, Killeen epitomized West Bell County farmers and ranchers as a leading financial and shipping center for cotton, cattle, and wool. (Courtesy of the Killeen Area Heritage Association.)

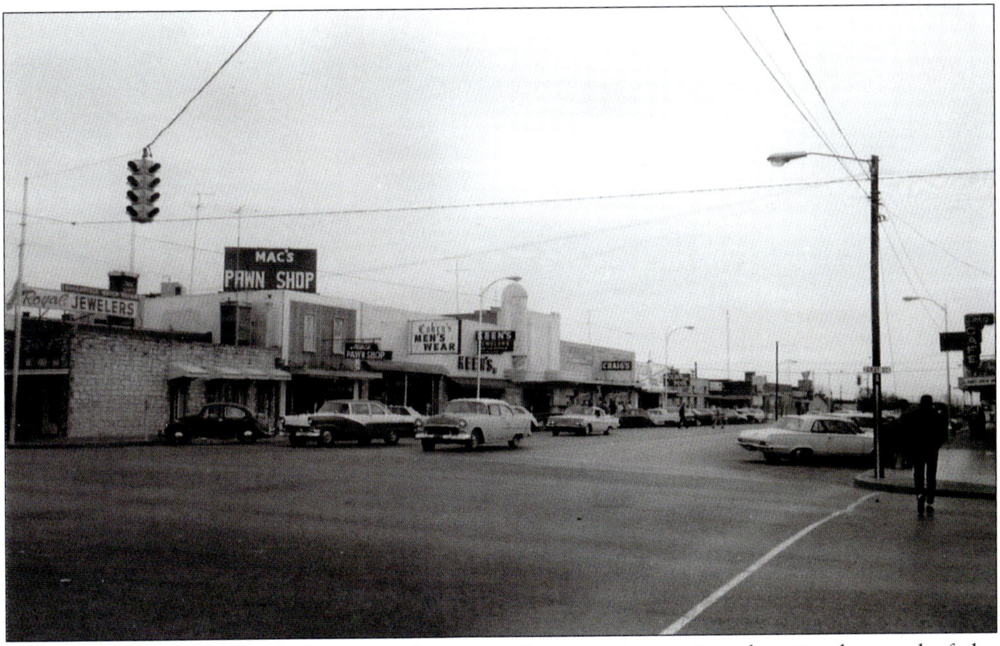

The City of Killeen focused its revitalization efforts on improving the visual appeal of the downtown historic district to attract more pedestrian traffic. To make the area a more inviting and walkable space, the city repaved streets, built sidewalks, added a plaza, and offered facade grants to property owners of historic buildings. Here are two views of the corner of Avenue D and Gray Street looking east along Avenue D. Above, is a view from the 1960s showing a variety of mixed-usage businesses. Below is the same view as a revitalized district of restored buildings in 2015. (Above, courtesy of the Killeen Area Heritage Association; below, authors' collection.)

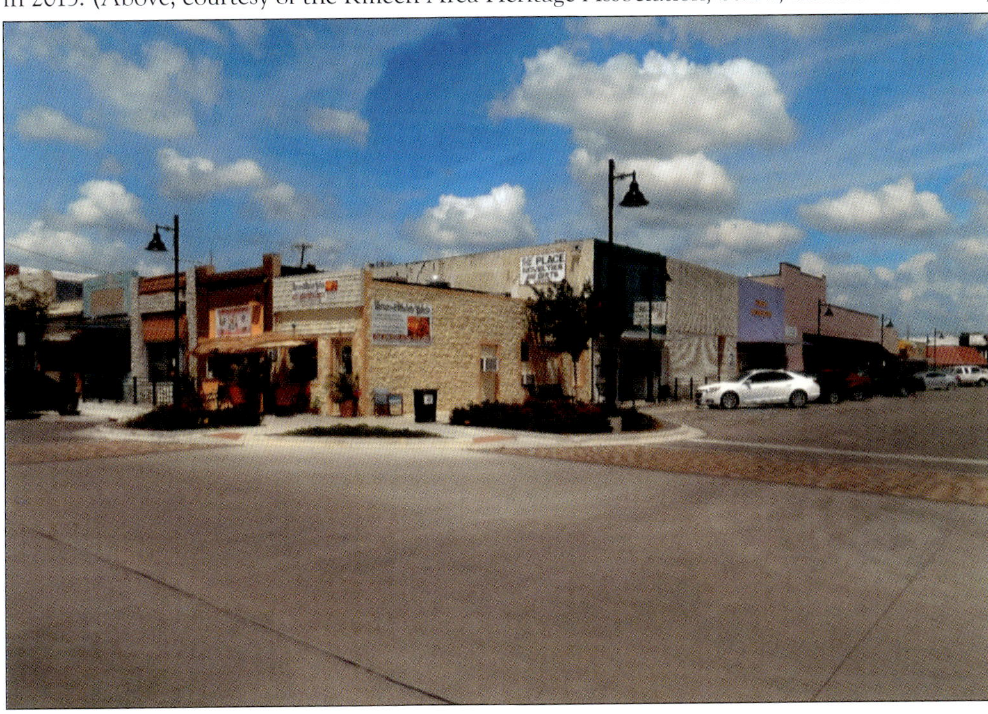

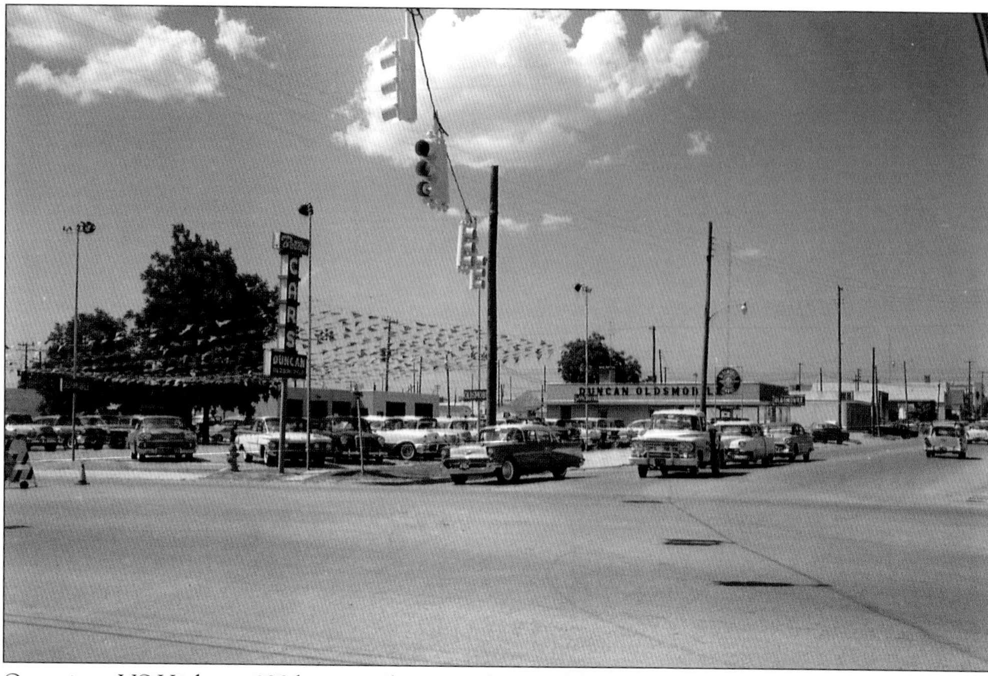

Over time, US Highway 190 became the main thoroughfare leading into Killeen. The area along US Highway 190 nearest the heart of the business district attracted businesses that primarily served the large community of military personnel stationed at Fort Hood. Today, numerous new and used automobile dealerships stretch along the modern US Highway 190, constructed in the 1970s. Duncan Brothers Oldsmobile, above, was one of the automobile sales agencies to open in Killeen after World War II. Connell Chevrolet, below, became one of the oldest family-owned businesses in Killeen. (Both, courtesy of the Killeen Area Heritage Association.)

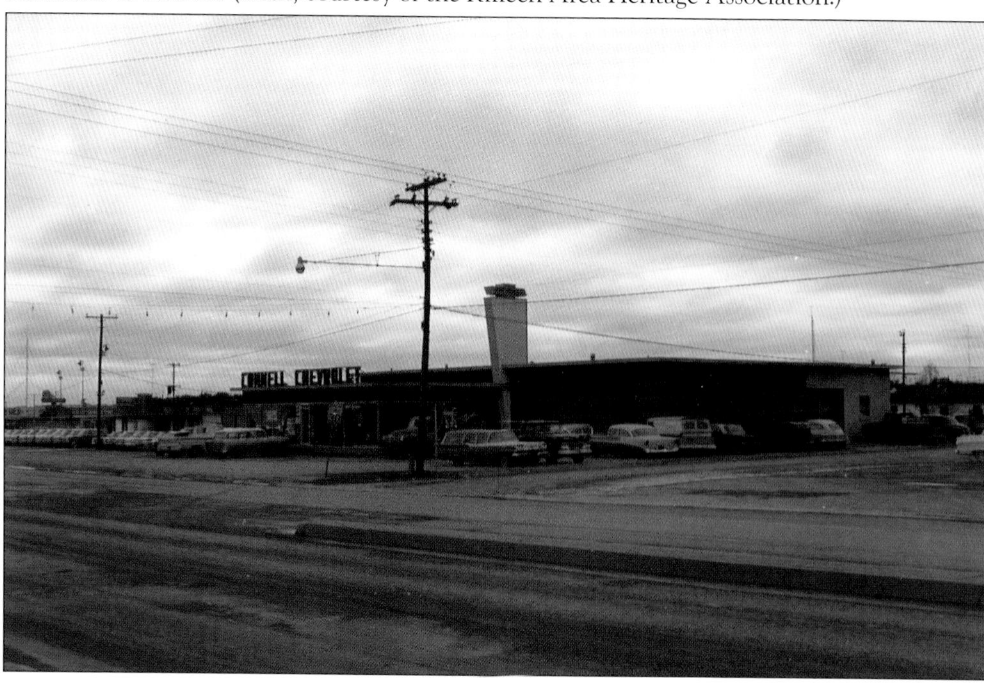

Three

Salado

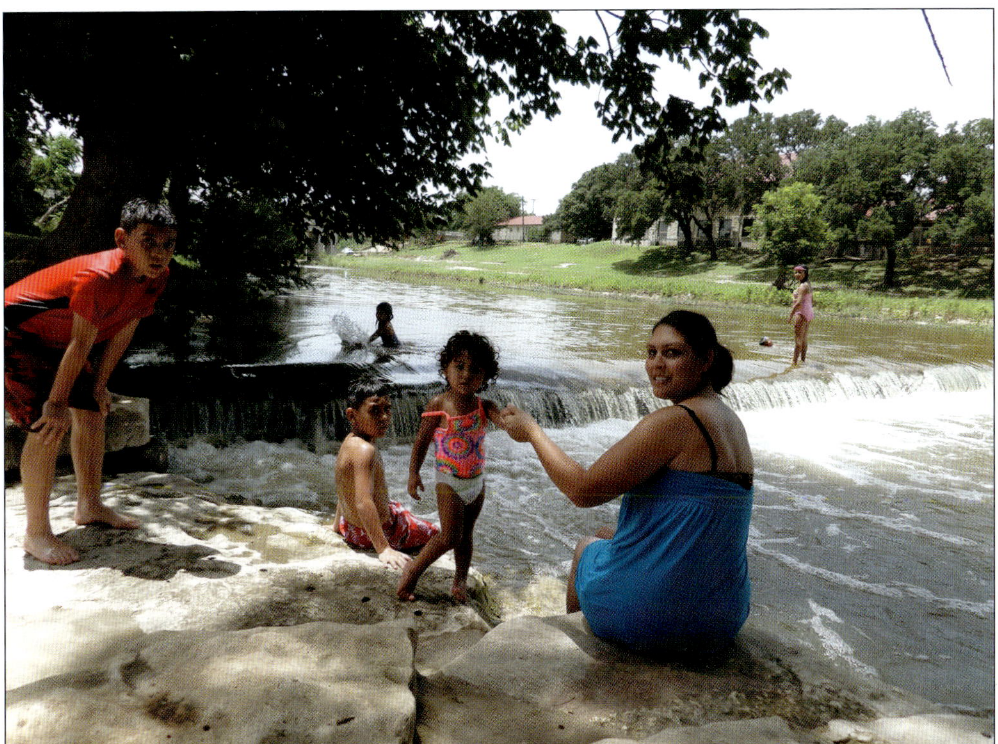

Every summer, the clean cool water of Salado Creek draws members of the DeLaGarza and Ramos families from Temple to enjoy swimming, playing on the rocks, and picnicking. Traveling 15 miles from Temple to Salado for fun and family time is a tradition for the families. (Authors' collection.)

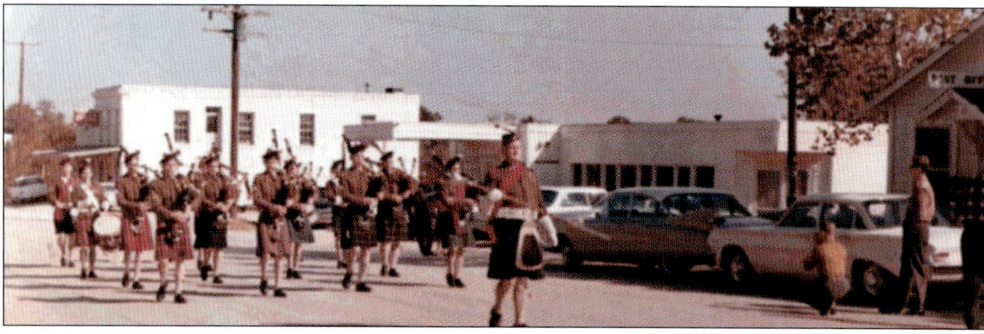

Lucile Robertson founded Gathering of the Scottish Clans as a fundraiser for the Central Texas Area Museum in 1961. More than 1,000 registered for the first event, and an undetermined number attended. Above, the highlight of the event is a parade on Main Street. Businesses in the background are on the east side of Main Street. From left to right are the grocery store, service station, Village Café, and post office. Guy and Florence Allamon ran the café. Gathering of the Scottish Clans and Highland Games celebrated its 50th anniversary in 2011. Pictured below in 2012 are volunteers who worked the gate and ticket sales at the event, held at Salado Civic Center. The women to the right represent three generations of their family. (Above, courtesy of the Central Texas Area Museum; below, authors' collection.)

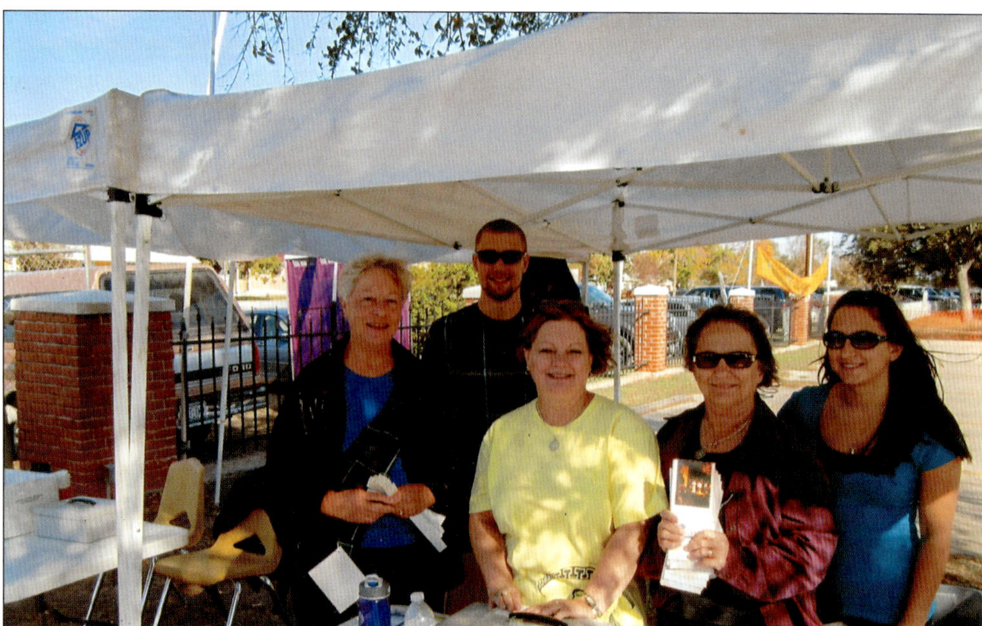

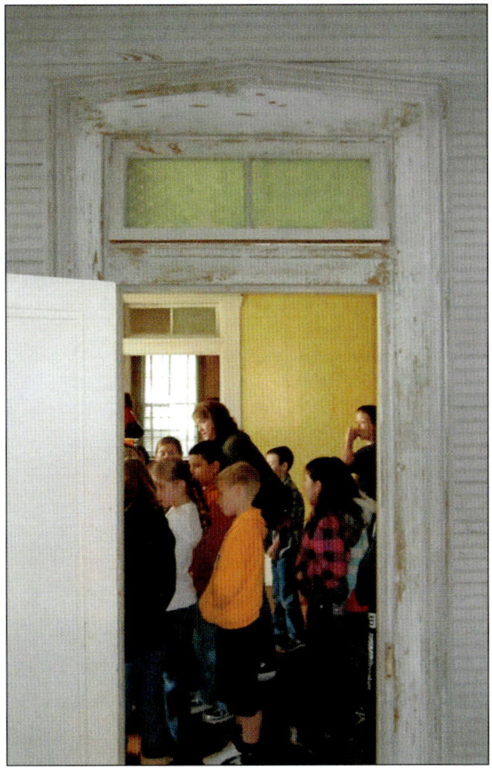

Students from Salado schools tour Col. E.S.C. Robertson's plantation each year as part of their Texas history lessons. They ask pertinent questions of the costumed docents, Robertson descendants, members of Salado Historical Society, and Sons of Confederate Veterans. The students tour the 1860 E.S.C. Robertson house, grounds, slave quarters, and barn. The photograph below is of Colonel Robertson's office in the two-story, 22-room house as it looked in 2010. (Right, authors' collection; below, courtesy of the Robertson Plantation.)

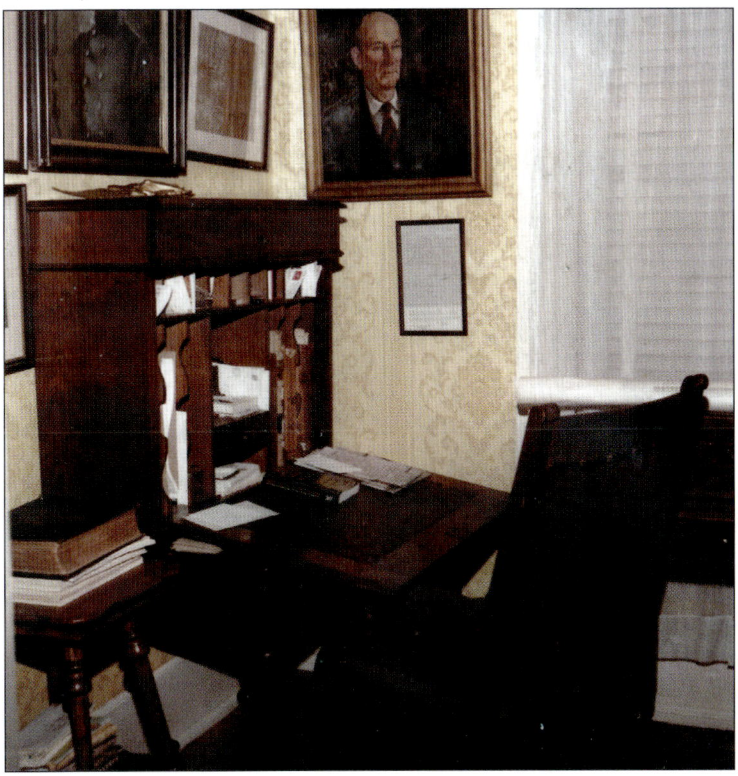

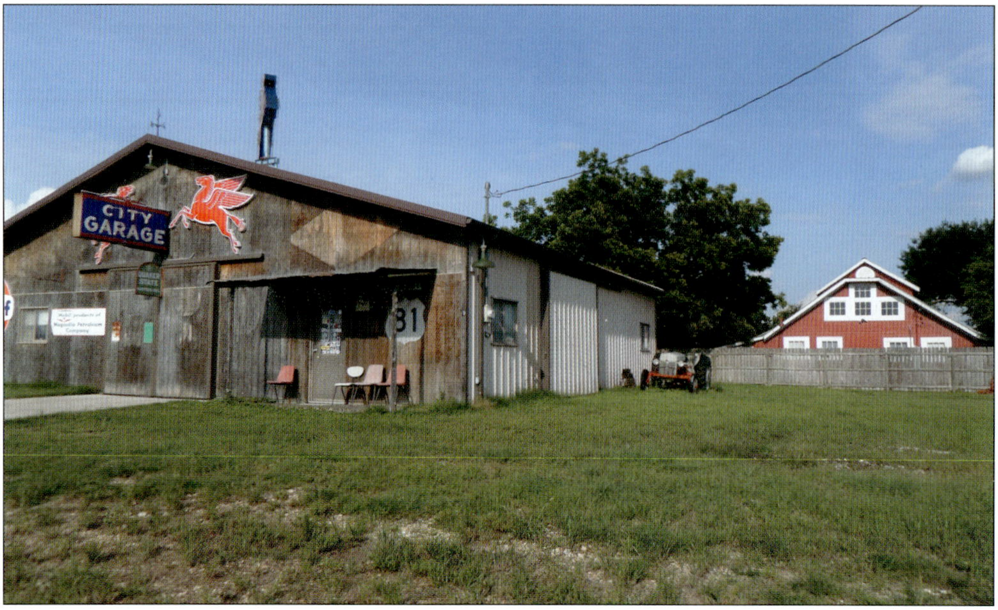

Pegasus, the winged horse of Greek mythology, rests atop the roof of Don Ellis's building that he uses for storage of vintage automobiles. The City Garage sign came from Calvert, Texas. Located on the east side of Interstate Highway 35, the building displays Ellis's collection of antique signs. (Authors' collection.)

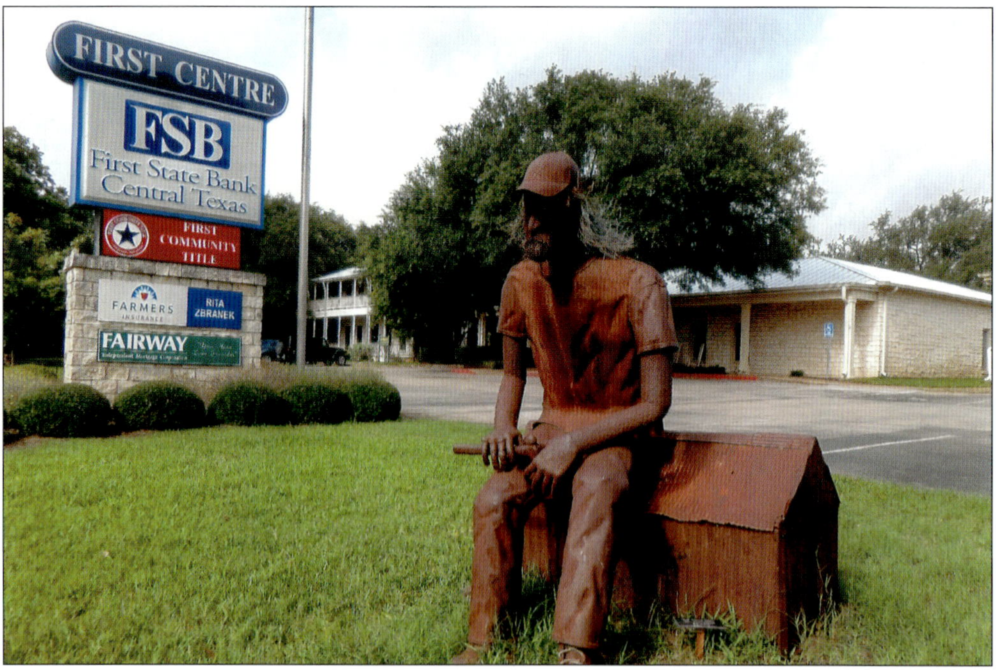

Among art on display throughout Salado is the sculpture *Self Made Man*, by artist Joe Barrington, who owns Red Star Studio in Throckmorton. This sculpture portrays a man holding a hammer and sitting on a barnlike structure that Barrington modeled after his father's welding shop. Known for his large-scale projects in welded steel, Barrington majored in sculpture at Midwestern State University in Wichita Falls, Texas. (Authors' collection.)

Salado College, established in 1859, opened to students in early 1860. The area surrounding the ruins of the school building is now a park that features a sculpture of E.S.C. Robertson, who led efforts to found the town and school. Placed in 1994, the sculpture is the work of Clay Dahlberg of Hunt, Texas. Robertson descendant Alice West, wife of flamboyant Texas millionaire Jim "Silver Dollar" West, contributed most of the $35,000 needed to commission the statue. The front iron gates, dedicated to Mary Marshall on June 3, 1995, bear the name "Salado College 1859." At the dedication ceremony, Jon Burrows was keynote speaker. Pictured here are, from left to right, Cile Robertson Ambrose and Liz Carpenter (both Robertson descendants), unidentified, Jon Burrows, and Jim Bowmer. (Right, authors' collection; below, courtesy of the Central Texas Area Museum.)

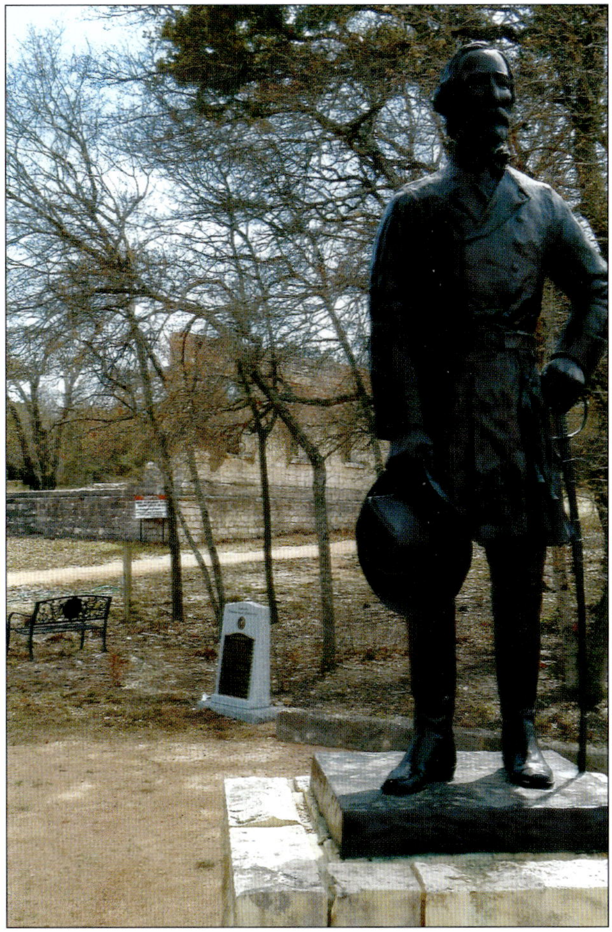

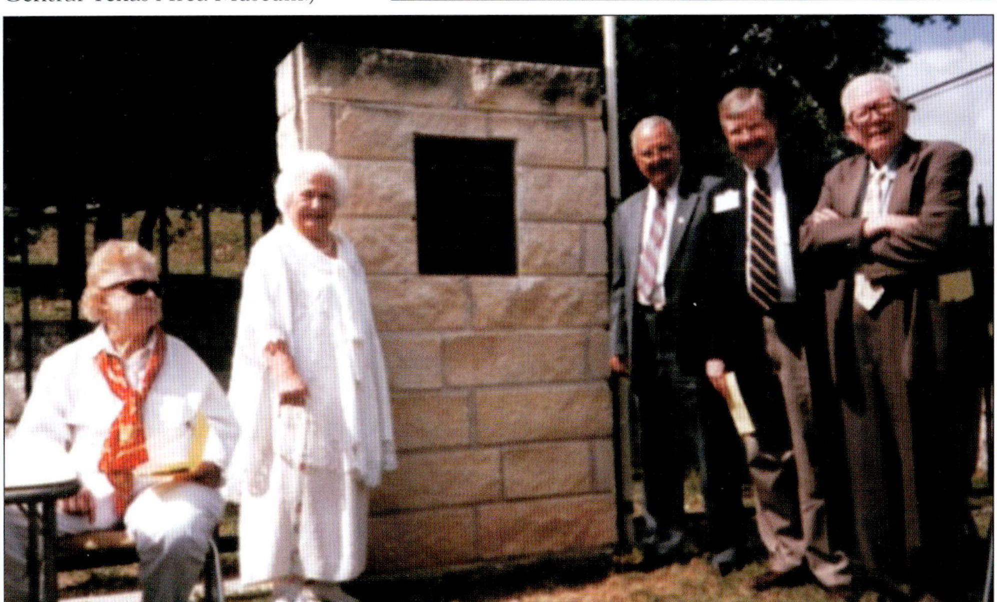

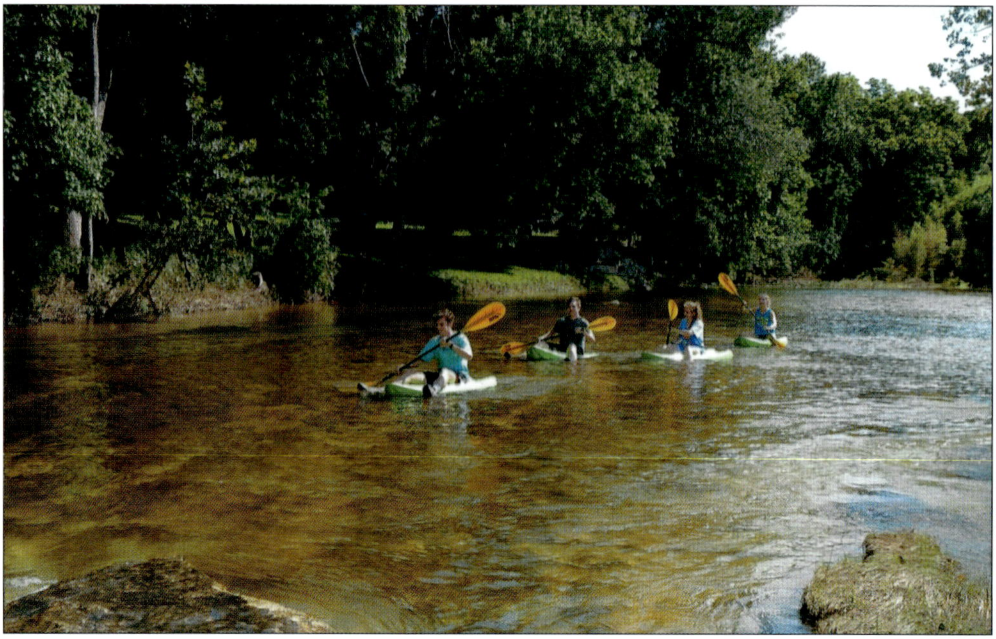

Since the town of Salado was established in 1859, Salado Creek and its springs provided for recreation. LaZy-Day Camp, opened in 1959 by Chester Critchfield, provided swimming, canoeing, archery, fishing, hiking, and nature study. In recent years, canoeing and kayaking have become popular recreational pastimes. Lucile Robertson and her sister Ivy Armstrong operated Camp Tejas at the springs on Salado Creek on the Robertson property. Damming the springs provided a large swimming hole for the young girls who attended the camp. Above, youth enjoy kayaking in 2015. Below, the *Serena* mermaid statue rests at the site of a spring east of Main Street in 2012. (Both, authors' collection.)

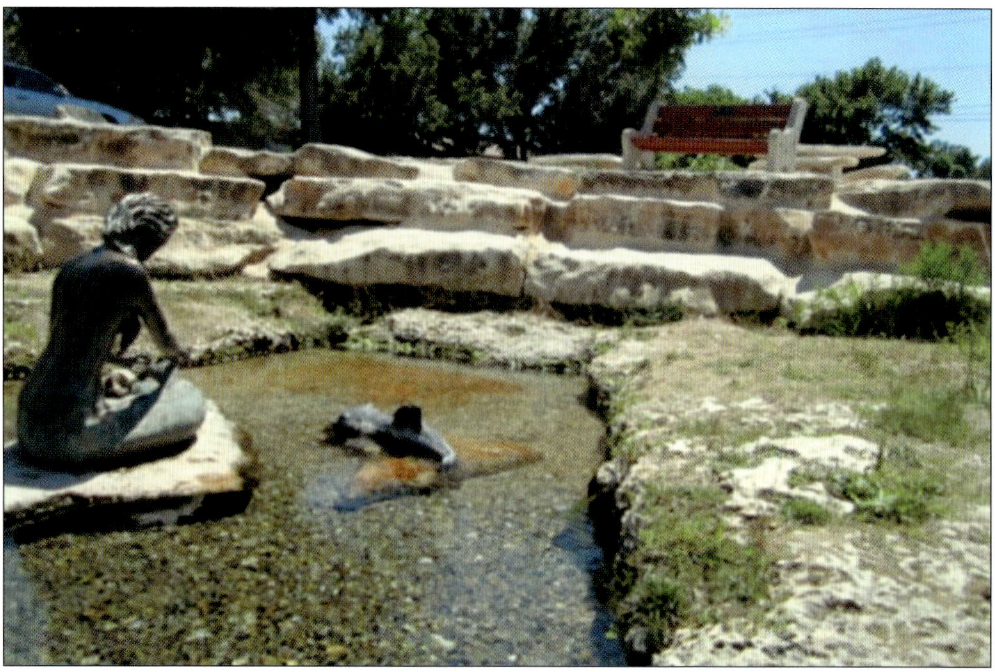

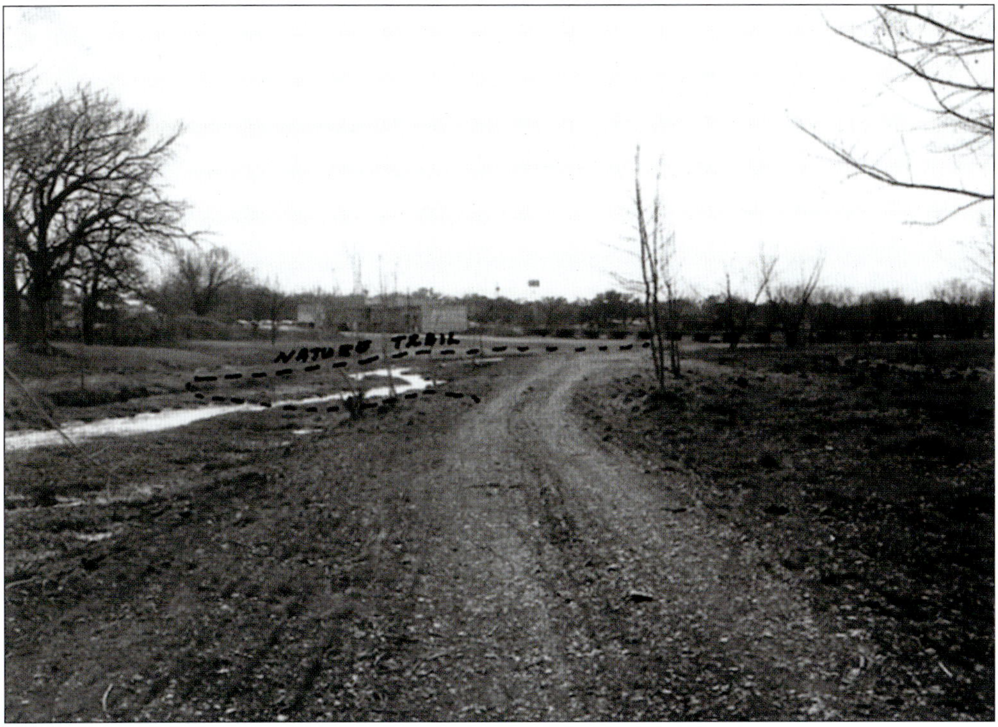

In 1971, the community developed this area along Salado Creek to serve as a recreation area. Development included roads, landscaping, and a rock wall at Pace Park. Above is the north side of Salado Creek in 1971. The general area is shown below in 2014. The concrete bridge, built in 1922, appears in the background of both photographs. (Above, courtesy of the Central Texas Area Museum; below, authors' collection.)

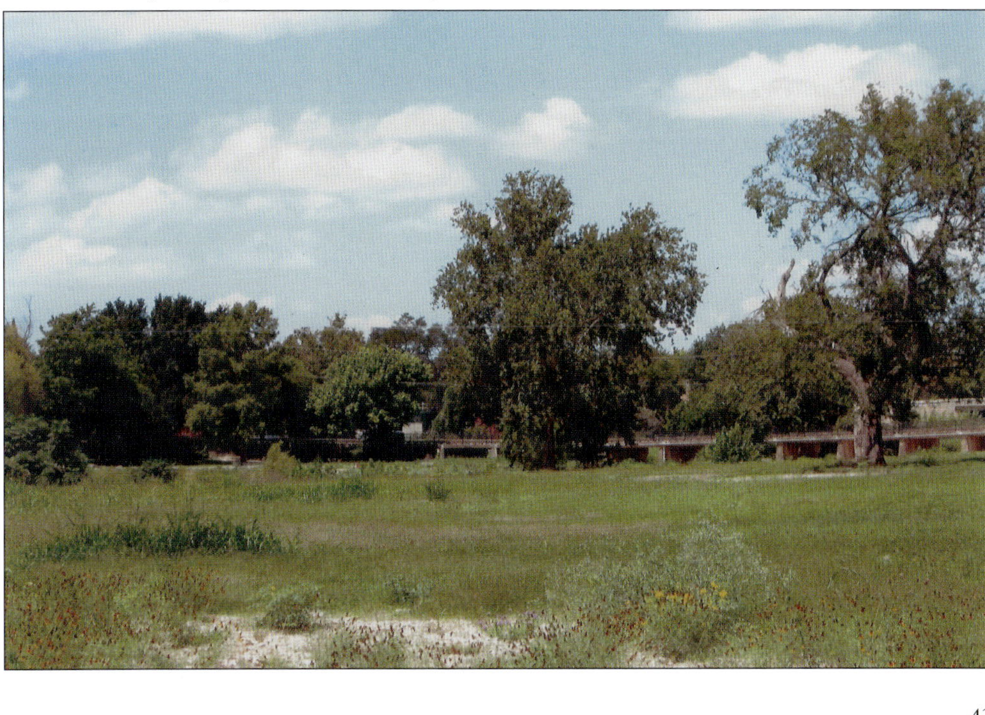

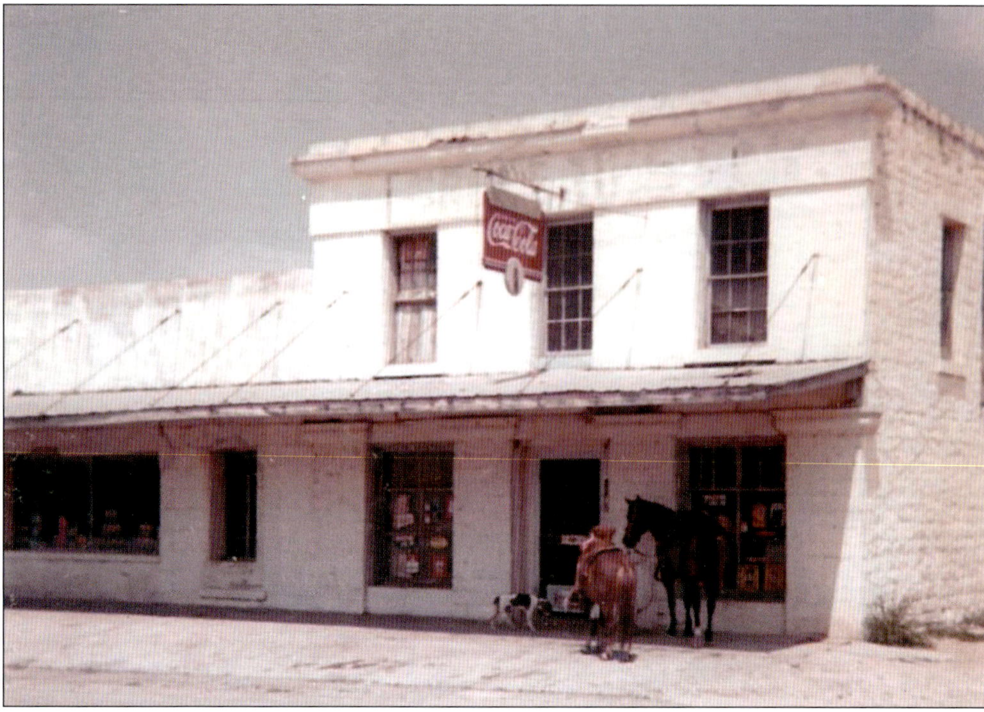

Roy and Lois Watson Shepperd ran a grocery store in the old rock two-story W.R. Berry building on the northeast corner of Main and Royal Streets. They rented the building from Earl and Ruth Guest. The Shepperds purchased local produce such as eggs and butter to sell in their store. Today, Sirril Art Gallery occupies the second floor. Below is the building as it appears in 2015. (Above, courtesy of the Central Texas Area Museum; below, authors' collection.)

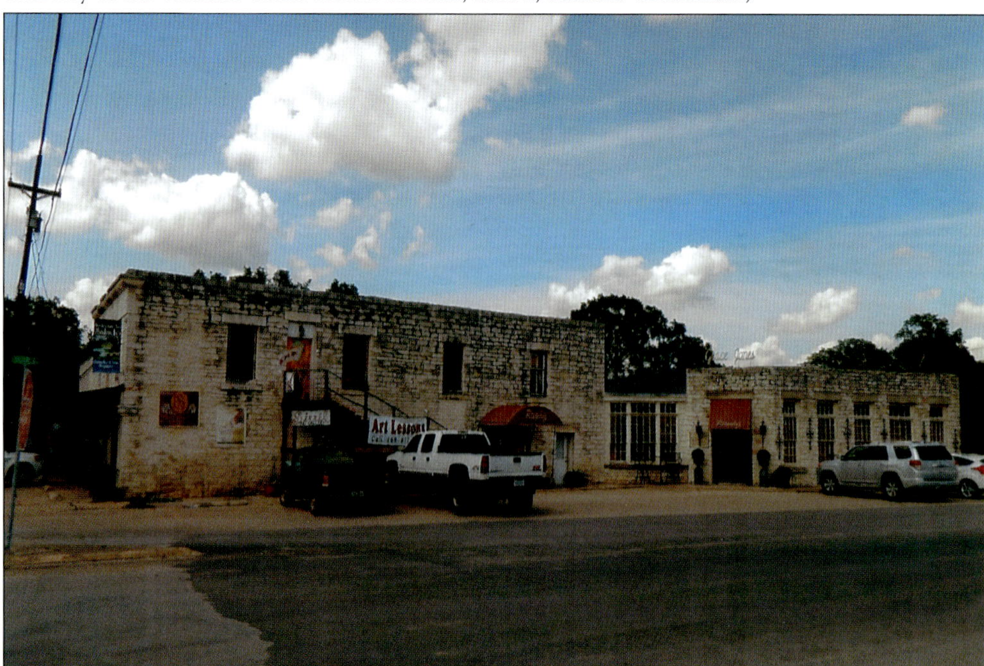

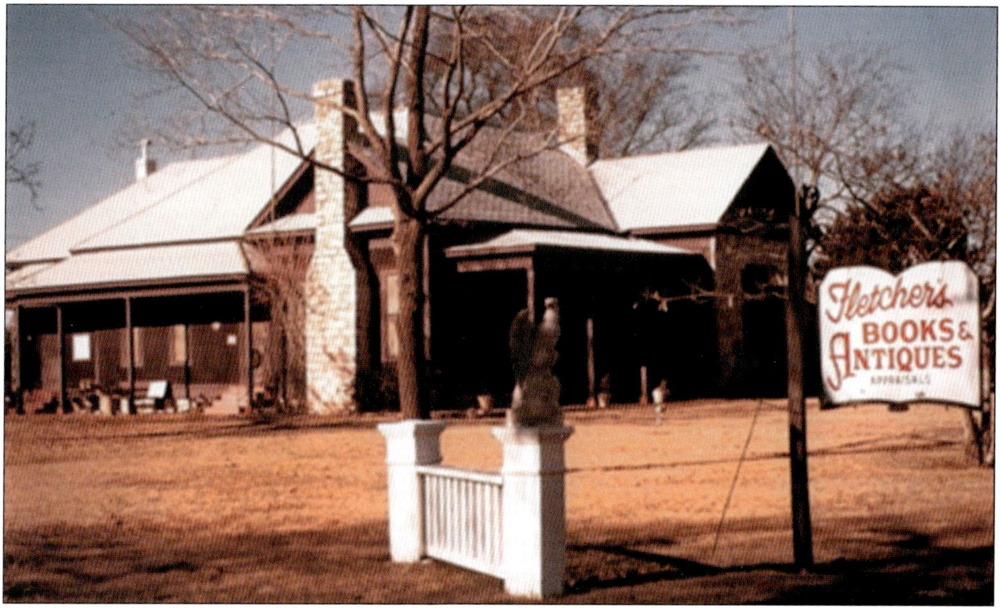

In 1954, Thelma and Herbert Fletcher opened Fletcher's Books and Antiques on the west side of Main Street in the old Vickery house. The Fletchers were experts on early Texas documents, rare books, and Texas history. They founded Anson Jones Press in 1929 in Houston. Herbert Fletcher remodeled the barn and used it for his Anson Jones Press office. Below, Stamp Salado currently occupies the old barn and is an excellent example of adaptive reuse. This usage of older buildings preserves the structures and helps retain the historic charm of Salado. Three windows and a small shed are additions to the old structure. (Above, courtesy of the Central Texas Area Museum; below, authors' collection.)

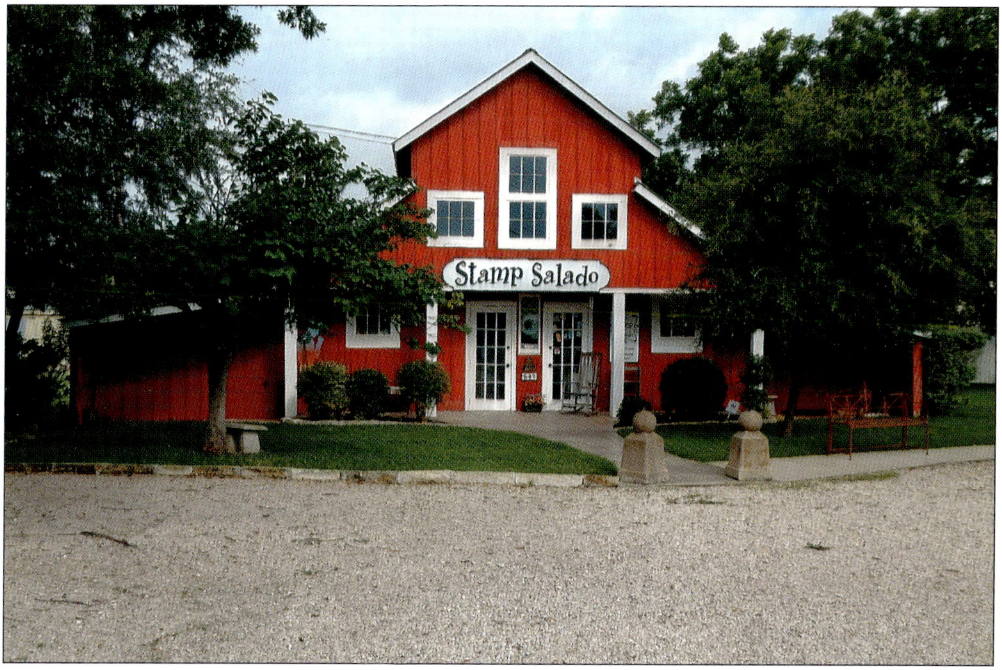

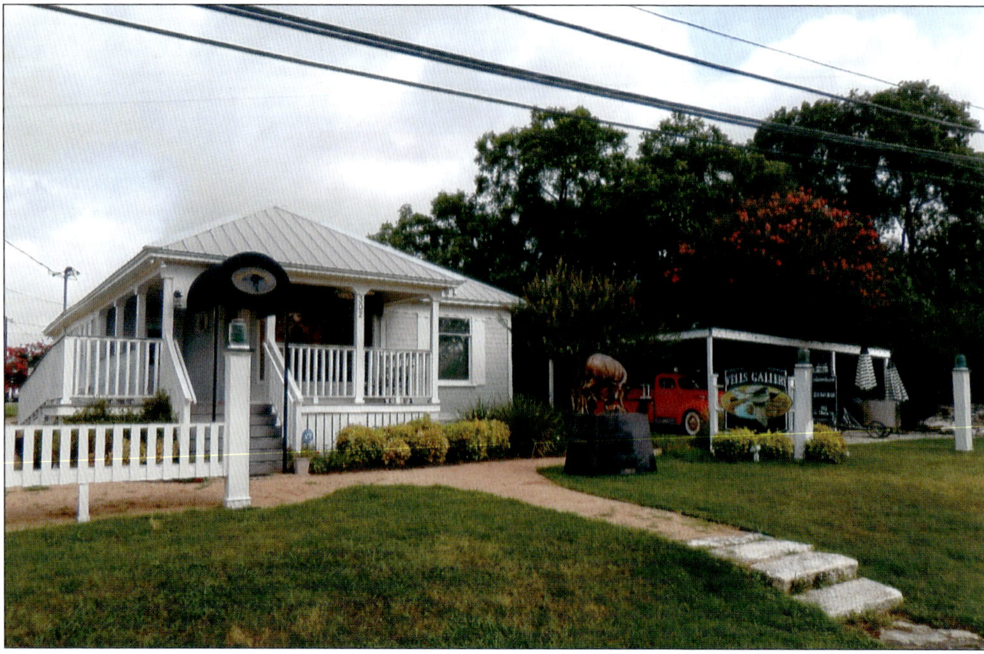

In 1990, nationally recognized sculptor, oil and watercolor painter, and author Ronnie Wells moved to Salado with his wife and business manager, Patricia, and opened Wells Gallery on South Main Street. After 24 years at that location, the couple moved their gallery to a new location on North Main Street, above, where his bronze sculpture *Twins* prominently stands in front of the studio. In the photograph below, Wells is at work creating a clay model sculpture of Buffalo Hump, famed warrior chief of the Penateka band of the Comanche Indians. His interest in the life of Buffalo Hump inspired this sculpture. (Both, authors' collection.)

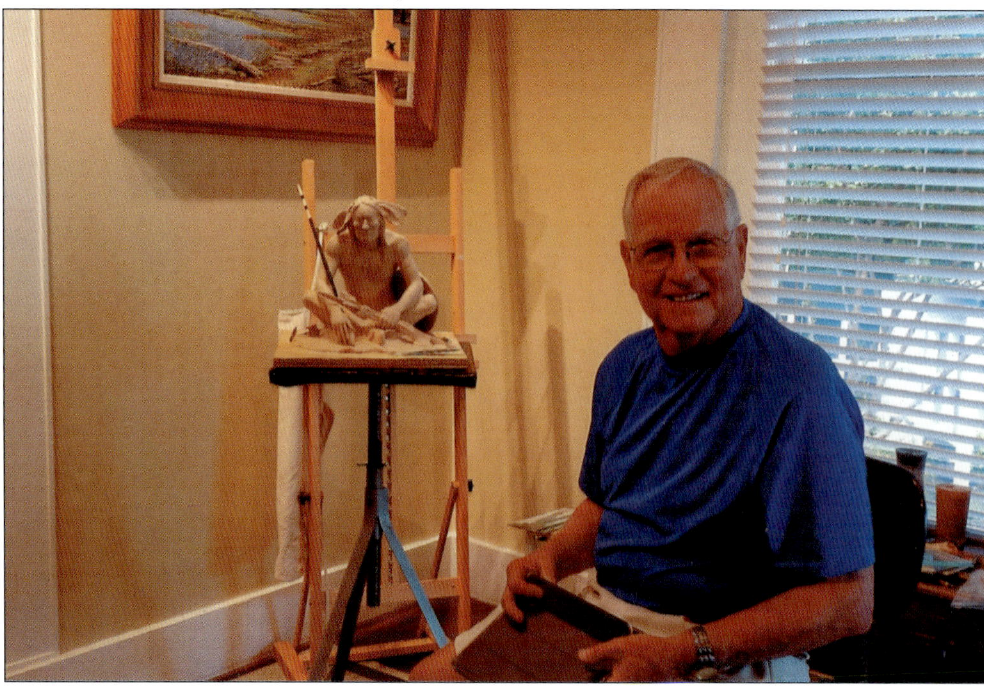

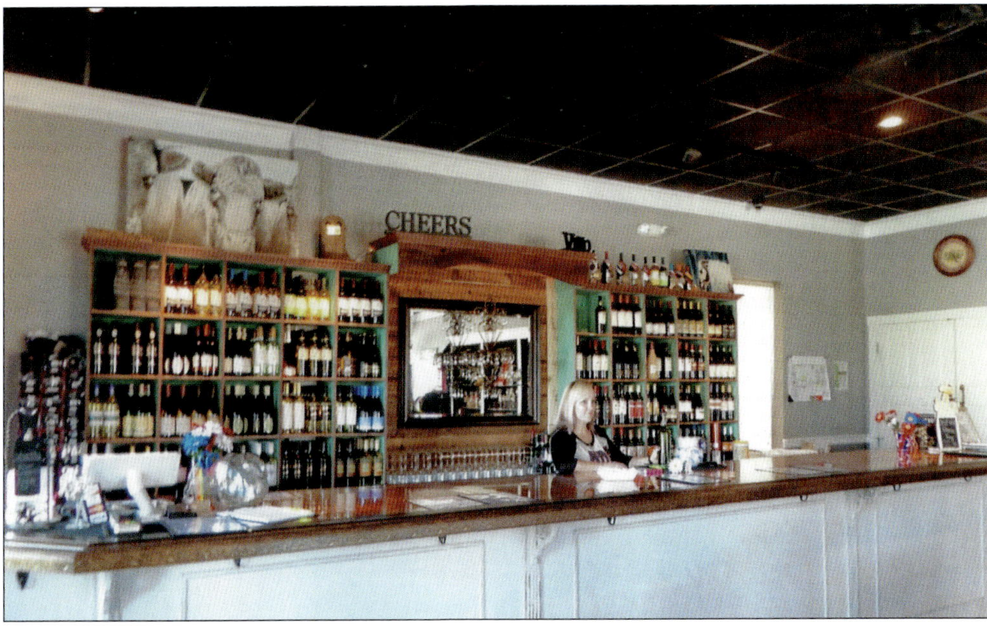

Early Salado deeds restricted the sale of intoxicating liquor in quantities less than a quart. Prohibition of all spirits ended in 2008 when town laws changed, allowing businesses such as Salado Creek Winery & Vineyard to open. The winery is the first award-winning winery in Bell County and one of two wineries in Texas making wine out of citrus fruit. Dystiny serves behind the bar. (Authors' collection.)

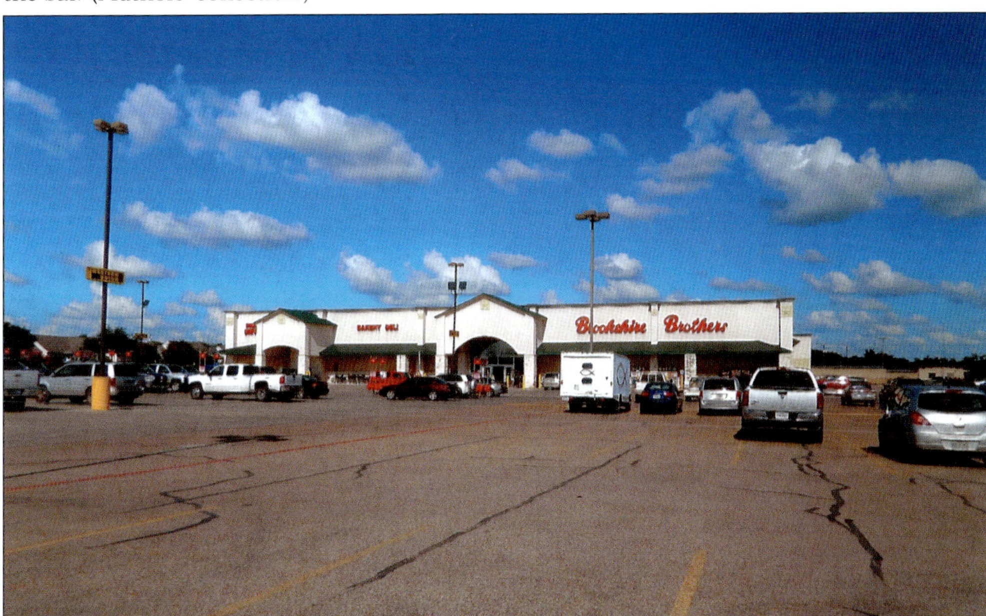

In 1921, Tom and Austin Brookshire founded Brookshire Brothers in Lufkin, Texas. Employee-owned since 2006, the grocery chain focuses on offering quality goods and services with a steadfast belief in family and community. In that spirit, the Salado store participates in Neighbors Helping Neighbors, providing food to the needy. The store, at its present location since 2010, is Salado's only grocery store. (Authors' collection.)

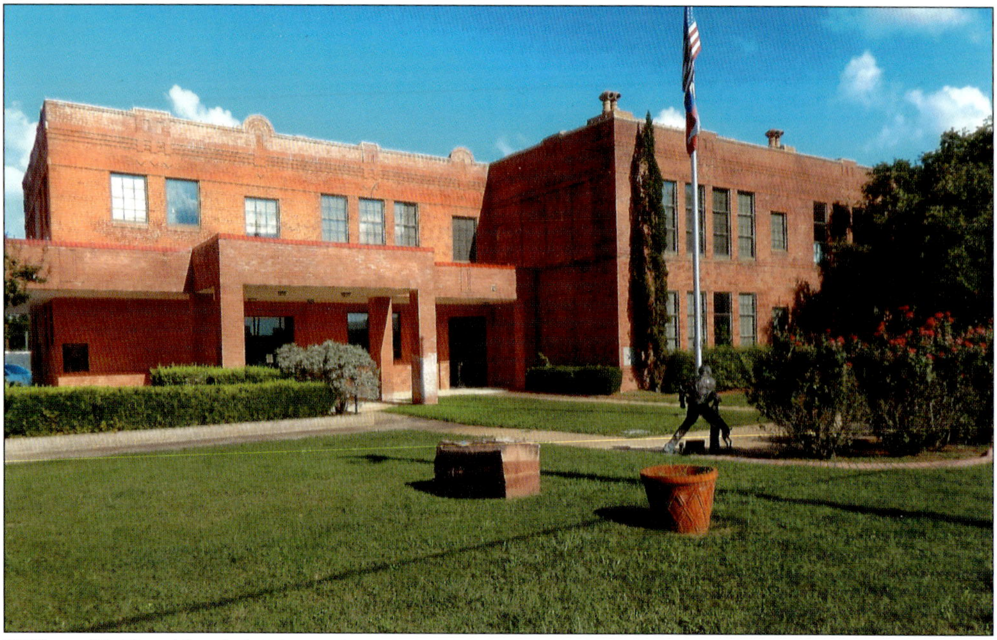

William K. Hamblen left Maury County, Tennessee, for Texas in 1834 at age 17. He was a Church of Christ minister. An advocate of education, he became a Salado College trustee and in 1871 petitioned for the establishment of a second school in Salado. When Salado needed a site for a new school in 1924, Hamblen descendants donated their homestead for the school. Burial sites of the couple are behind the school building. A metal fence surrounds the nine graves in Hamblen Cemetery, below, located a short distance off North Main Street. The earliest marked grave is that of the 26-year-old daughter of W.K. and Alice Hamblen, Vesta Hamblen, who died in 1899. Salado Historical Society maintains the cemetery. (Both, authors' collection.)

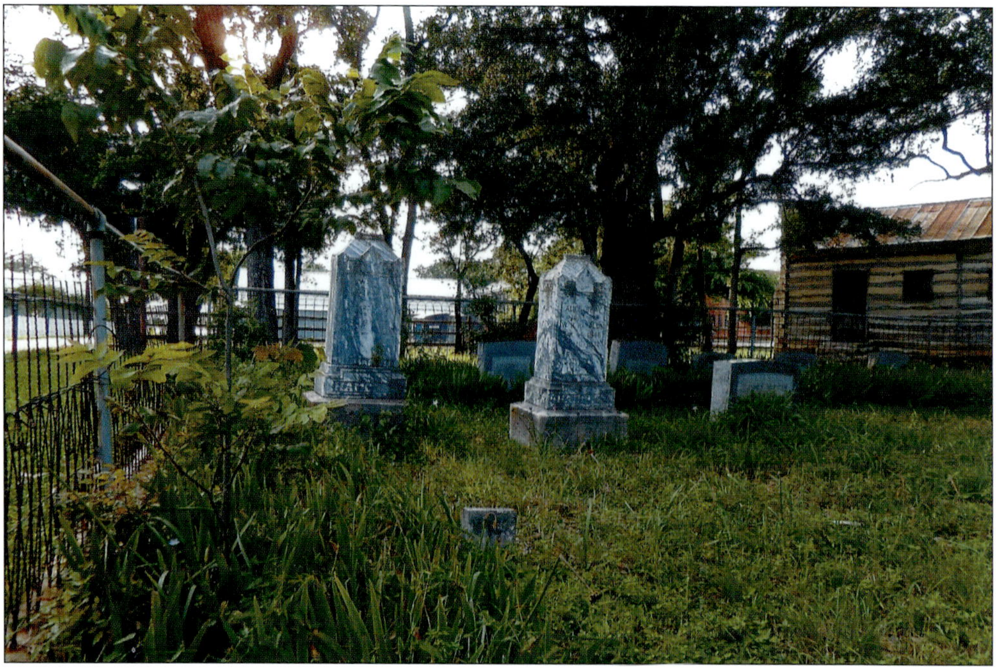

Four

TEMPLE

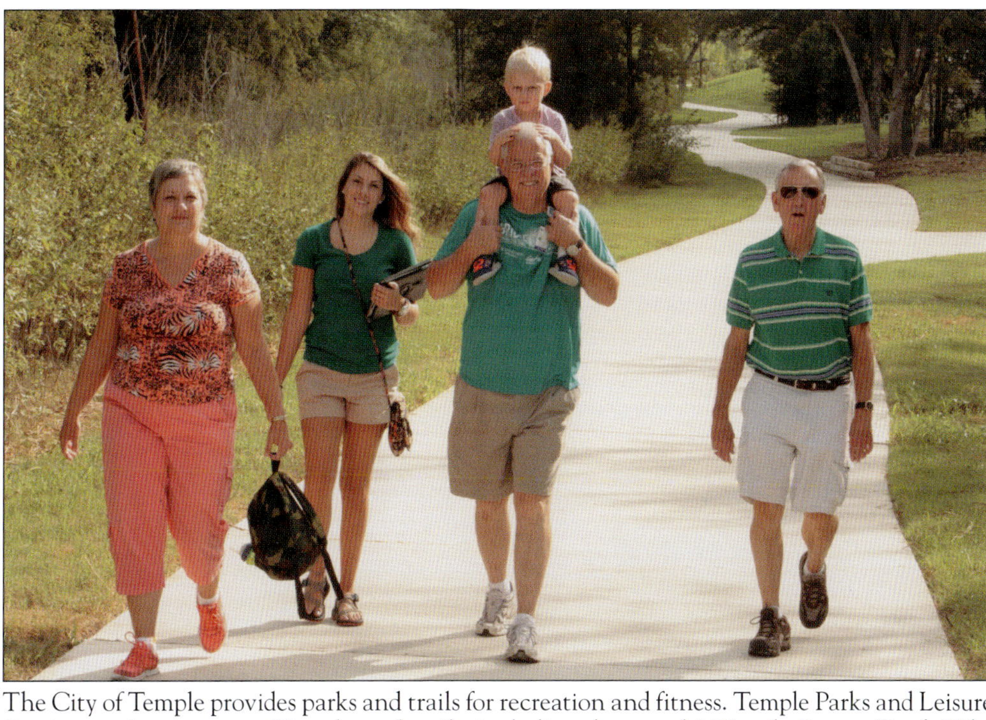

The City of Temple provides parks and trails for recreation and fitness. Temple Parks and Leisure Services maintains some 70 parks and trails, including the paved 1.20-mile Pepper Creek Hike and Bike Trail on West Highway 2305. The trails accommodate pets, joggers, bicyclists, nature lovers, and those looking for serene surroundings. (Courtesy of the City of Temple Parks and Recreation Department.)

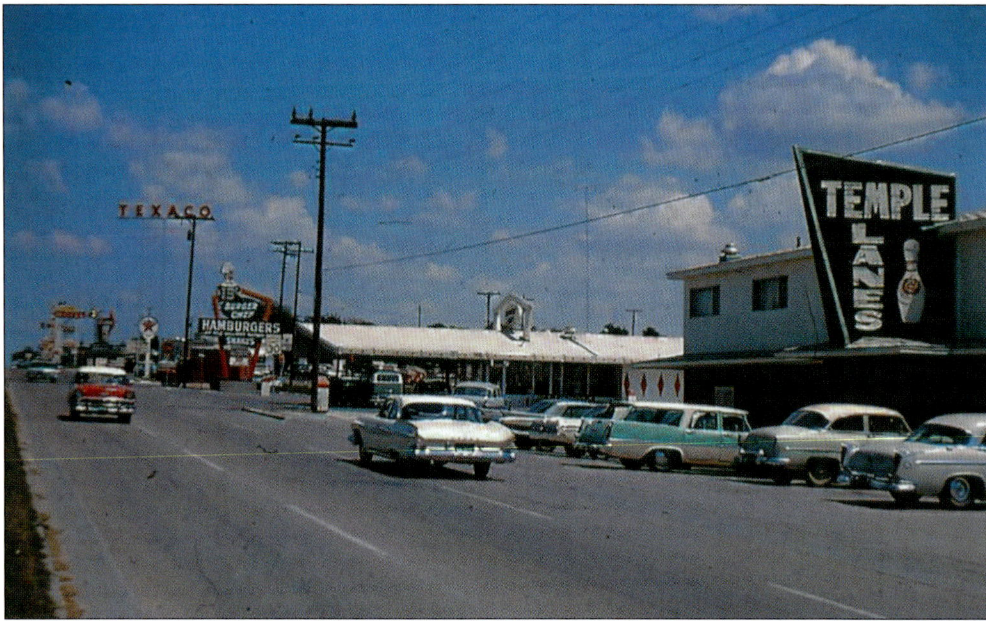

This street scene shows businesses on the east side of Interstate Highway 35 on South General Bruce Drive. The building in the foreground served as a bowling alley for many years until Grammy award–winning Tejano singer Little Joe Hernandez acquired the building to use as his studio and museum. The businesses are gradually being demolished to accommodate widening of Interstate Highway 35. (Courtesy of the Temple Public Library.)

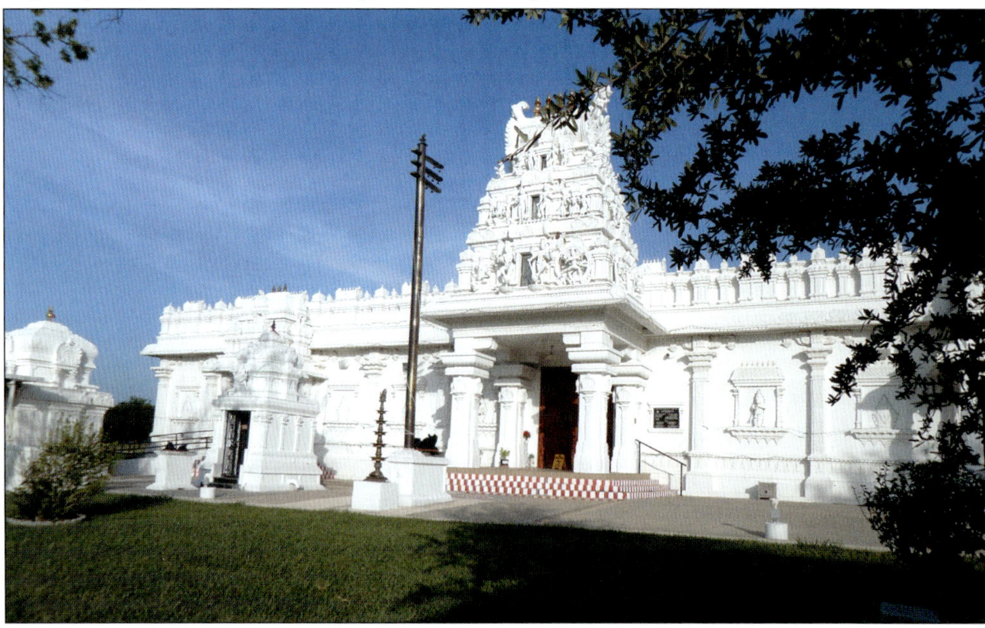

Sitting on 12 acres in south Temple, the 5,000-square-foot Hindu Temple of Central Texas opened in 2001. The Hindu community joined forces to build the complex, which took six years and $2 million to complete. Since its construction, devotees do not have to travel to San Antonio, Dallas, or Houston for meetings and celebrations. A cultural center opened on the grounds in 2005. (Authors' collection.)

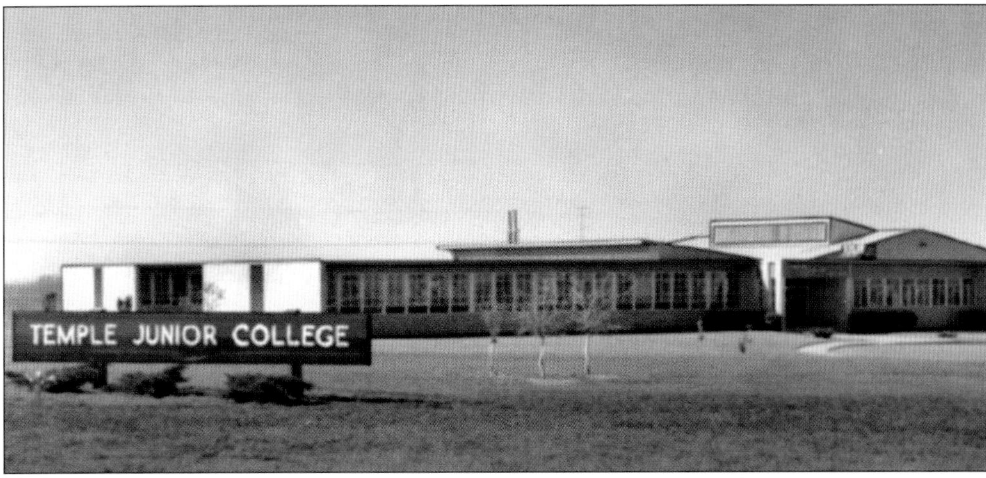

Temple Junior College opened its doors in the fall of 1926 in the basement of Temple High School. Considered a positive alternative to larger educational institutions, junior college afforded youth the opportunity to advance their education and prepare for university life. In 1957, the school moved to its present location on South First Street. The name of the school changed to Temple College in 1996. (Courtesy of the Temple Public Library.)

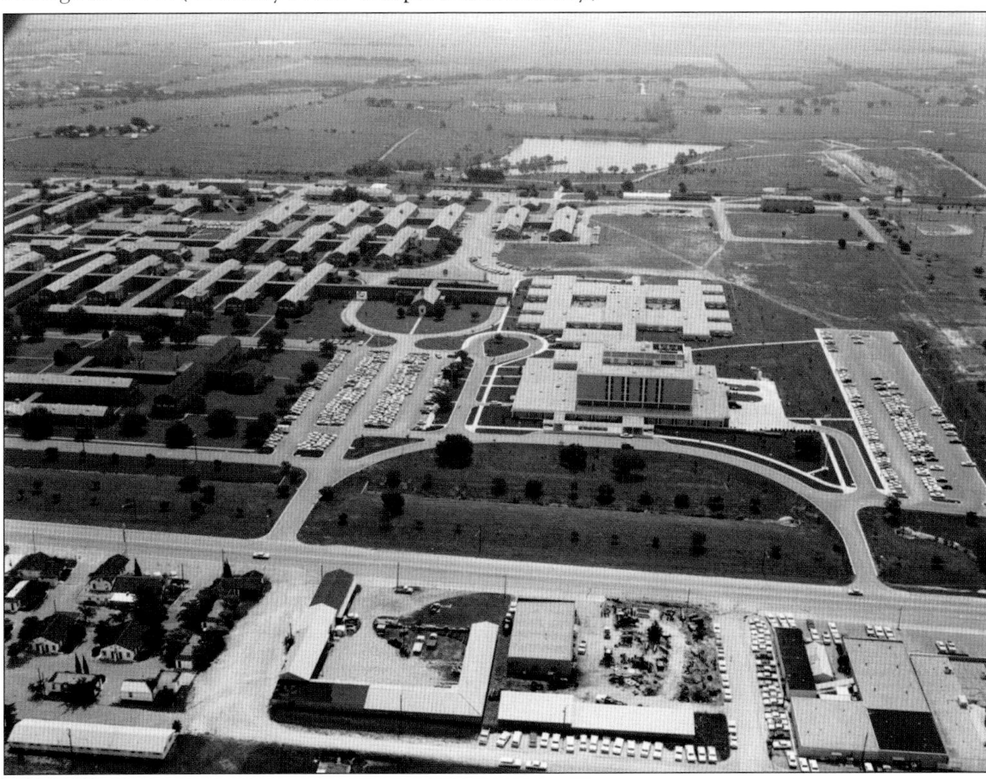

The Temple Veterans Hospital opened during World War II to provide medical care to soldiers injured during the war. The hospital grew to include a teaching hospital, a 408-bed domiciliary, and the 160-bed State Veterans' Home. As part of the Central Texas Veterans Health Care System, the Temple hospital serves more than 252,000 veterans. The original wooden barracks in this 1980s photograph no longer exist. (Courtesy of the Temple Public Library.)

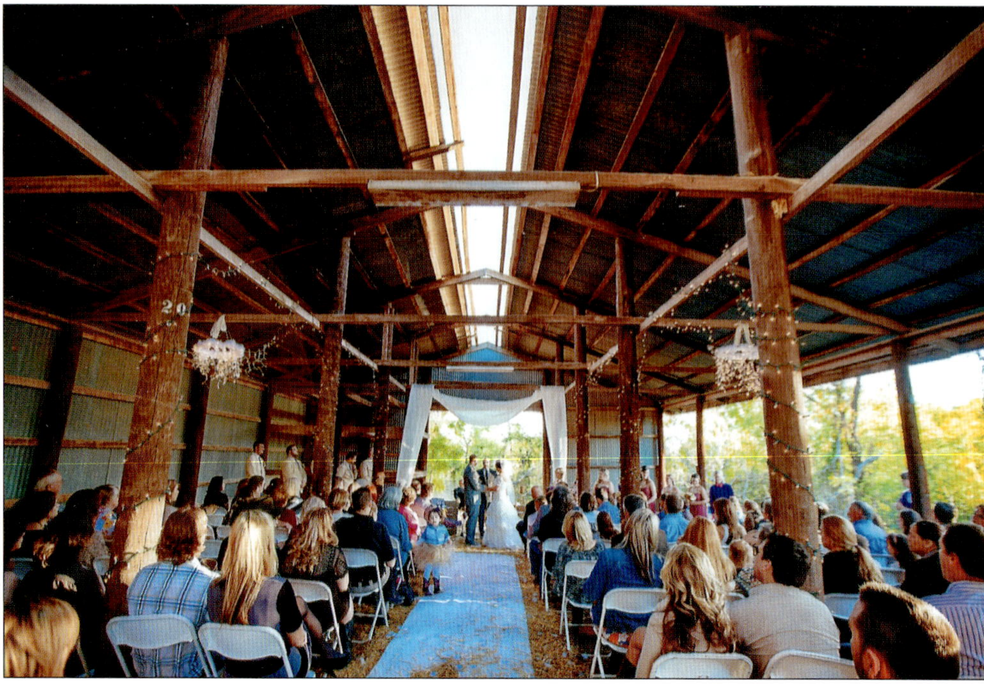

Ara Chelsea and Corey McGregor married at their dream location—Bend of the River Ranch in Temple. The couple described their wedding as homemade, since the couple, their friends, and family served as decorators, band, photographer, videographer, and everything in between. Bend of the River, owned and operated by City of Temple, sits on 30 acres donated by Bernice Talasek in 2011. (Courtesy of Steadfast Media.)

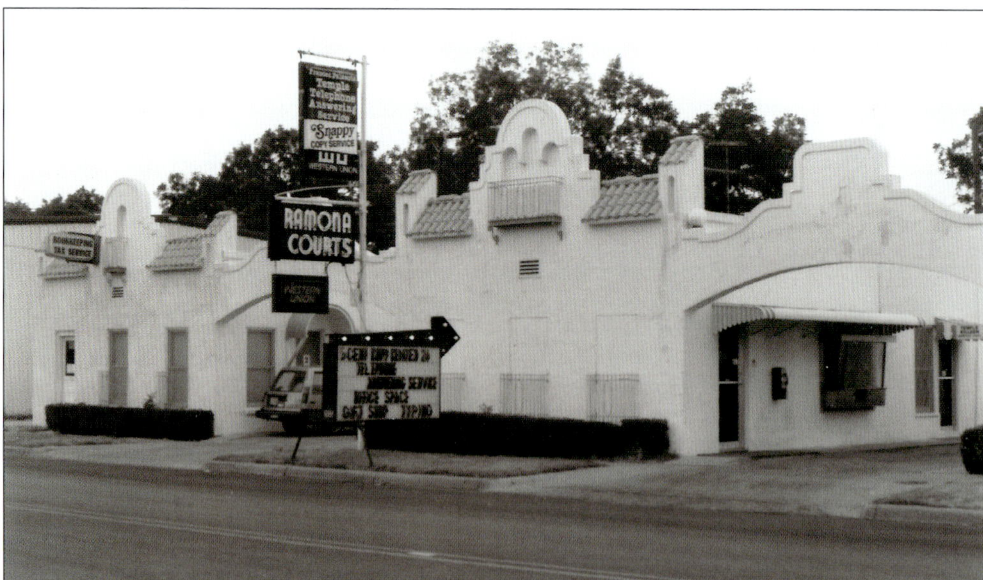

To satisfy the growing demand of the traveling public, in the 1920s and 1930s, tourist courts began to appear. One of the earliest tourist courts in Temple is Ramona Courts, shown here in 1986. Built about 1929, Ramona Courts is on Avenue G, near the old Scott & White Hospital. The lodging consisted of 12 one-story stucco tourist cottages surrounding a courtyard. (Authors' collection.)

Five

Throughout Bell County

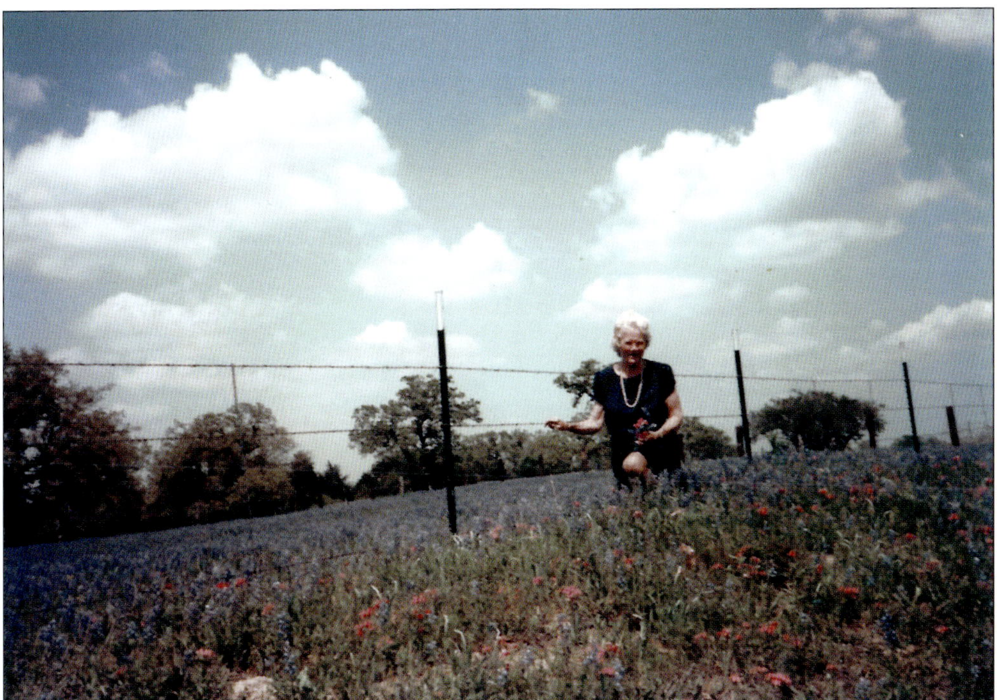

Spring brings a profusion of colorful wildflowers to the Central Texas prairie, and taking family photographs among the flowers is a Texas tradition. Bluebonnets, the state flower, are a favorite subject for photographs. Virginia Graff, at the age of 75, is pictured here in field of wildflowers. (Authors' collection.)

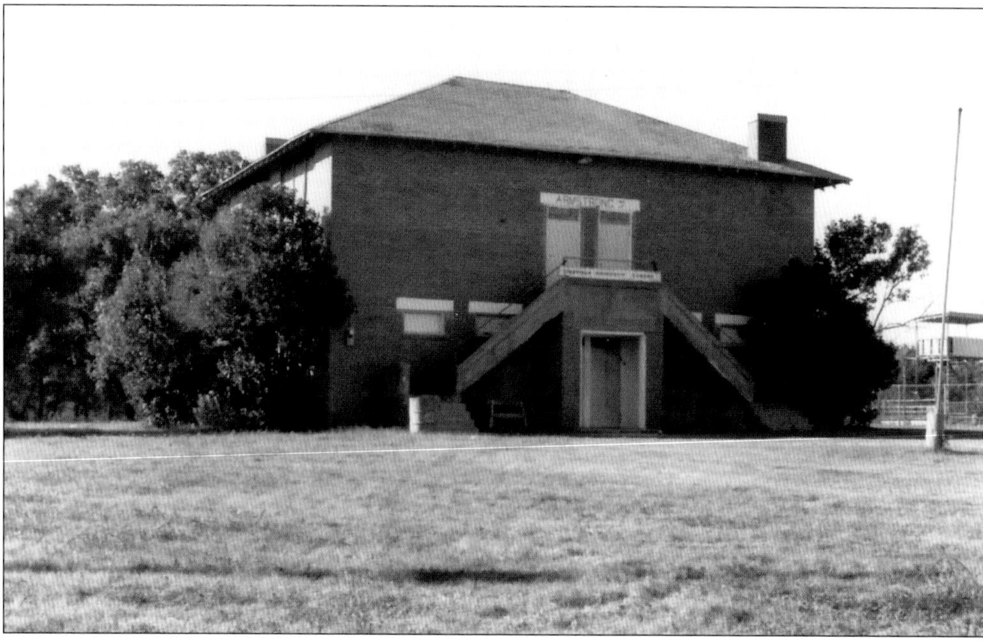

The Armstrong community of irrigated farms, an old mill site, and old pecan and live oak trees stretches along rich alluvial bottomland between the Lampasas River and Salado Creek in southern Bell County. The focal point of the community is the old two-story brick school building that opened on three acres in 1916. The school was the first rural high school in Bell County. Alvah Ferguson, brother of Gov. James E. Ferguson, was instrumental in establishing the school. In 2015, the former school building, pictured above in 1986, serves as a community center. The 1909 school at Bartlett, shown below in 1986, now serves as Bartlett Activities Center. Both are good examples of adaptive reuse. (Both, authors' collection.)

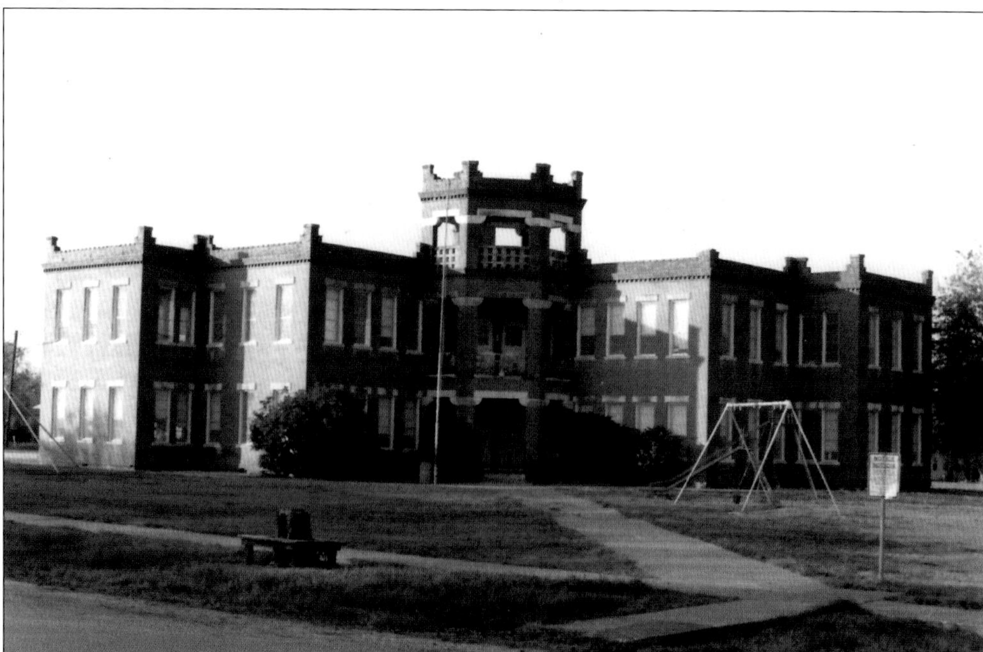

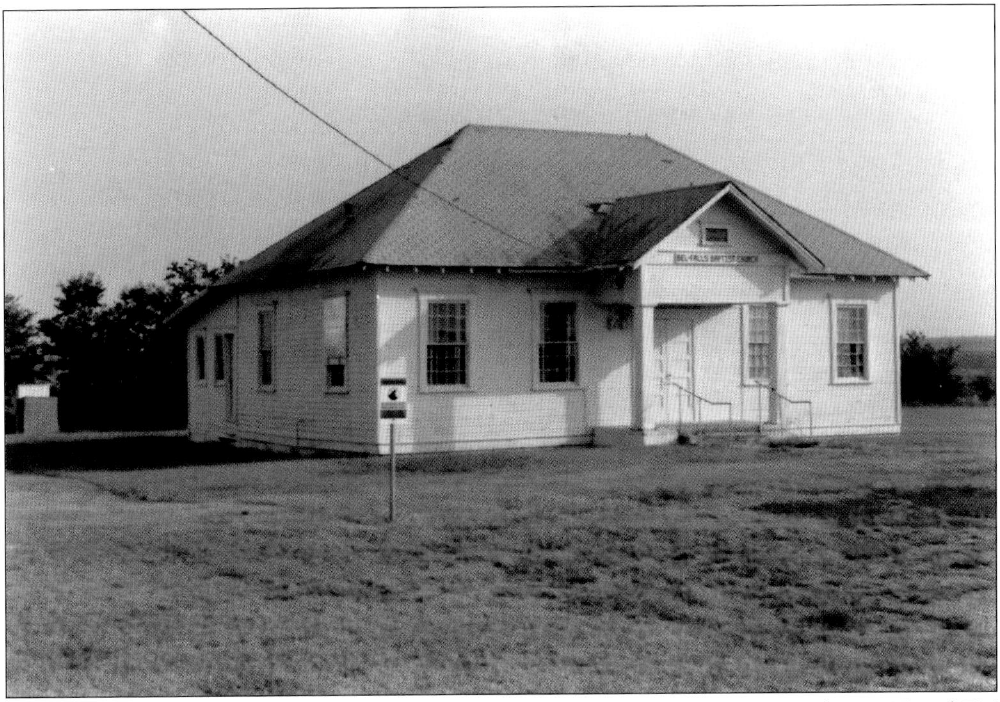

Belfalls is located in the northeastern section of Bell County at the junction of FM 935 and FM 438. The community is on the county line of Bell and Falls Counties, from which it derives its name. The town had two voting boxes, one for Bell County and one for Falls County. It is on the old Belton-to-Marlin Road. Belfalls is in the midst of the fertile blackland. Oats, wheat, corn, and cotton are grown in the area, and dewberries grow wild. Above is Belfalls Baptist Church in 1987. The church was later moved east of Temple and remodeled as a residence. Below is the old abandoned gin as it appeared in 1987. (Both, authors' collection.)

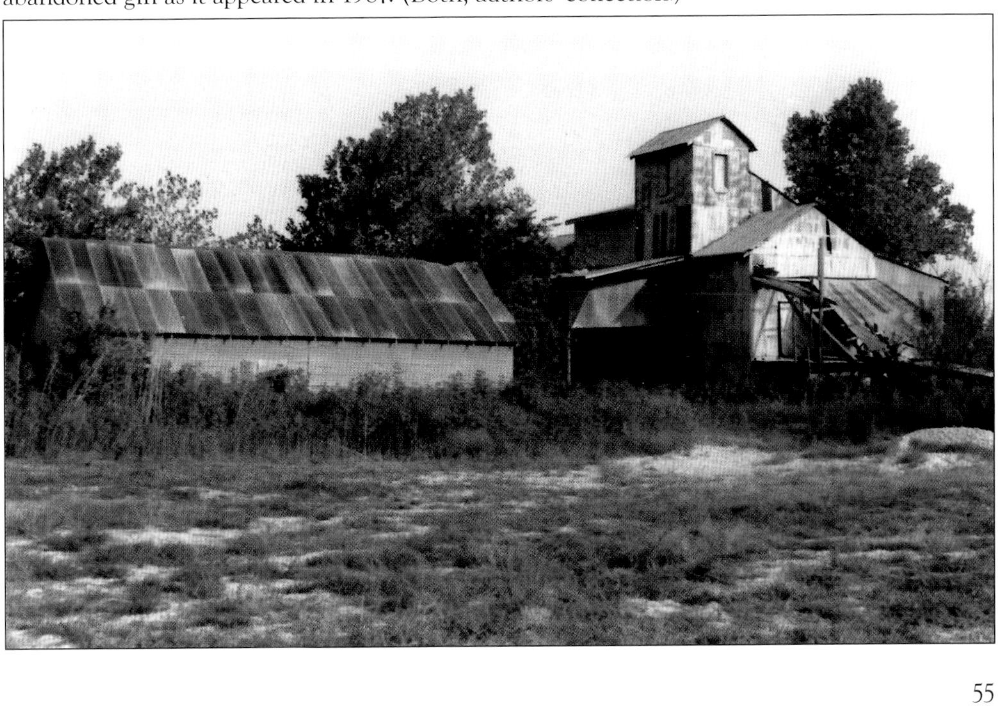

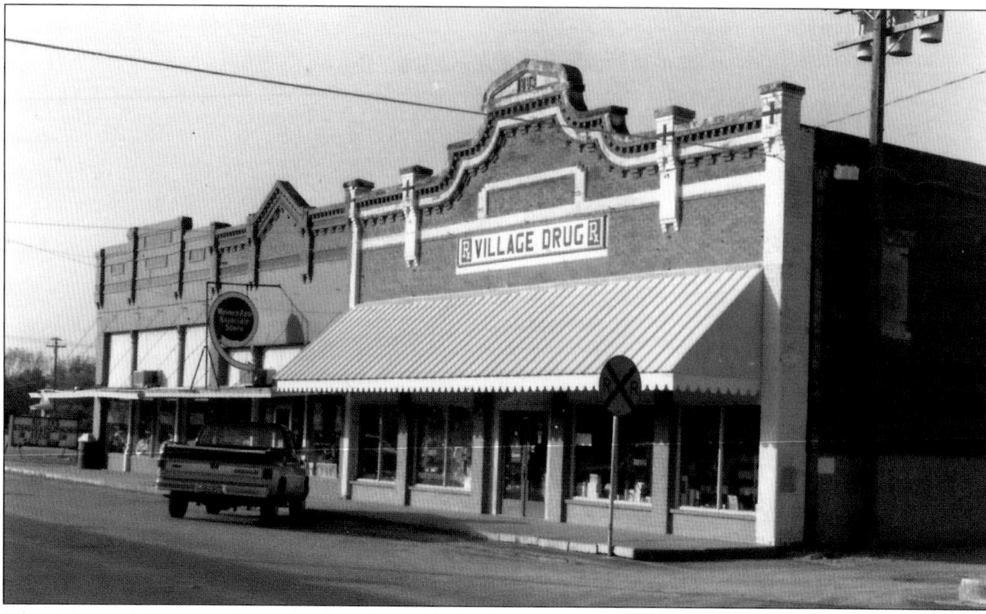

The Missouri-Kansas-Texas Railroad established the town of Bartlett in 1882. The town straddles Williamson and Bell Counties. The first post office was 165 feet from the Williamson County line and served a rural population of 600. The town became a shipping point for cotton and wool. The population of Bartlett reached 300 by 1884 and included a steam cotton gin. There were Baptist, Methodist, Christian, and Presbyterian churches. One hundred years ago, businesses in Bartlett included physicians, dentists, drugstores, hotels, attorneys, compresses, a blacksmith, three banks, a cotton gin, and a photographer. The businesses of the once-prosperous town above are on Clark Street. Below is an old business refurbished as a residence. Both photographs are from 1987. (Both, authors' collection.)

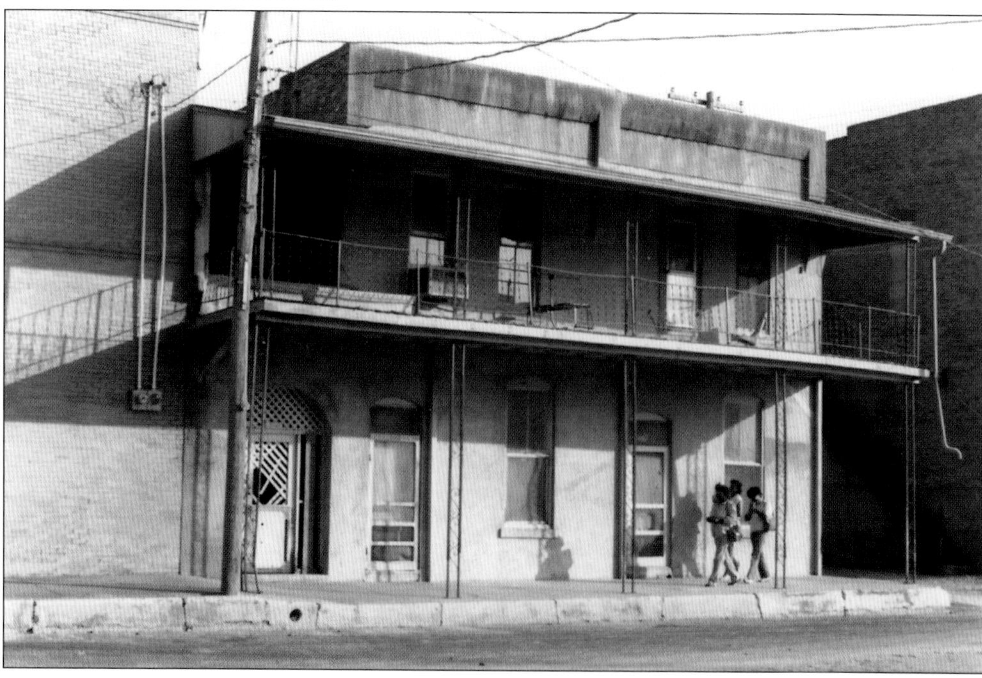

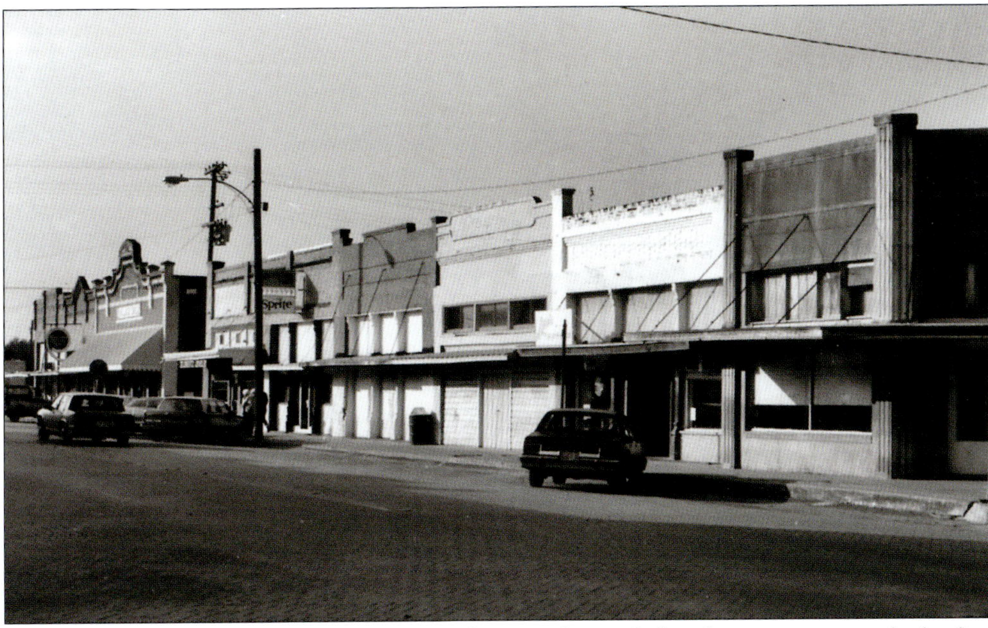

Bartlett had a population of 2,200 in 1915. The town boasted churches representing the leading denominations, electric lights, water works and sewerage, a weekly newspaper, a cottonseed oil mill and compress, a planing mill, and a laundry. In 2013, the population was 2,740, and the old buildings and stately houses in the once-prosperous town were abandoned. (Authors' collection.)

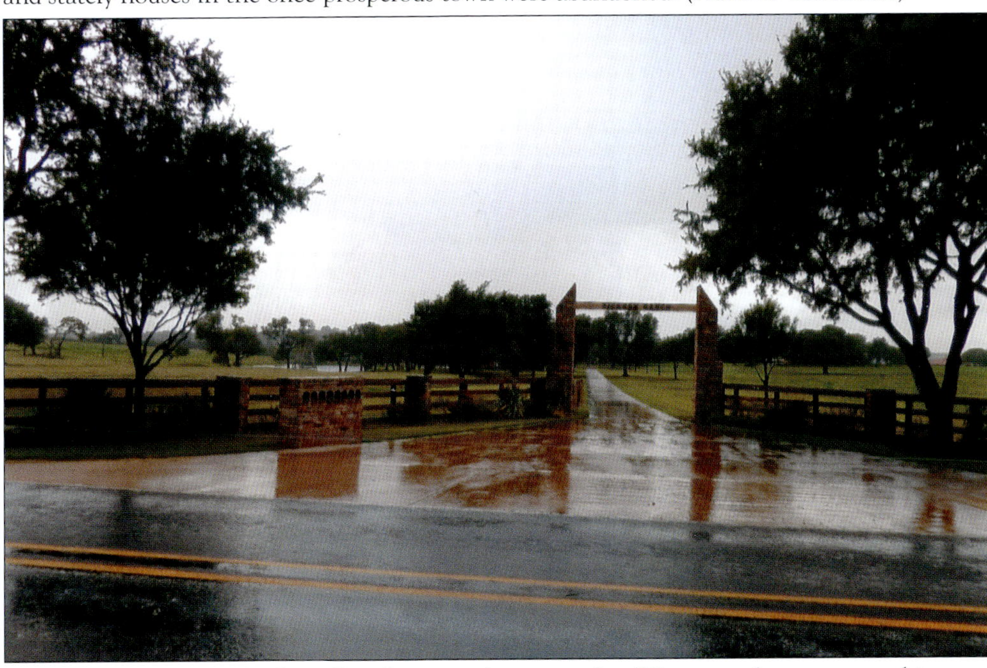

The ranch entrance at Dickson Ranch is a modest example of Texas ranch entrance architecture and includes a gate supported by two stone structures connected by a wood beam. The 400-acre-plus ranch, on Sparta Road west of Belton, sells several varieties of hay produced using the newest technology and inventions in farm equipment suited for hay production. The ranch is a sponsor of Belton's 4th of July Celebration. (Authors' collection.)

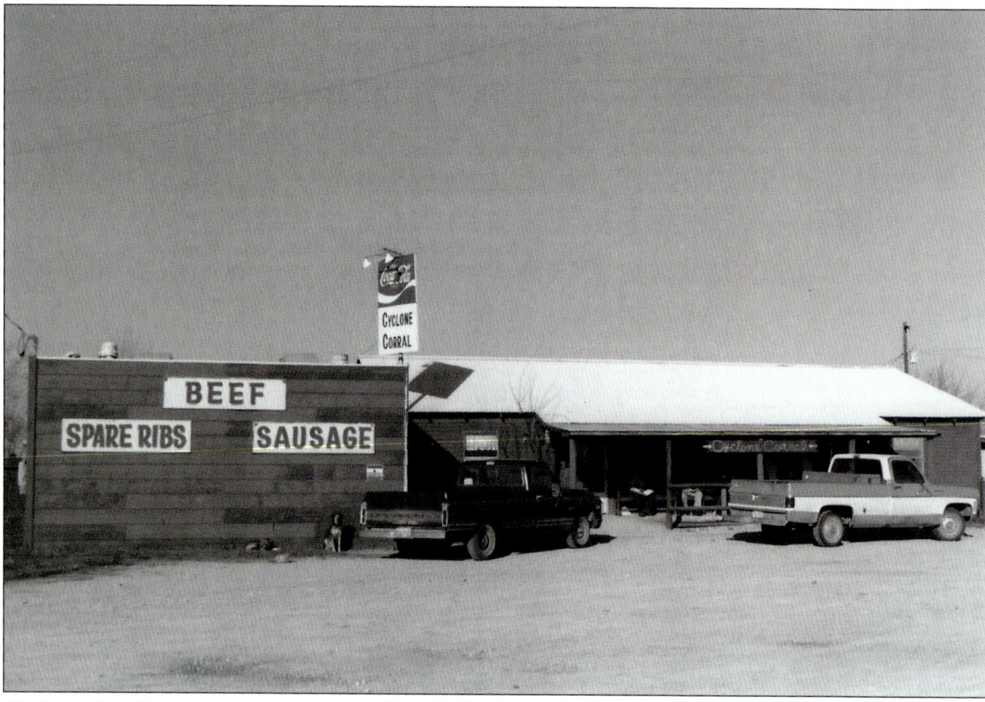

Cyclone is a farming community in East Bell County. A cyclone occurred at Cyclone on May 27, 1905, and caused considerable damage. The recently built Lutheran church was blown of its foundation a distance of 25 feet. Several other buildings were also damaged. No one was injured. Despite its name, the community had never known a severe windstorm before. In 1985, there was one business in Cyclone, the Cyclone Corral store (above). (Authors' collection.)

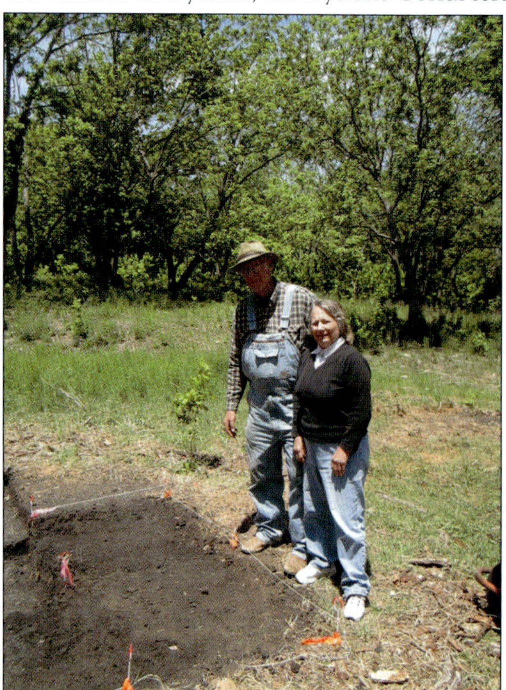

West of Salado is the Gault Site, a major Paleo-Indian base camp and stone tool manufacturing center during the Clovis Culture about 13,000 years ago. Recently discovered evidence of settlement roughly 13,500 years ago challenges the long-held belief that Clovis was the earliest human settlement in the Americas. Dr. Michael Collins of Texas State University discusses his work at the site with Nancy Kelsey in 2013. (Authors' collection.)

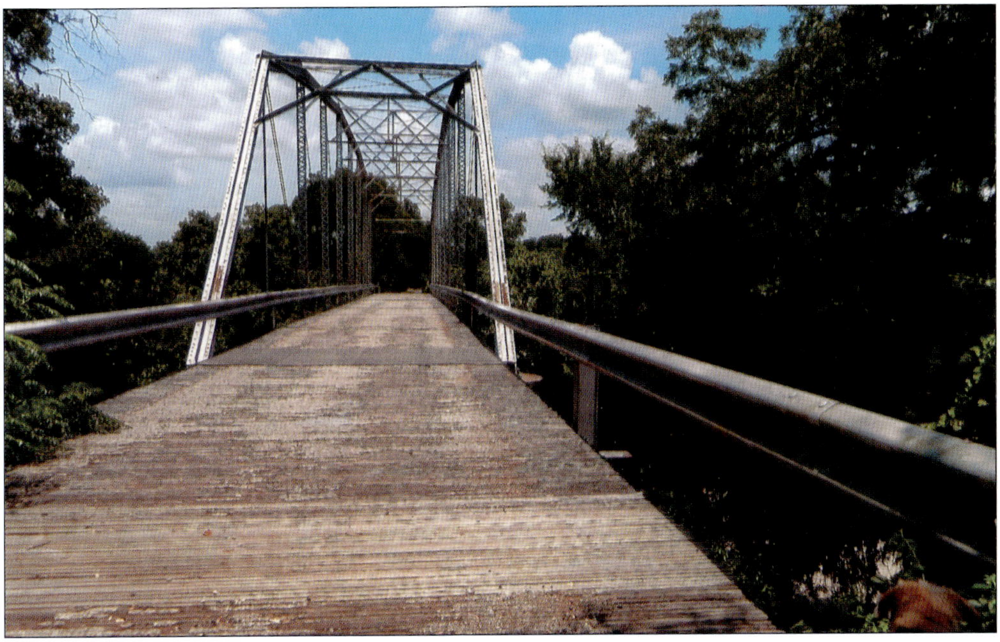

The Maxdale community is on the Lampasas River in West Bell County. The 1883 application for a post office described Maxdale as "a storehouse in the midst of a thin settlement." Wheat, oats, grain, and corn were the primary crops. All that remains of the community are a church, bridge, and cemetery. Hess & Skinner Engineering Company built the steel-truss bridge over the Lampasas River in 1914. Planking set edgeways added strength to the bridge floor. The bridge is no longer in use. Maxdale Cemetery was established about 1863 to serve the community of Pleasant Grove, located east of Maxdale. Joe Wilson, age 81, has mowed the cemetery for 20 years. He lives nearby and has family buried in the cemetery. (Both, authors' collection.)

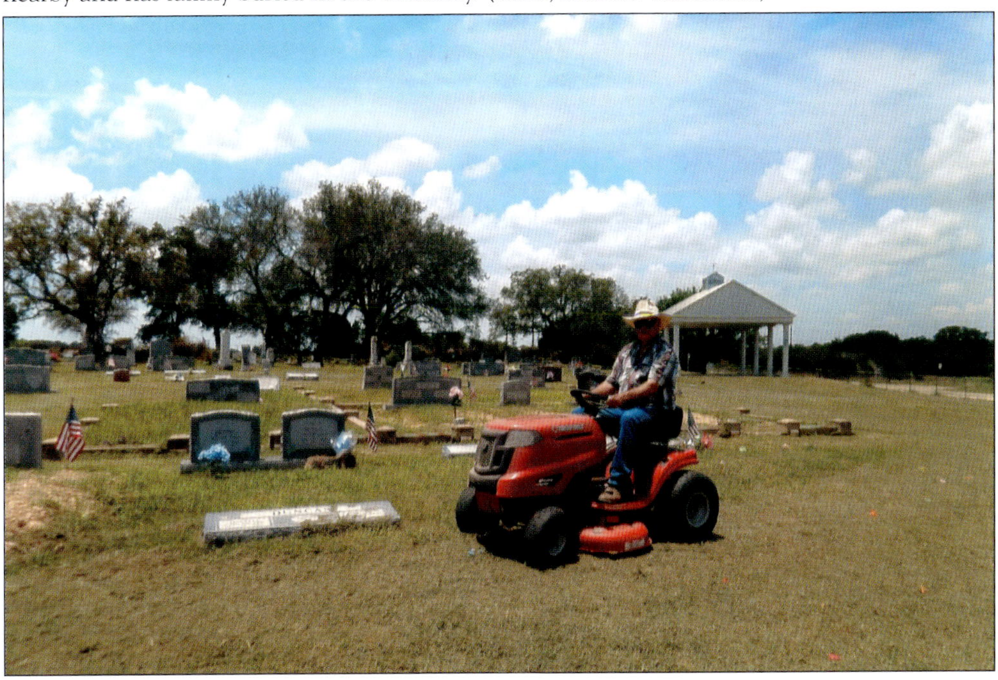

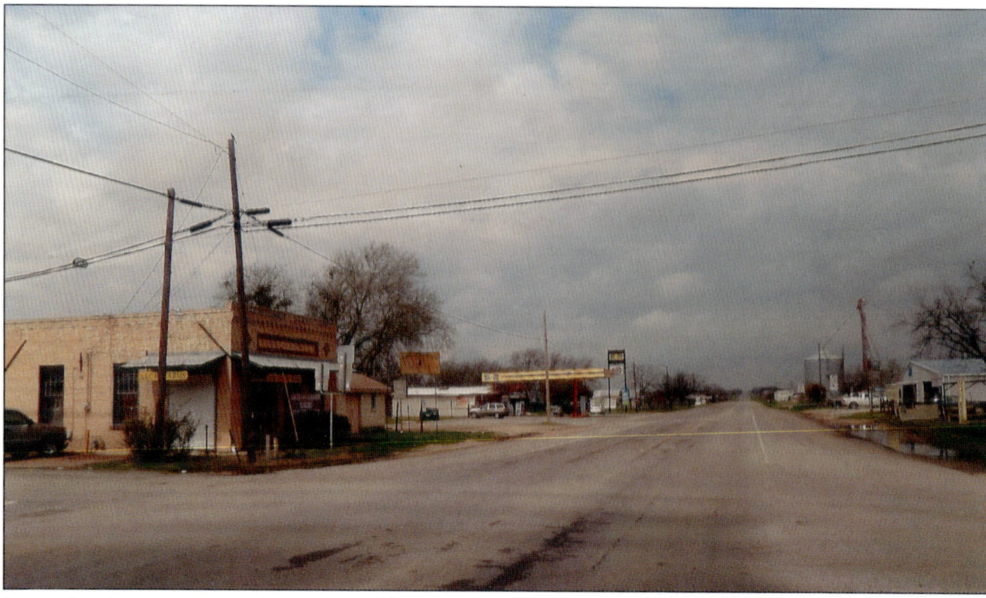

Named in honor of Santa Fe Railroad director Sampson Heidenheimer, the town of Heidenheimer is located about 4.5 miles southeast of Temple on US Highway 190. The railroad established the town in 1881, when the railroad came to Bell County from Galveston. The lands surrounding Heidenheimer are of the blackest and richest variety, suitable for growing cotton and corn. The population of Heidenheimer in 1925 was 250. In 1948, the population was 125, and there were seven businesses, three churches, and two schools. By 1990, the population was 144, and businesses declined to two. The above photograph shows downtown Heidenheimer in 2015. Pictured below in 1986 is the Bel-Hi Grocery, which sold groceries, ice, newspapers, and Fina gas. (Both, authors' collection.)

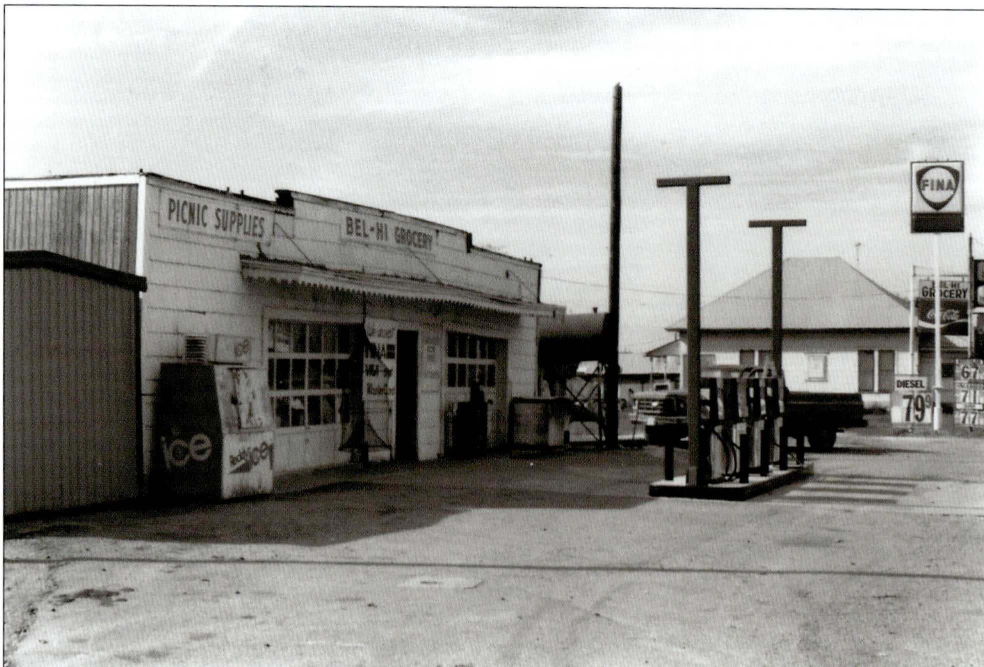

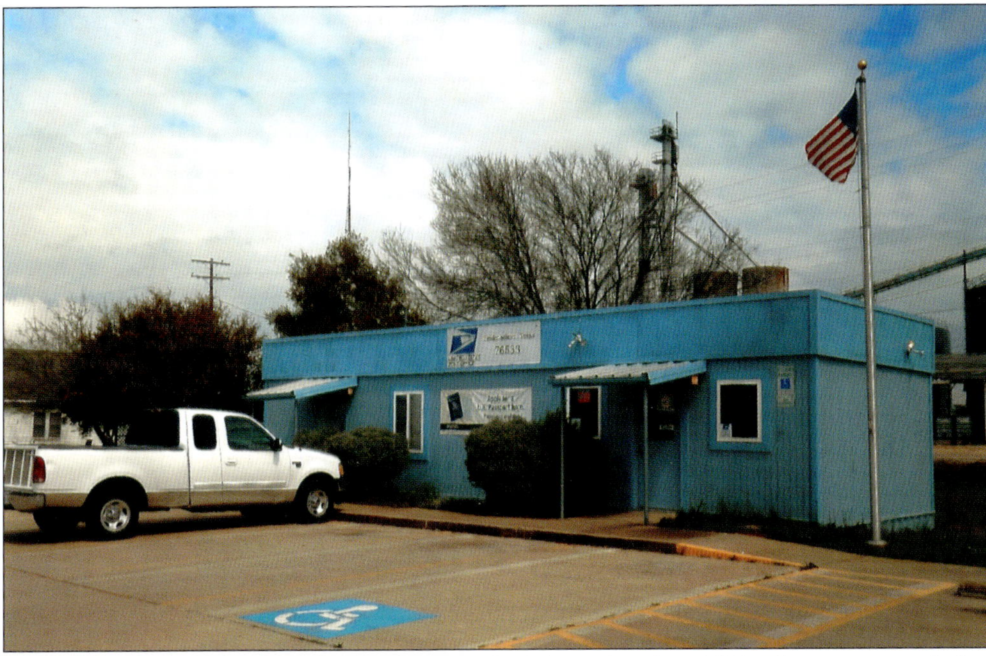

Heidenheimer was established with the arrival of the railroad in 1881. The community's first post office opened the same year and served between 2,000 and 3,000 people, 142 of these living within half a mile of the post office. Presently, the post office on US Highway 190 occupies a blue prefabricated unit and serves a rural population. (Authors' collection.)

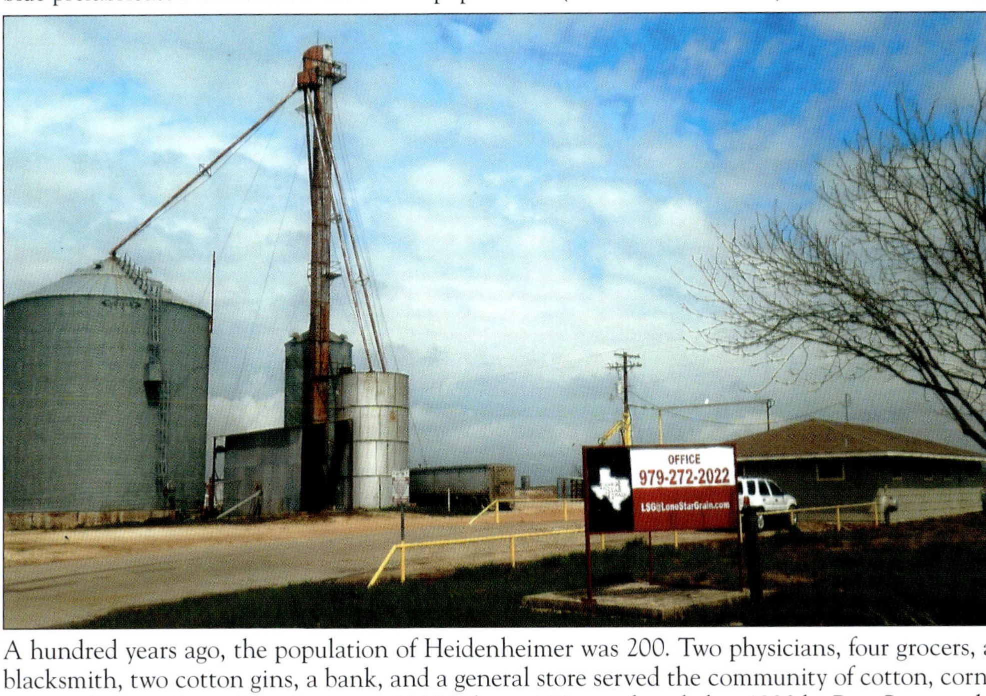

A hundred years ago, the population of Heidenheimer was 200. Two physicians, four grocers, a blacksmith, two cotton gins, a bank, and a general store served the community of cotton, corn, and oat farmers. Lone Star Grain, on US Highway 190, was founded in 1990 by Pete Scarmardo and serves the farming community. The grain elevator is one of five owned by the company in Central Texas. (Authors' collection.)

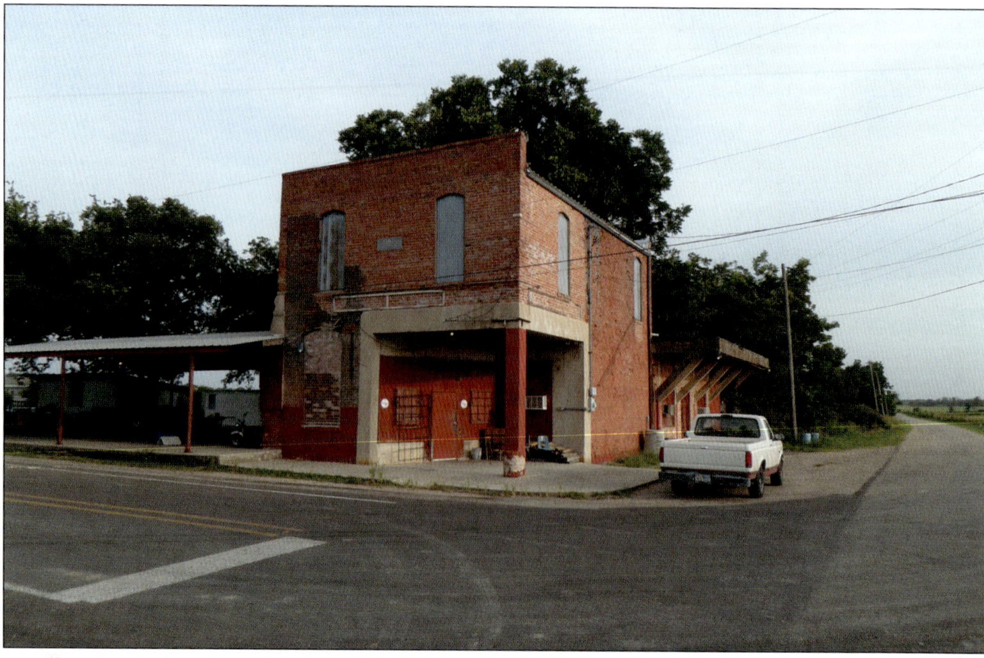

Pendleton, until 1908 known as Pendletonville, was founded in 1882 by the Gulf, Colorado & Santa Fe Railroad. William Gilmore owned the land where Pendleton was to be located, but he refused to sell to the railroad. George C. Pendleton, later lieutenant governor, who had a store in Old Howard, bought Gilmore's land and sold it to the railroad and moved his stock of goods to Pendletonville. The photograph above captures the remains of the last occupied brick building in Pendleton, the Leon Masonic Lodge No. 193, built in 1931. The building demonstrates the deterioration of the town in 2015. Pendleton Cemetery, shown below, sits on a prominent hill about one mile from town. On the distant horizon, a train approaching the town can be seen. (Both, authors' collection.)

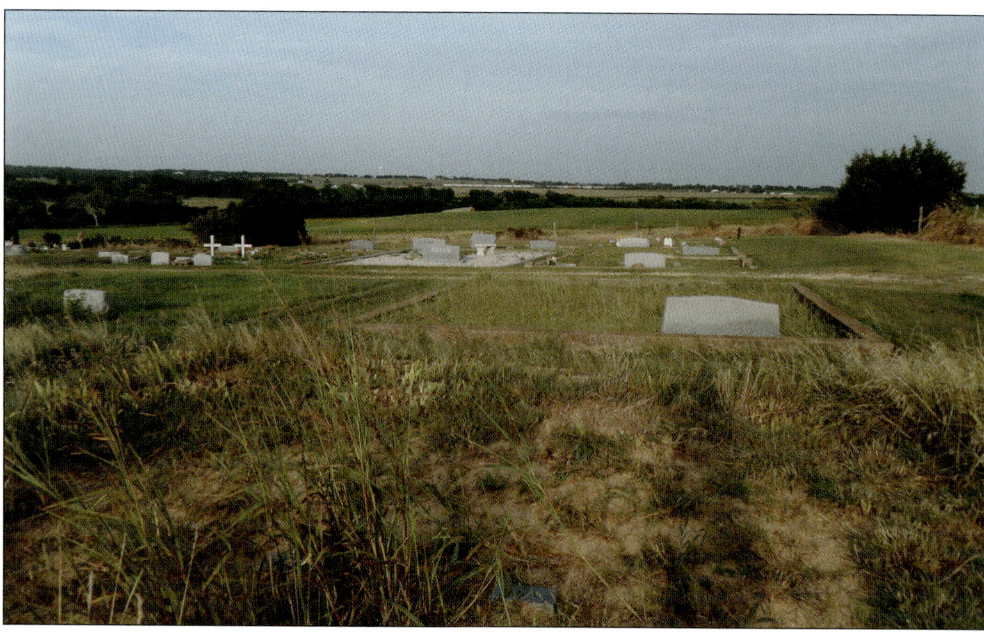

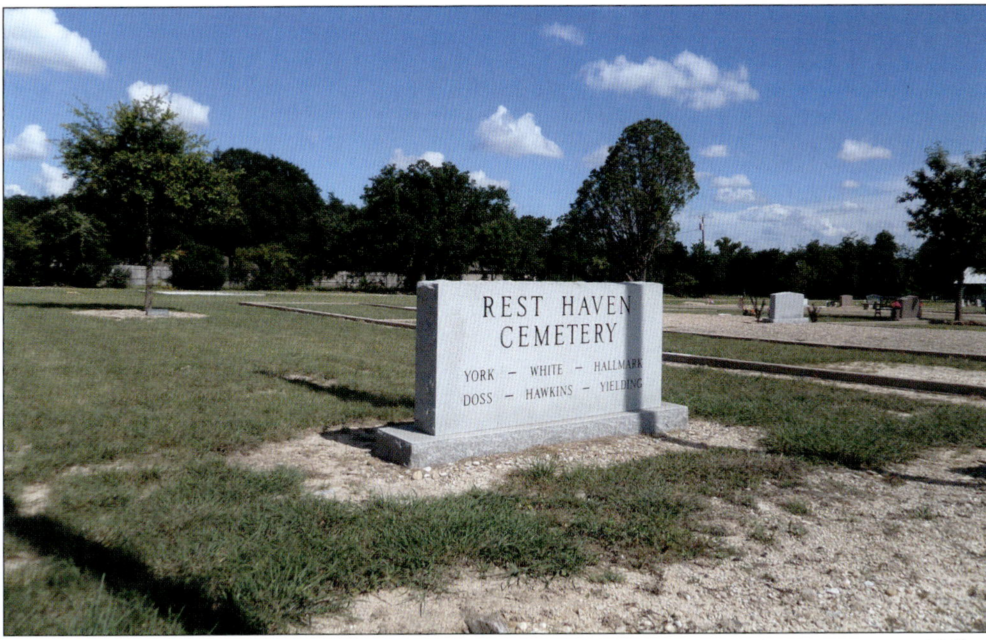

Construction of Belton Lake in 1953 forced the removal of 1,087 graves from Tennessee Valley, Denman-Walton, Liberty Hill, Hawkins, York, White, and Yielding Cemeteries. Newton and Luckey Funeral Home, under contract with the Corps of Engineers, moved, plotted, and marked each grave at the new 10-acre Resthaven Cemetery, located about two miles south of Belton at Shanklin Road and Interstate Highway 35. The contractor placed granite markers to designate main sections of the cemetery, completed gravel streets, installed a water system with faucets throughout the cemetery, placed cattle guards at entrances, and planted shrubbery. The old tabernacle moved from Tennessee Valley Cemetery, below, provides shelter at the cemetery. (Both, authors' collection.)

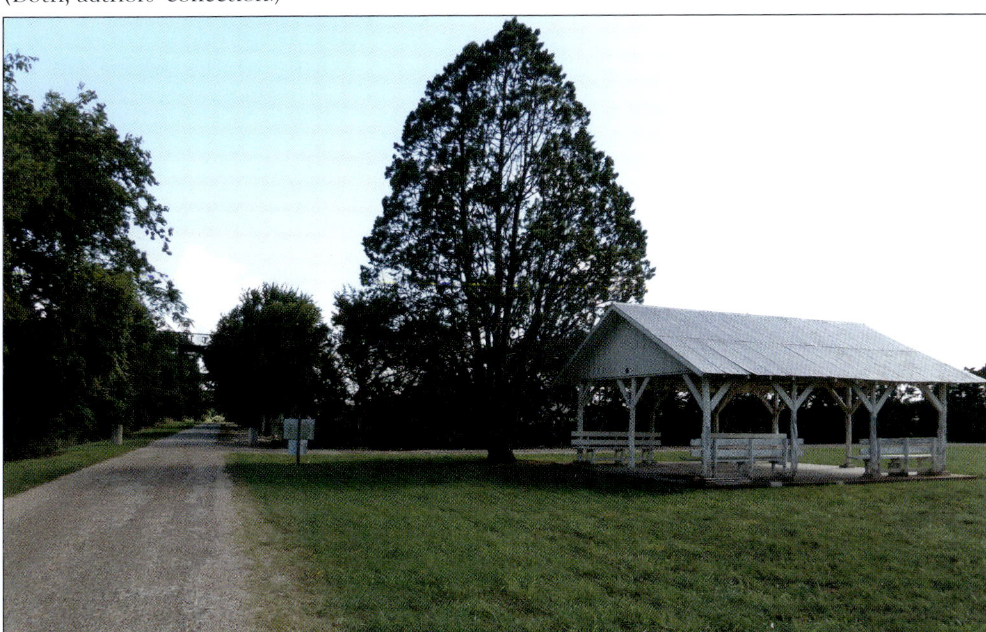

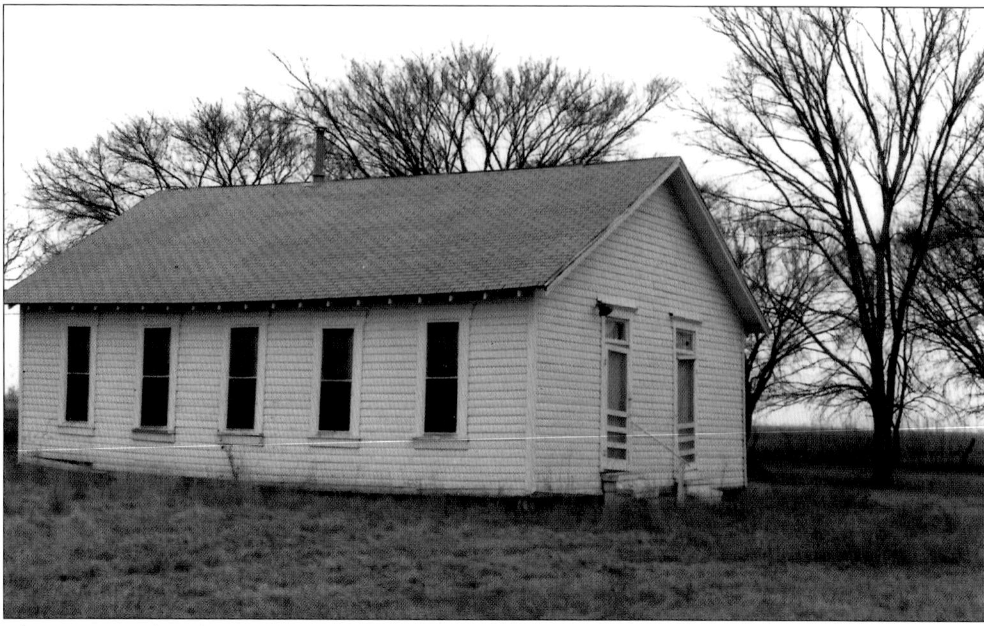

The country church is probably the most common social institution found in rural America. A declining rural population had a direct impact on the support and membership of churches in farming communities. The Bell County countryside has numerous neglected, abandoned, and forgotten rural churches, such as Stockton Methodist Church, above, located on Siler Road in the farming community of northwestern Bell County. The photograph was taken in 1987. Pictured below in 1990 is Willingham Springs Baptist Church, in southwestern Bell County. Over the years, attempts have been made to revitalize the church. (Both, authors' collection.)

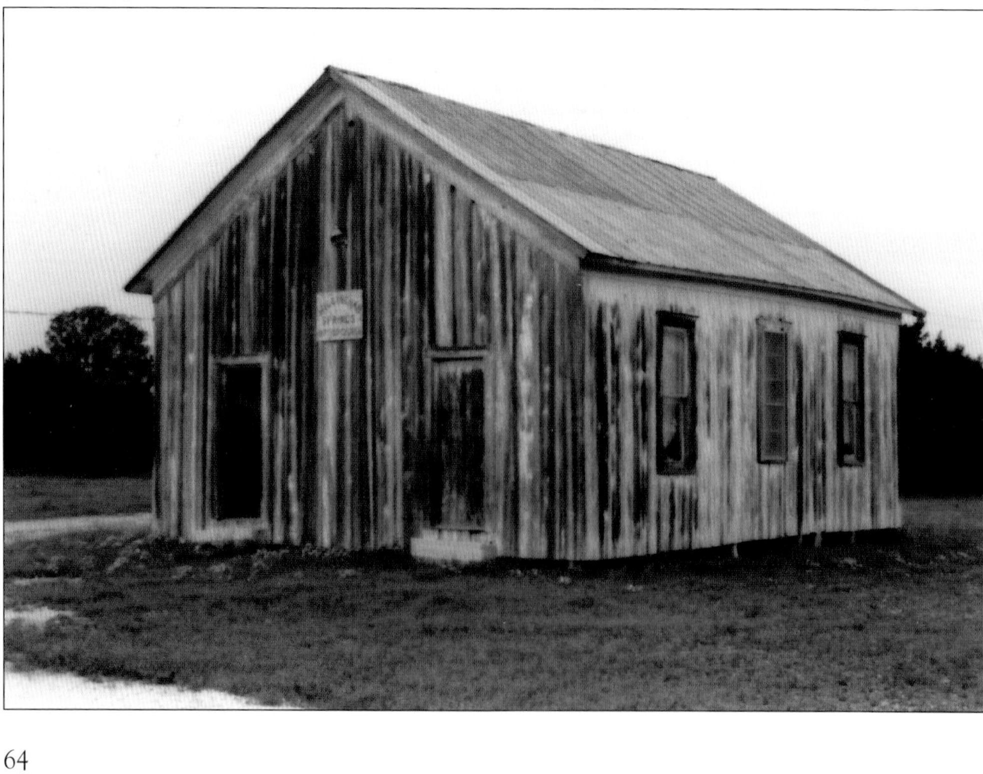

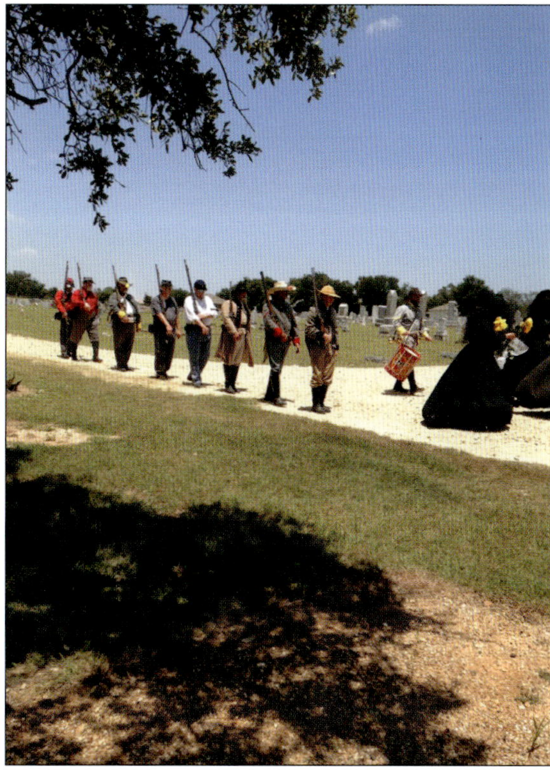

Margaret Sprott's ancestors lived in Texas during the Republic of Texas and the Confederacy. She was a member of United Daughters of the Confederacy. When she died in 2014, her son carried out her wishes with a service honoring her heritage. Members of the Order of Confederate Rose dressed in mourning clothes placed yellow roses at her grave. She received a 21-gun salute. (Authors' collection.)

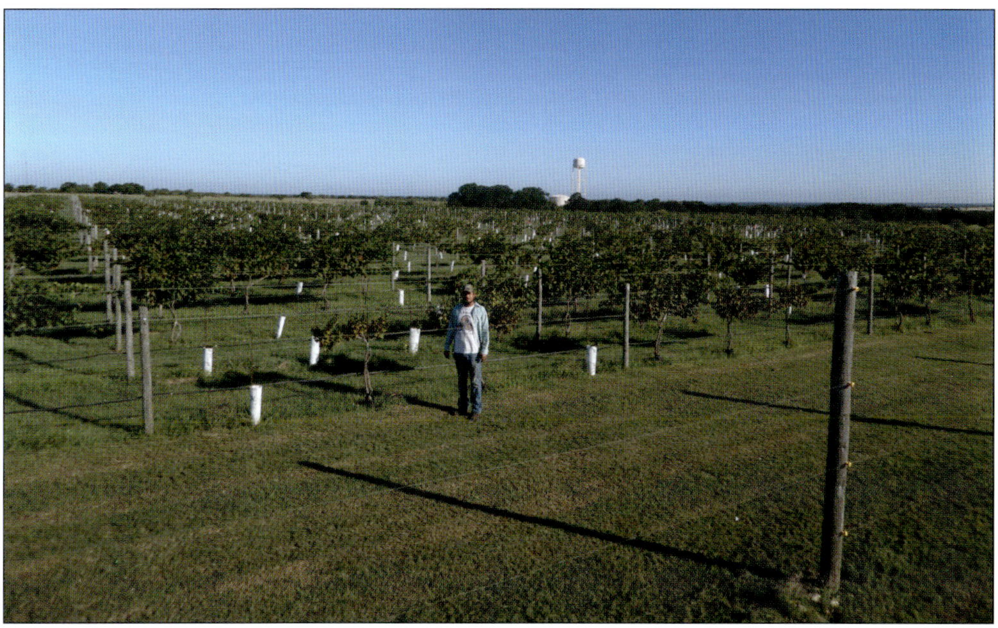

In 1881, when Daniel Taylor opened the Moffat distillery, capable of producing 50 gallons of whiskey and consuming 25 bushels of corn daily, Moffat residents objected to the distillery using the name "Moffat." Attitudes and taste changed in the 129 years after Taylor bottled his "corn squeezins." In 2010, the 3 Texans Vineyard was established. Today, Bacchus rules the spheres of Moffat. Oscar Resendiz, pictured here, works at the vineyard. (Authors' collection.)

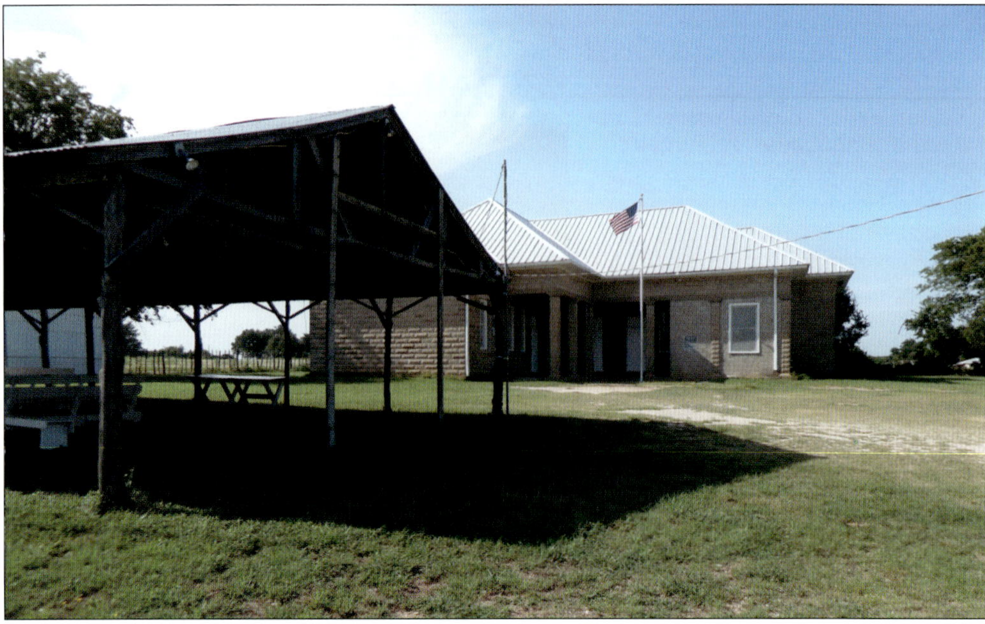

Moffat, on the Leon River 13 miles north of Belton, is one of the oldest towns in the county. For many years, harvesting posts from nearby cedar breaks was a thriving industry. The cedar industry also supplied Christmas trees. In 1878, there were 60 students attending school in Moffat. A new school erected in 1881 burned in 1886. Now used for community activities, the building pictured above was originally a school built around 1910. The Upton family owns and operates Lone Star Burgers out of a metal trailer at their home in Moffat. They have lived in their home for three years and opened the business in early 2015. The mother and father do the cooking, and the children take food orders. There are four outdoor umbrella-covered tables. (Both, authors' collection.)

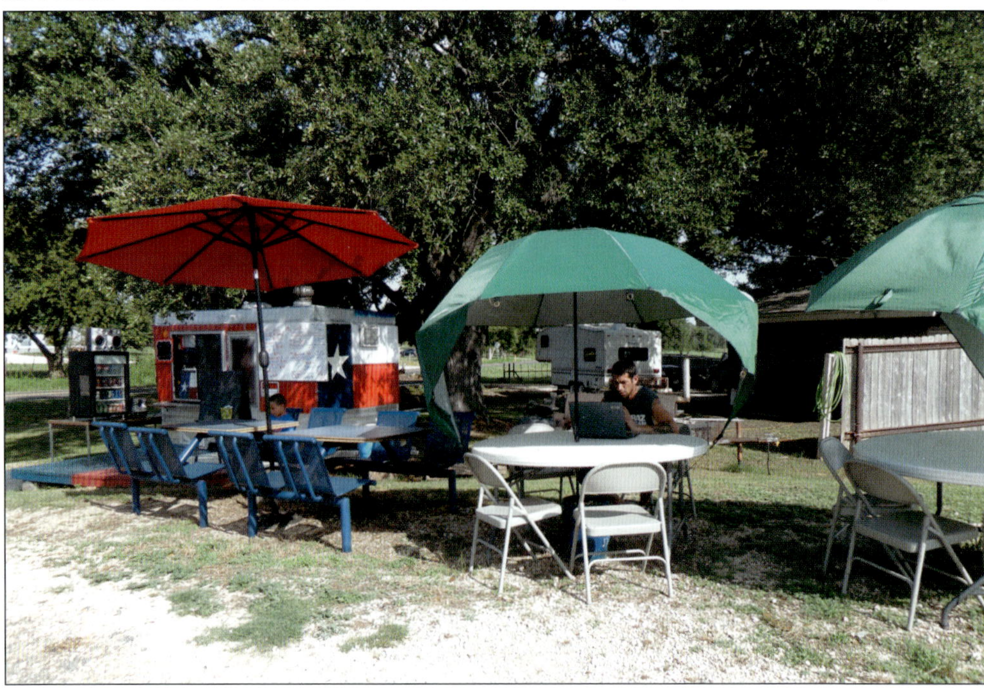

A new kind of Christmas tree business opened when Marilyn and Bob Garber purchased a 12-acre farm near Moffat in 2000. They restored the farmhouse and turned the historic property into a Christmas tree business, Silo Christmas Tree Farm. A silo located on the farm was the inspiration for the name. Besides selling Christmas trees, the Garbers conduct field trips on the property. (Authors' collection.)

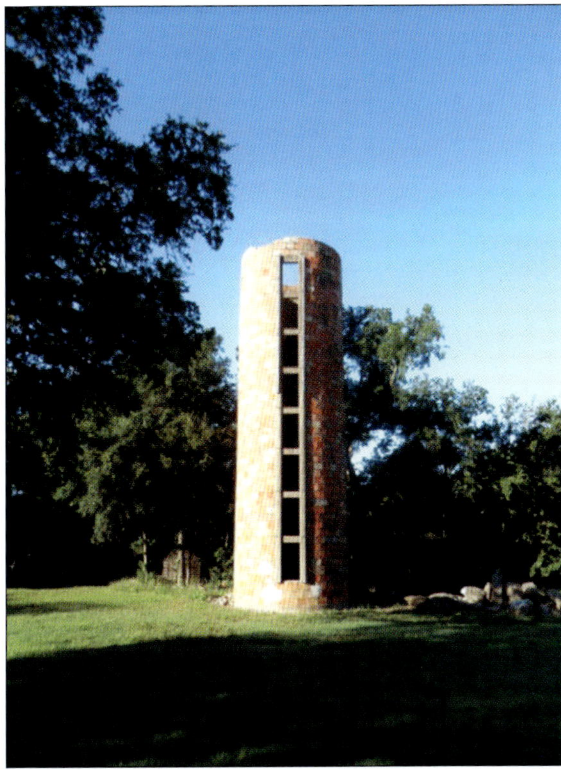

Military exercises take place regularly in Bell County. Convoys such as this one on State Highway 36, near Rogers, are a familiar sight. The Texas Highway Department designated State Highway 36 as a memorial to the 36th Division in 1944, and the 67th Texas Legislature funded marking the road in 1981. (Authors' collection.)

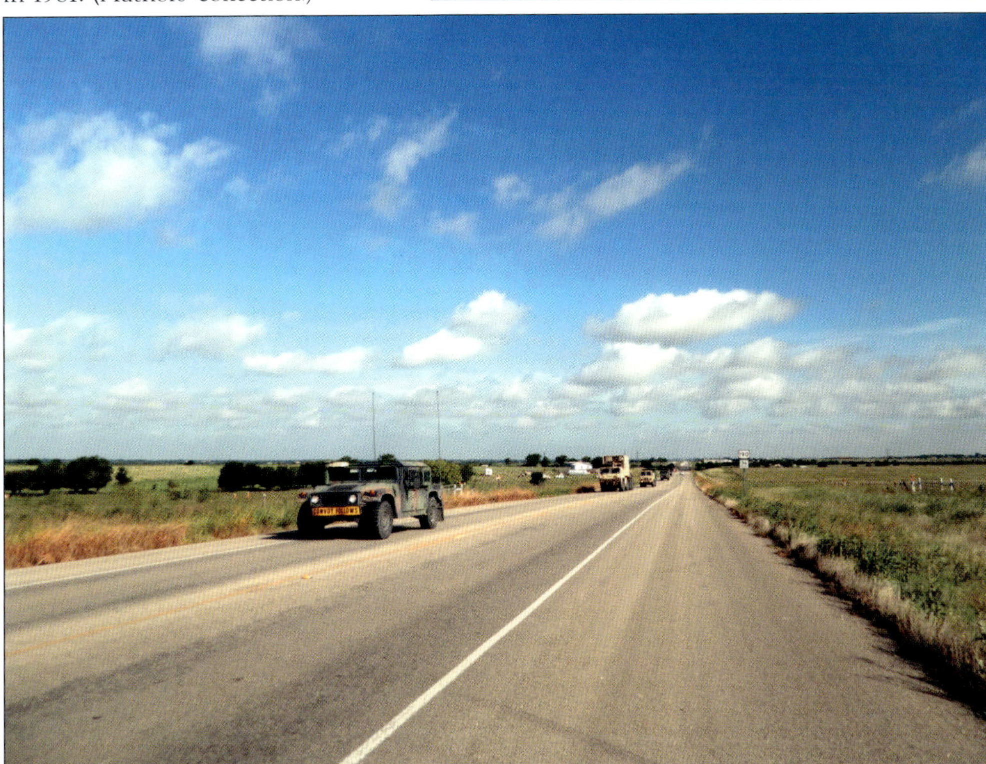

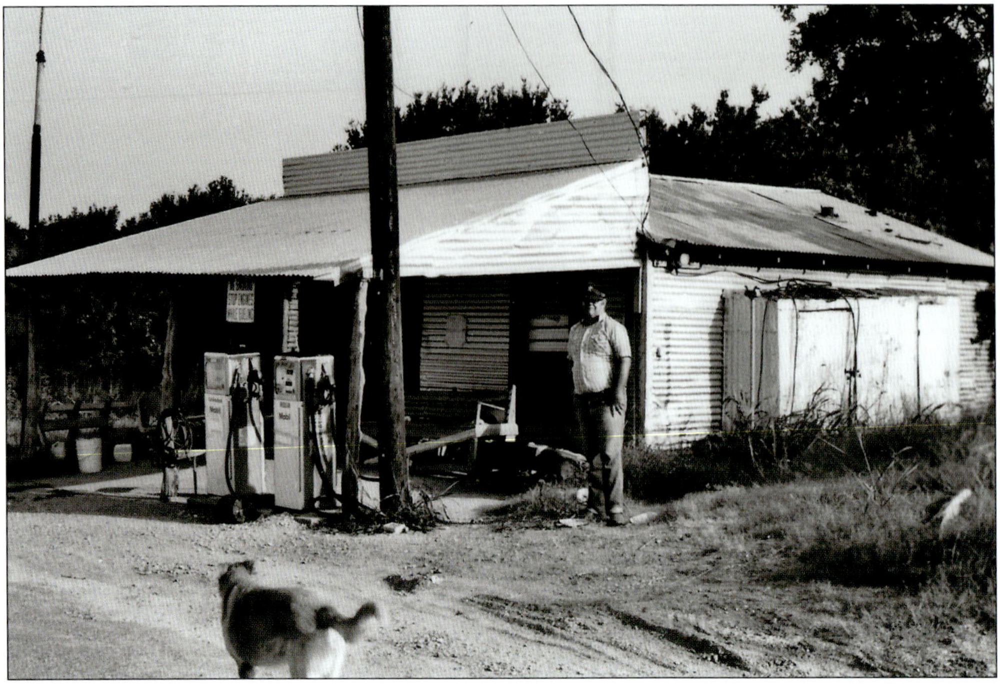

The farming community of Oenaville is located on FM 3369 in East Bell County. There are at least three versions of how Oenaville received its name. One version is Oenaville was named for Oena Griffin. Another version says that Oenaville was given its name when Cullen D. Johnson was appointed postmaster there in 1872. He had the new post office christened Oenaville after a town in his native state, probably in Alabama. Another version is that a young man, who came from another state, named the area Oenaville after his girlfriend Oena. In 1914, Oenaville boasted a population of 200 and included five general stores and the Ewing Drug. Above, Roy's Garage, built about 1946, is pictured here in 1987. Below, the Shell convenience store, across the street from Roy's Garage, now sells gas at Oenaville. (Both, authors' collection.)

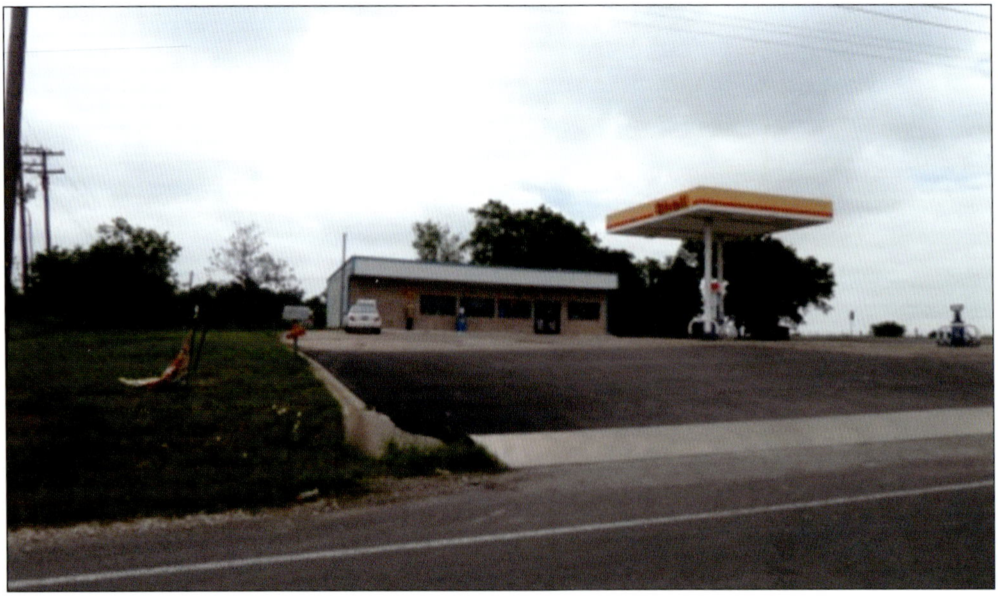

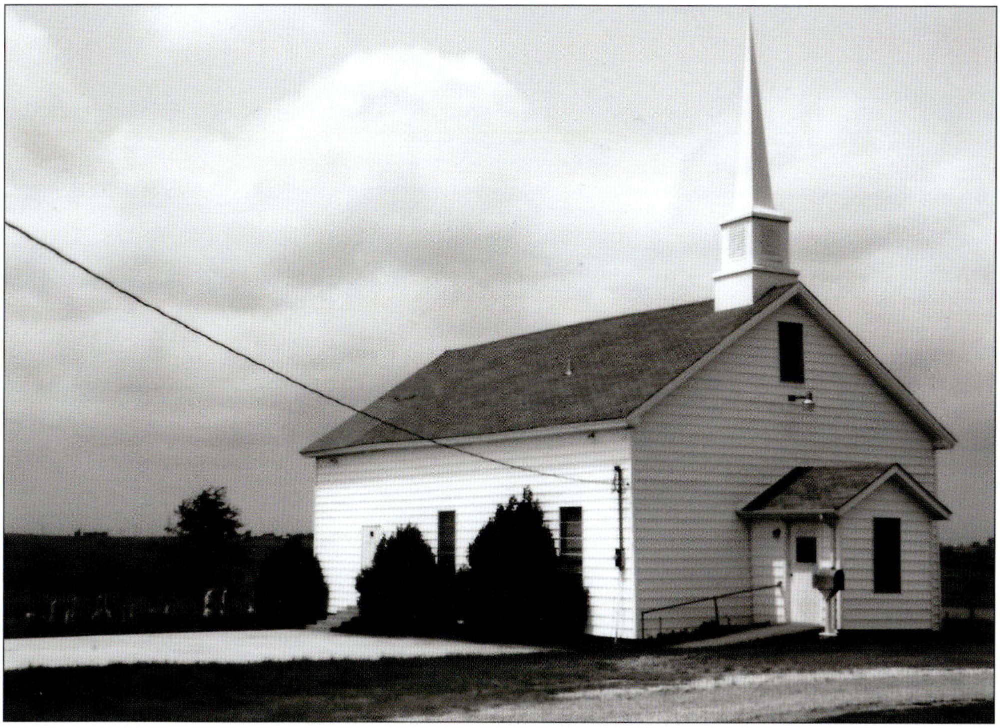

The farming community of Dyess Grove received its name from John Dyess, an early settler. F. Simonton and Peter Houston operated stores in the community in the 1890s and the Smith brothers in the 1920s. The gins of Jacob & Little and McVeigh served the community. Dyess Grove Baptist Church organized in 1895, and a church was built in early 1896. The photograph is from 1987. (Authors' collection.)

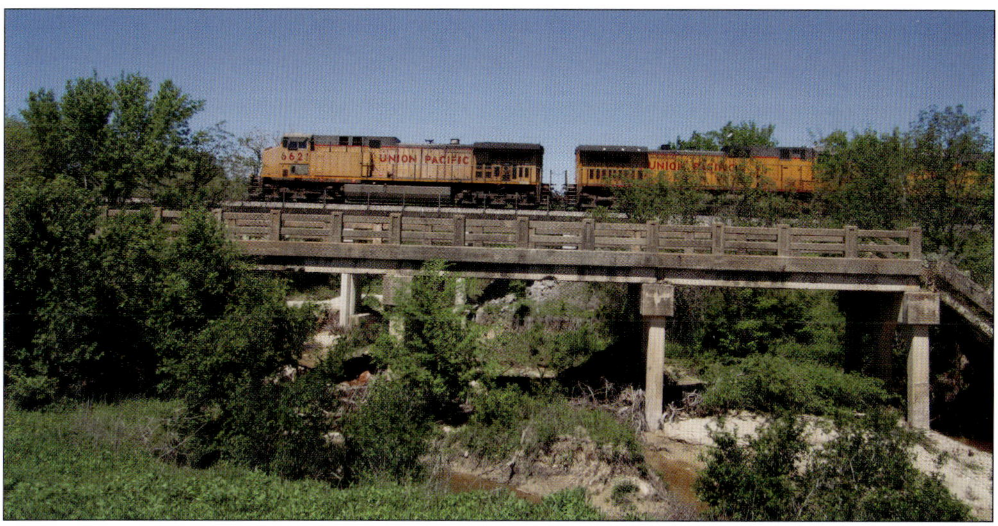

Trains first traversed Bell County in the early 1880s. Across the county, trains are seen carrying items such as coal and military equipment. Traveling over the route of the railroad tract laid in 1882, this photograph shows a modern train behind an old highway bridge on the road that paralleled the track. The north end of the highway bridge has collapsed and is visible to the right. (Authors' collection.)

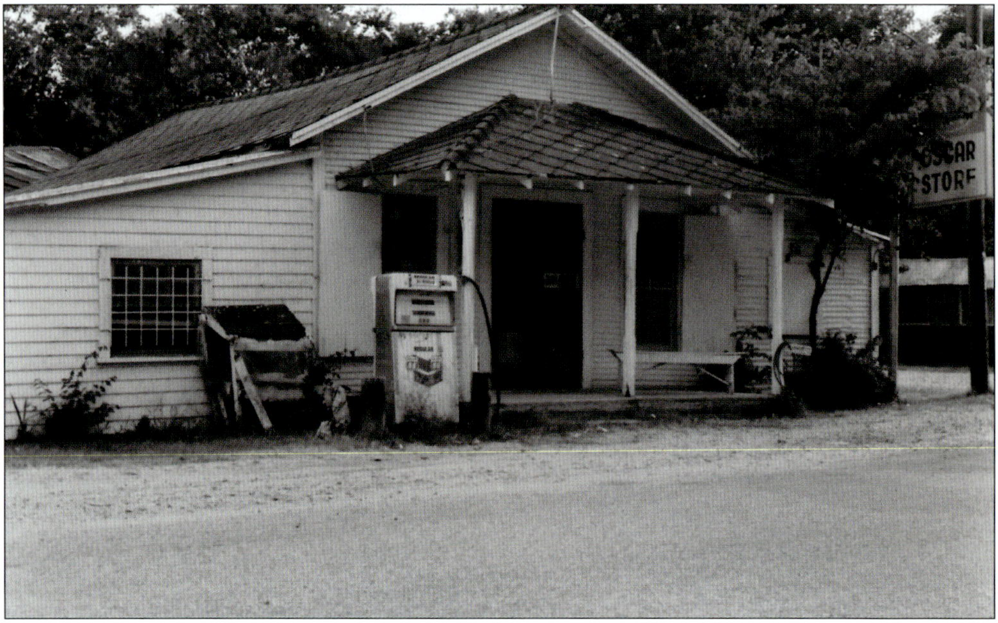

First known as Jones's Gin, Oscar developed around a gin owned by W.H. Jones. In 1891, this East Bell County farming community consisted of a gin, mill, school, and church, all within a quarter of a mile of each other. Rudy and Grace Schiller ran Oscar Store, established in 1934. Oscar Store became popular in the 1970s for family gatherings and turkey shoots. After the store, pictured above in 1986, burned to the ground in 2005, Thomas Maddux took advantage of the historic and nostalgic nature of the old structure and rebuilt on the site of the old store. The new Oscar Store, below, opened in 2009 and includes a restaurant, bar, and meeting rooms. (Both, authors' collection.)

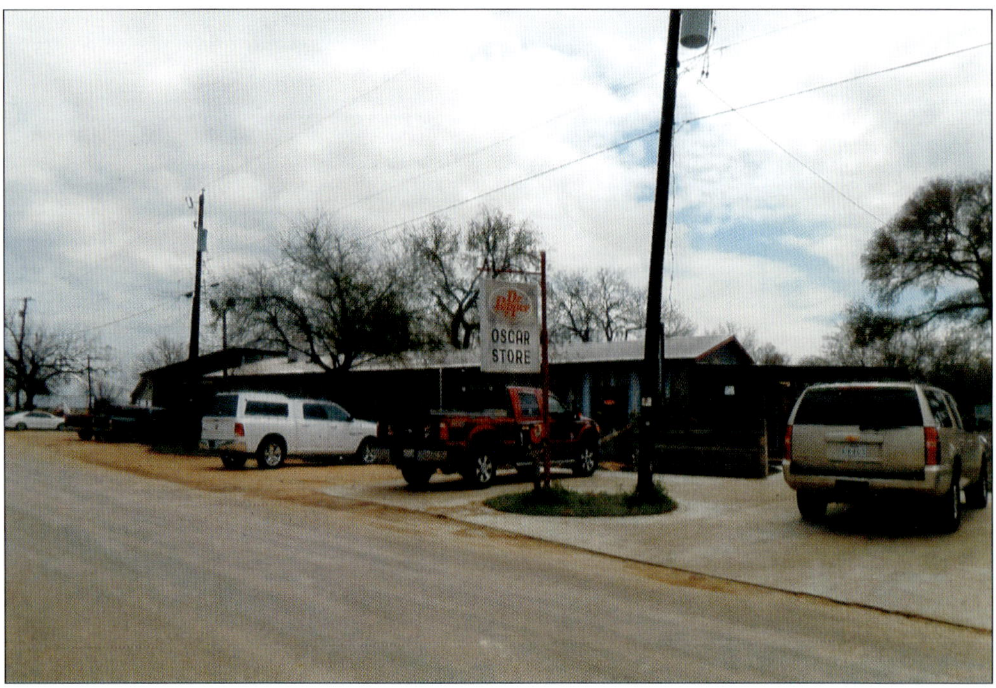

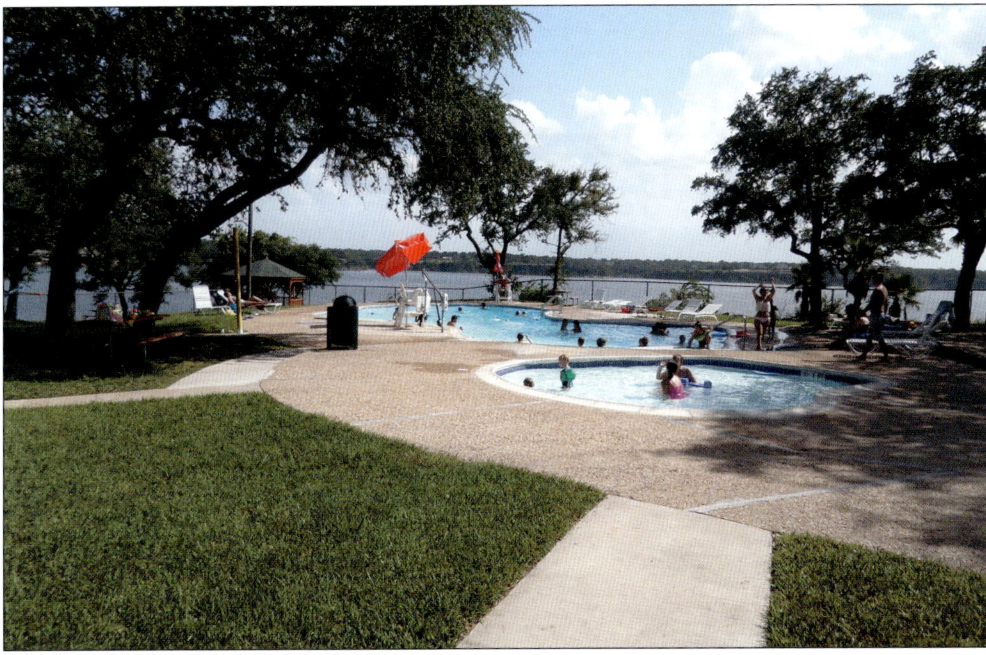

Morgan's Point Resort, a multimillion-dollar development, was established in the early 1960s as a resort on Belton Lake. Promoted as the "Switzerland of Texas," the resort included a swimming pool, playground, lake fishing and swimming, and a golf course. The population in 2013 was 4,223, up 41 percent since 2000. A police department was established in 1986. Today there are 17 police officers. The above photograph offers a view of the swimming pool and Belton Lake. Below is the building shared by the police and fire departments. (Both, authors' collection.)

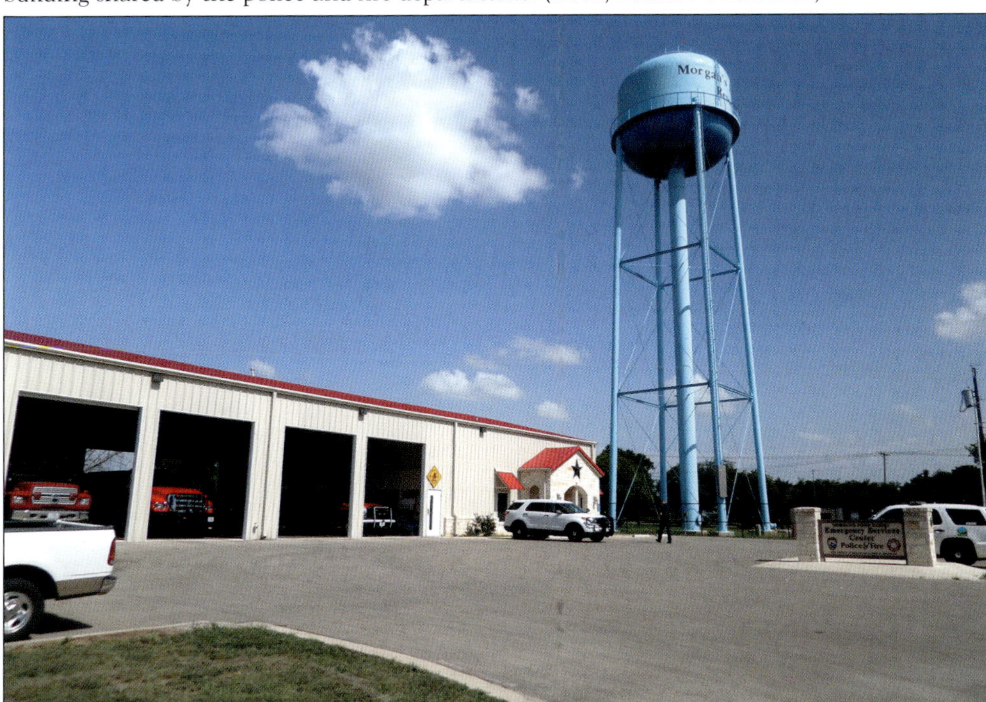

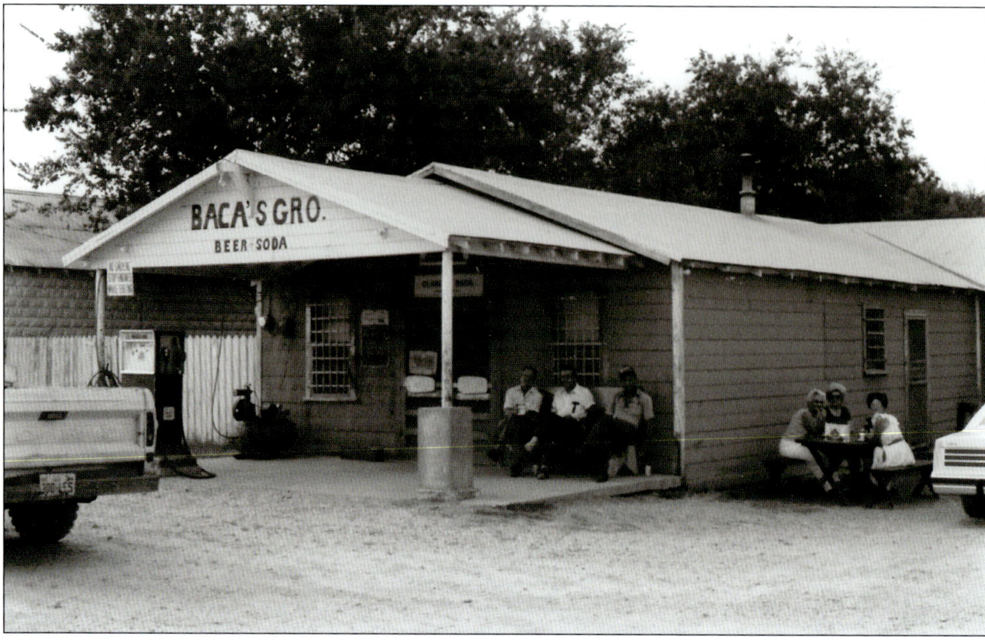

Ratibor, named after a community in the Czech Republic, is located eight miles east of Temple on State Highway 53 and two miles north of Seaton on FM 2086 in East Bell County. John Naivar opened the first store at Ratibor in 1912. That same year, Tom Talasek built a gin. The center of social activity for the predominately Czech farming community centered on a country store built in the 1940s. In 2003, Edwin and Judy Pechal acquired the historic Baca Store and renovated the structure to a family-oriented restaurant with a dining room, party room, and patio. Above is the Baca's Grocery Store in 1986. Below are the 1912 store and the remodeled Baca's Grocery store in 2015. (Both, authors' collections.)

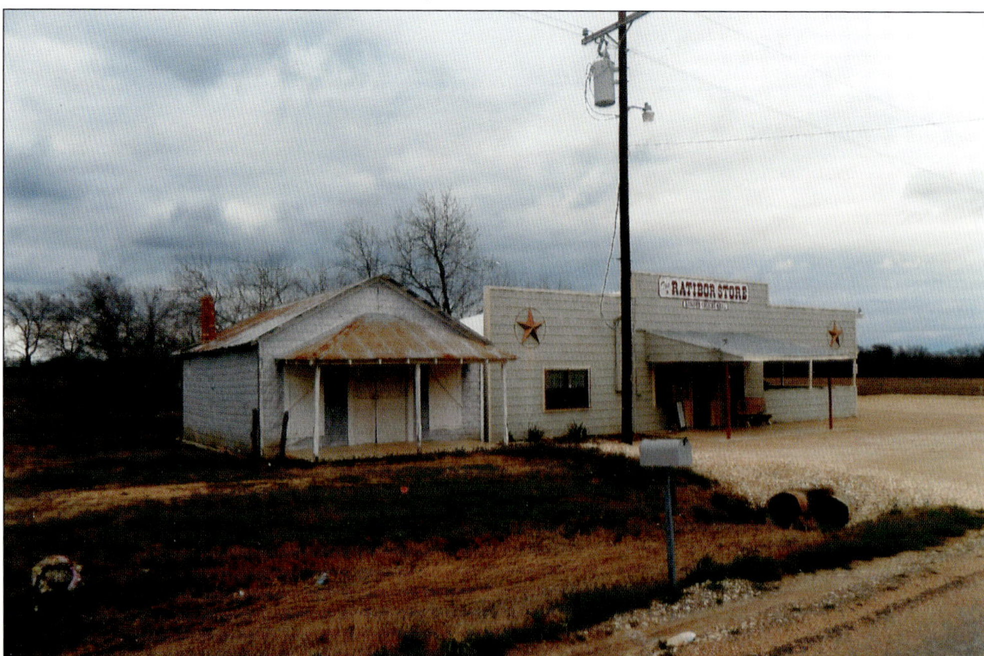

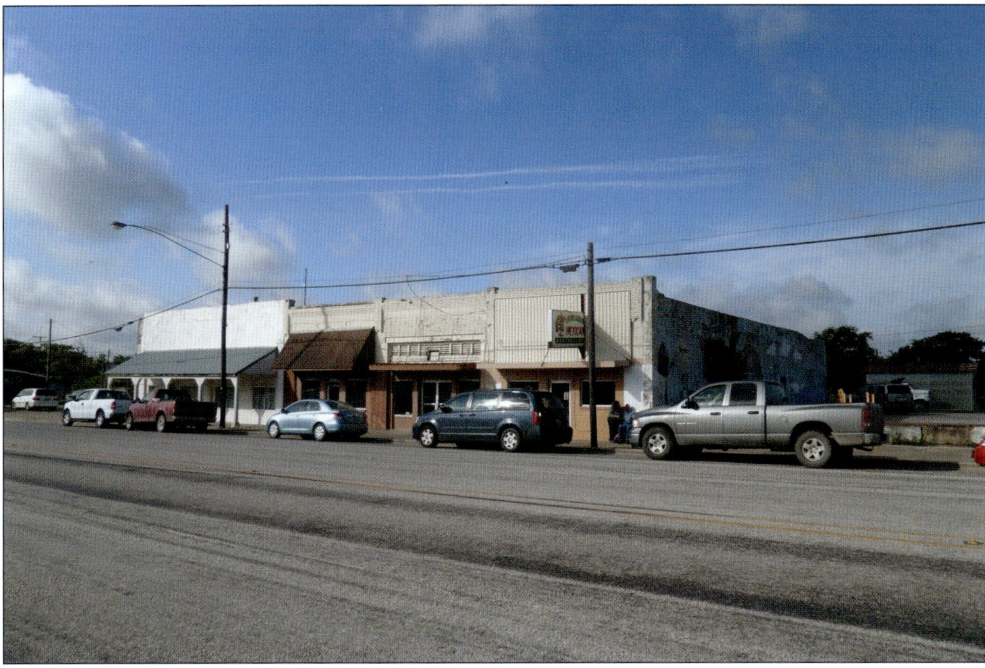

Rogers, on Highway 36 in east Bell County, was founded in 1881 by the Santa Fe Railroad and named in honor of Galveston capitalist John D. Rodgers. The town was known as Rodgers until 1908, when the name changed to Rogers. The original townsite included 24 blocks. Possibly one of the first oil wells drilled in Bell County, prior to the oil and gas craze that over took the entire country in the late 1910s and early 1920s, was drilled near the Rogers State Bank corner about 1890. This well produced a small amount of oil. In 1917, there were three churches, three banks, four cotton gins, and four physicians at Rogers. The two photographs feature Rogers in 2015. (Both, authors' collection.)

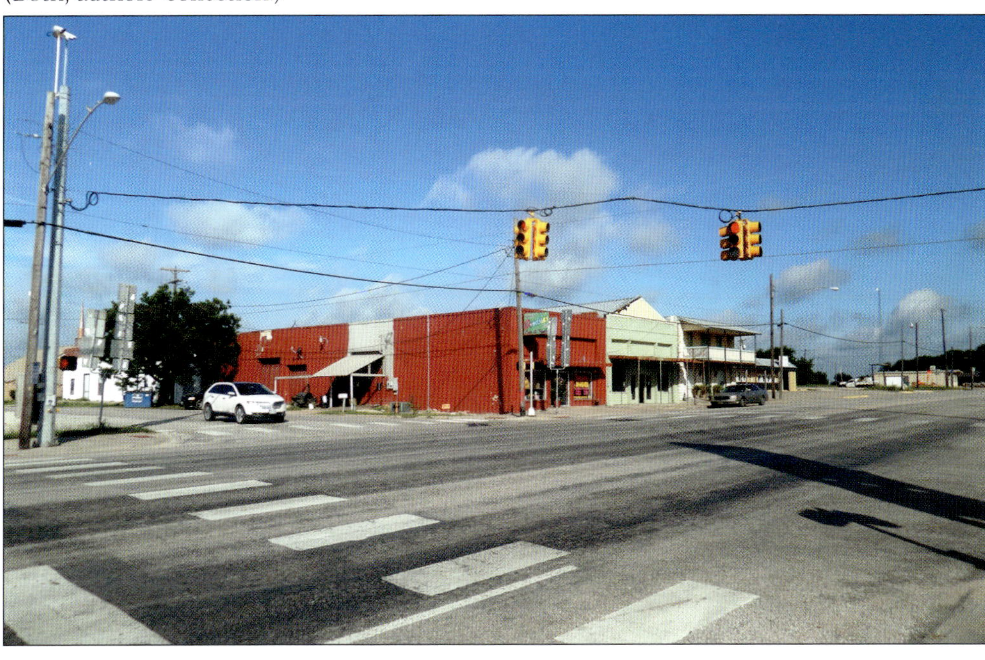

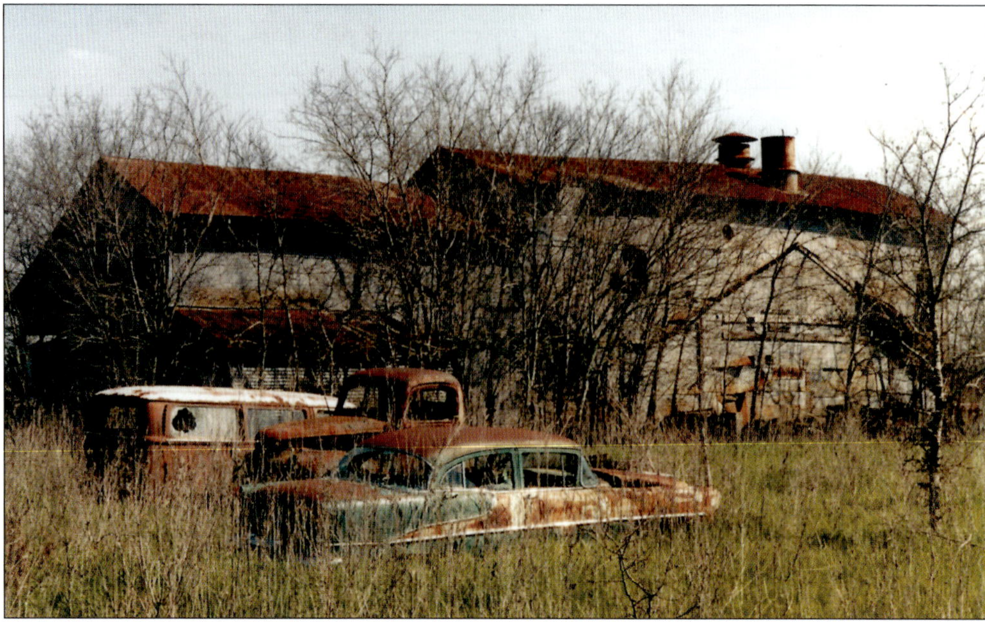

The cultivation of cotton and processing its byproducts into commercial goods were major economic investments in Bell County. Every town and most communities had at least one gin. Cottonseed oil mills were in operation and produced cooking oil and livestock feed from cottonseed. One hundred years ago, there were three cotton gins and a cottonseed oil mill at Bartlett. Bartlett processed an estimated 50,000 bales a season. There were six gins at Oenaville and four at Rogers. The boll weevil, cotton root rot, and falling prices devastated the cotton industry in Bell County. Cottonseed oil mills closed and gins were abandoned. The Edgeworth gin, pictured above in 2003, in East Bell County fell into ruin, and the Seaton gin is pictured below in the process of being torn down. (Both, authors' collection.)

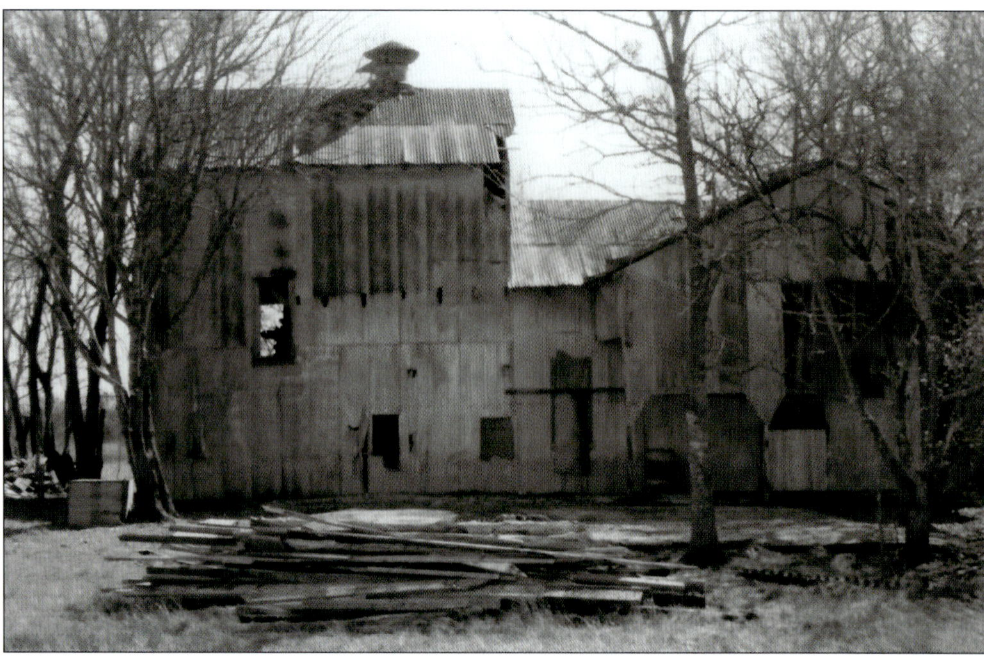

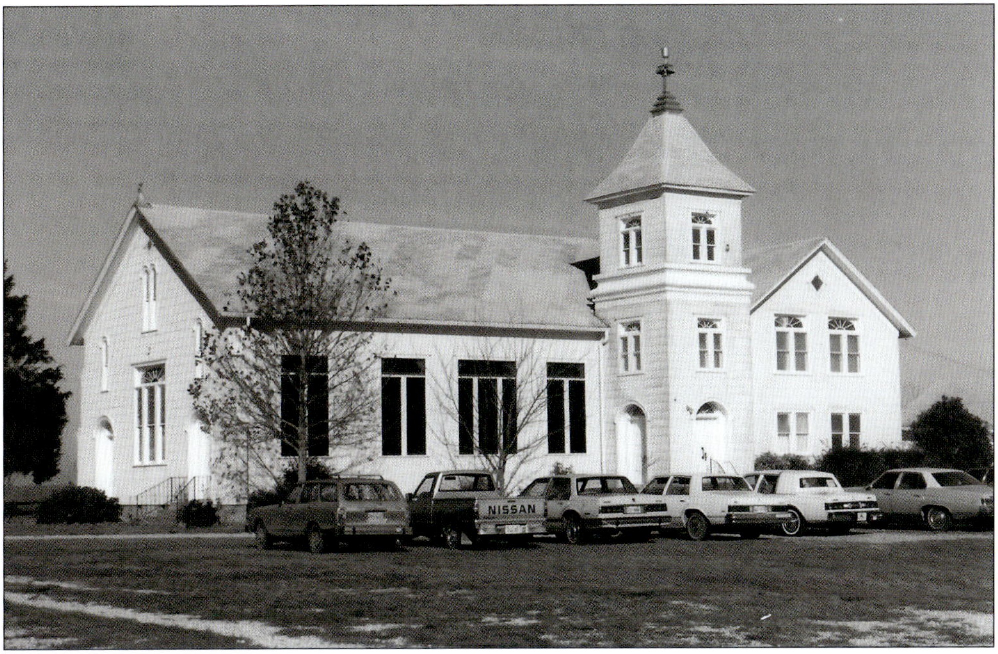

Named in 1924 for John Zabcik, the farming community of Zabcikville is located 15 miles east of downtown Temple on State Highway 53. When the new concrete State Highway 53 was completed in 1932, the opening celebration was held at the newly completed store of Frank Zabcik. After the ceremonies marking the opening of the highway, a barbecue and dance were held on the new concrete road. Ocker Brethren Church has served the community since 1892. Rev. Ron Winsman has been at Ocker Brethren Church since early 2001. Green's Sausage House, famous for its kolaches, provides a meat market, bakery, café, and deer processing. Sold in the store are kolaches, meat kolaches, jerky, bacon, sausage, and specialty meats. The business has been family owned and operated in Zabcikville since 1946. (Both, authors' collection.)

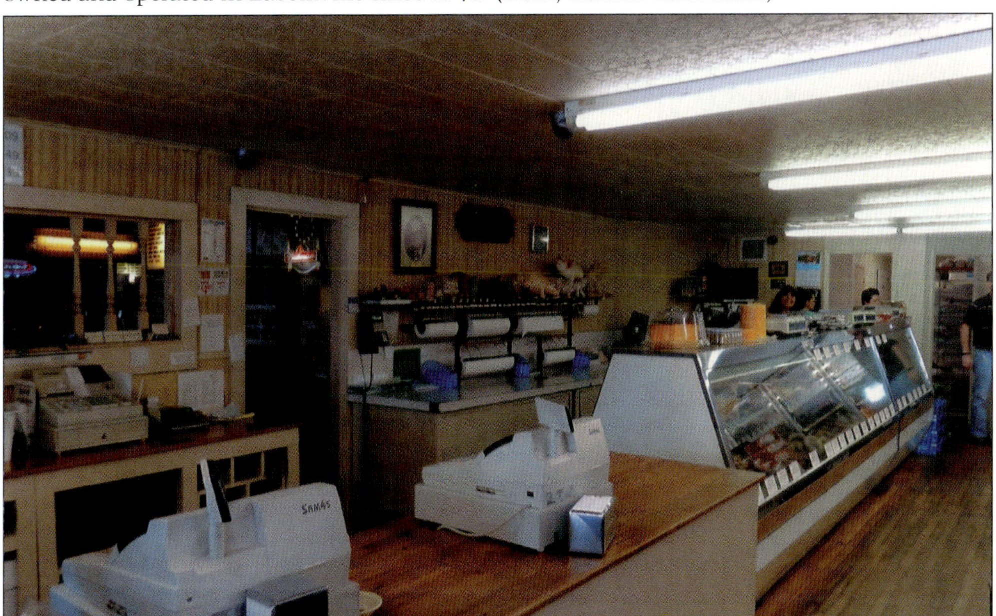

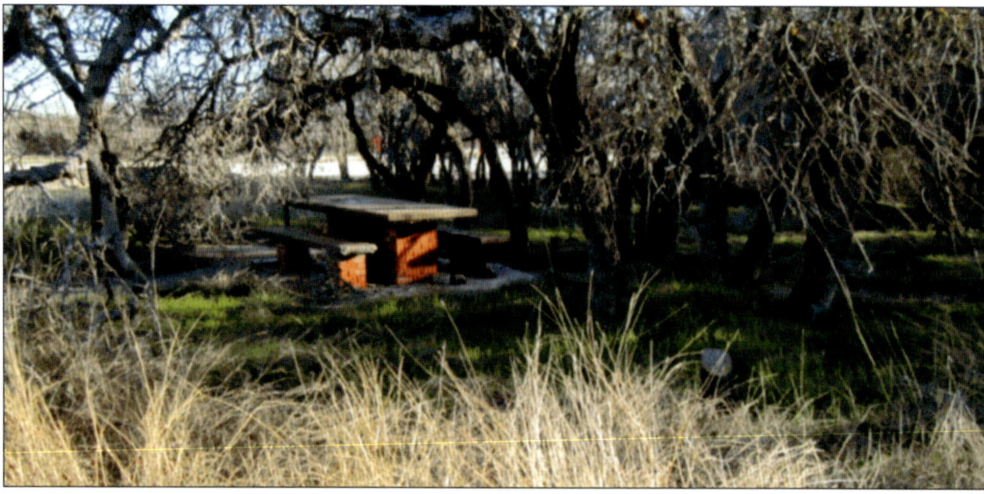

The Works Progress Administration (WPA) funded a $2,200 modern roadside park on the north side of the Lampasas River in 1939 on US Highway 81. The park, pictured above, has been unused for several years and is in a deteriorated condition. A roadside park opened in 2008 about two miles south of Salado on Interstate Highway 35. The facility is one of Texas's 80 safety rest areas. With an architectural design inspired by the mills that once stood along Salado Creek, the roadside park below, with facilities on both sides of the freeway, features a storm shelter, separate truck and automobile parking, a playground, picnic tables, and restrooms. (Both, authors' collection.)

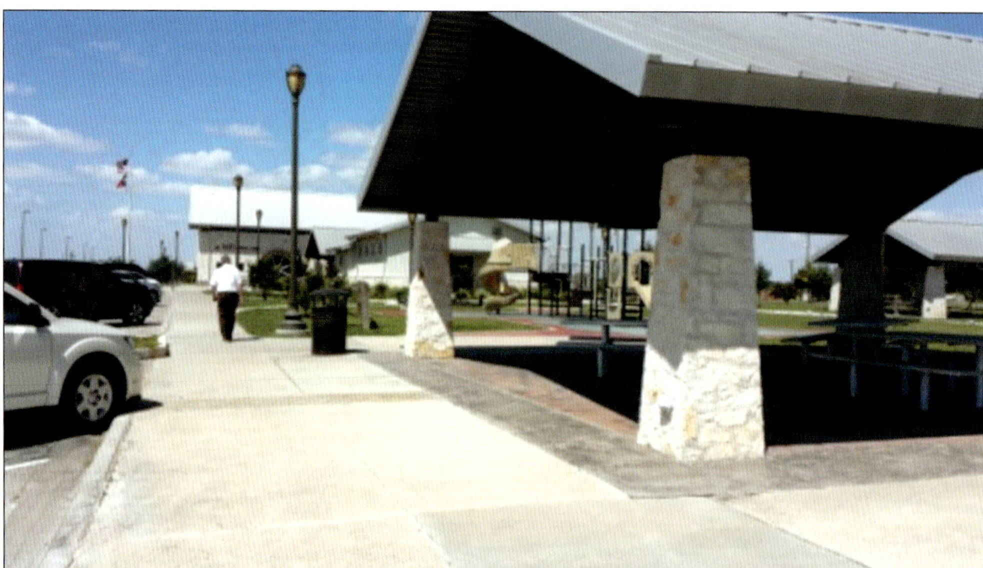

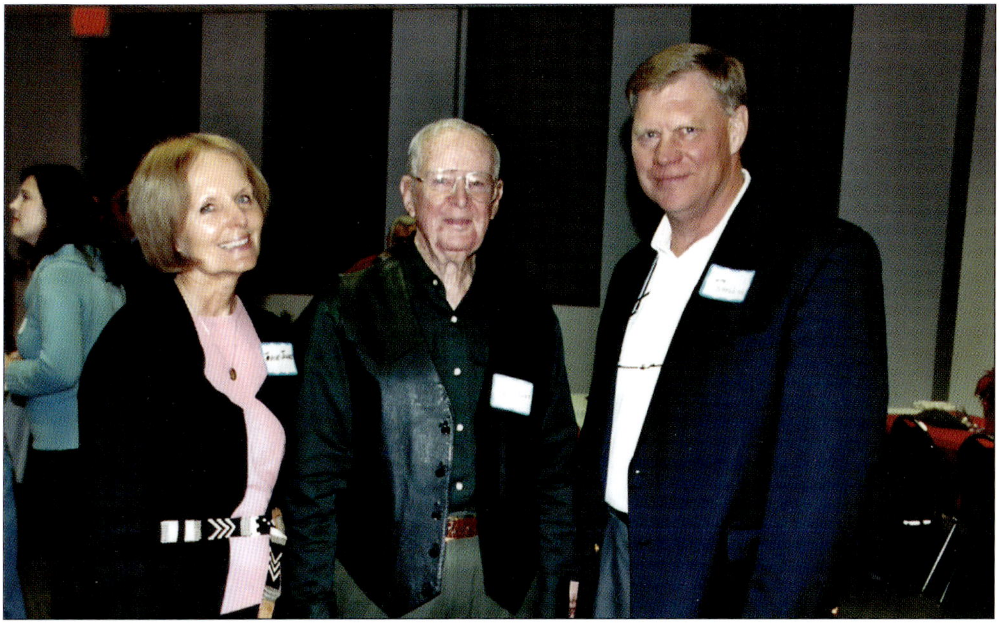

Longtime supporters of efforts to preserve and promote Bell County's history pictured here are, from left to right, Joyce Jones, Jack Jones, and Pete Stebbins, during an event in Salado at Christmas 2005. Joyce Jones is a college professor, and her late husband, Jack Jones, was a World War II flying ace. Pete Stebbins is a member of Salado Historical Society Board of Directors. President of Salado Historical Society in 2005, Maurice Carson sang and played the guitar at the event. He and his wife, Charlene Carson, are members of Salado Historical Society, and she serves as the archivist for the Salado Historical Society Board of Directors. (Both, courtesy of the Bell County Historical Commission.)

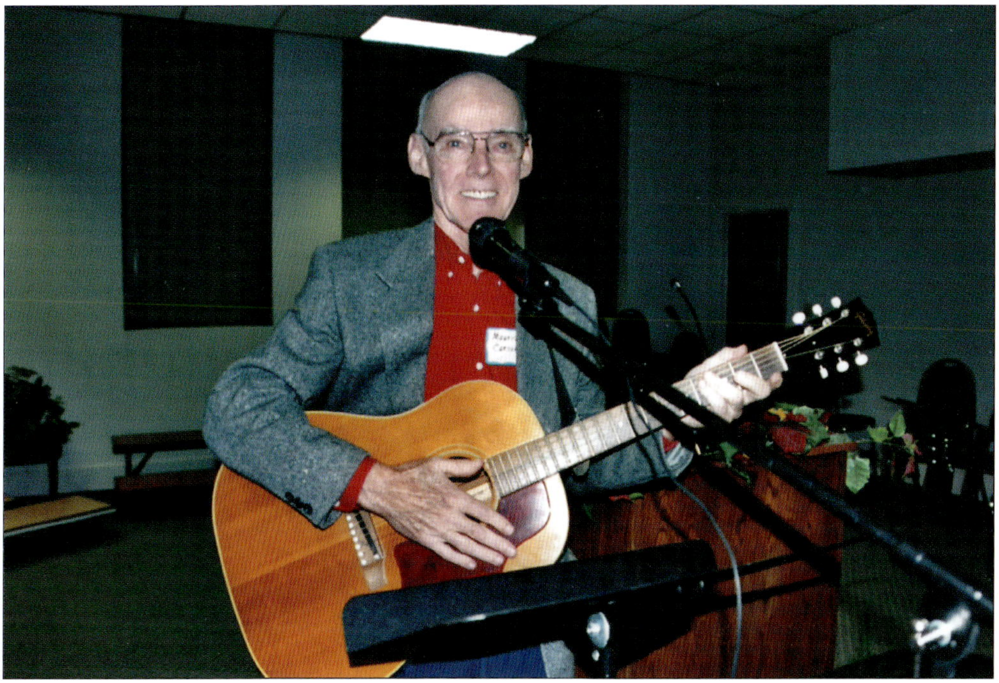

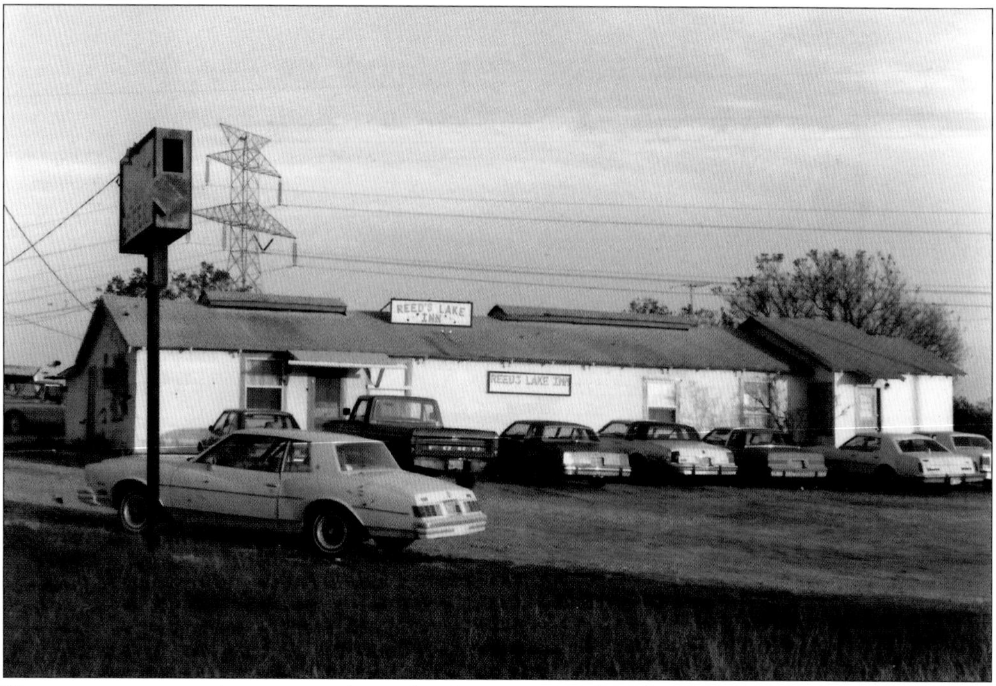

There was a time in American culture that businesses such as bars, taverns, honky-tonks, dance halls, juke joints, and beer joints, primarily focused on the sale of alcoholic beverages and other sources of sinful pleasure, played an intricate part in the social life of a community. With the passage of stricter laws prohibiting driving under the influence, many well-patronized Bell County honky-tonks met their demise, including Reed's Lake Inn (above) in East Bell County and Karl's Place (below), located south of Holland. Both photographs are from 1987. (Both, authors' collection.)

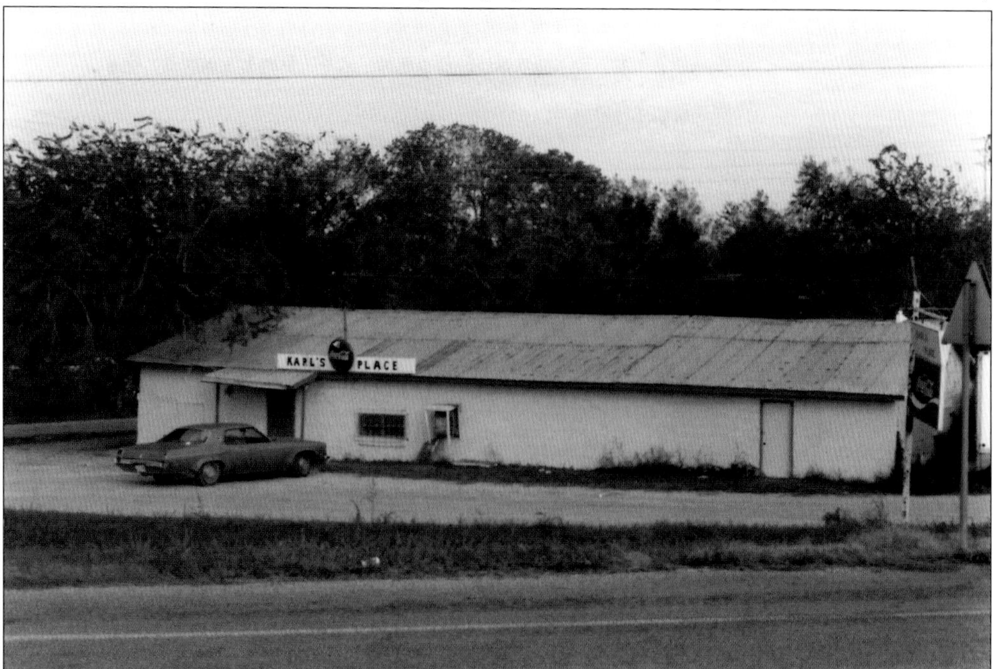

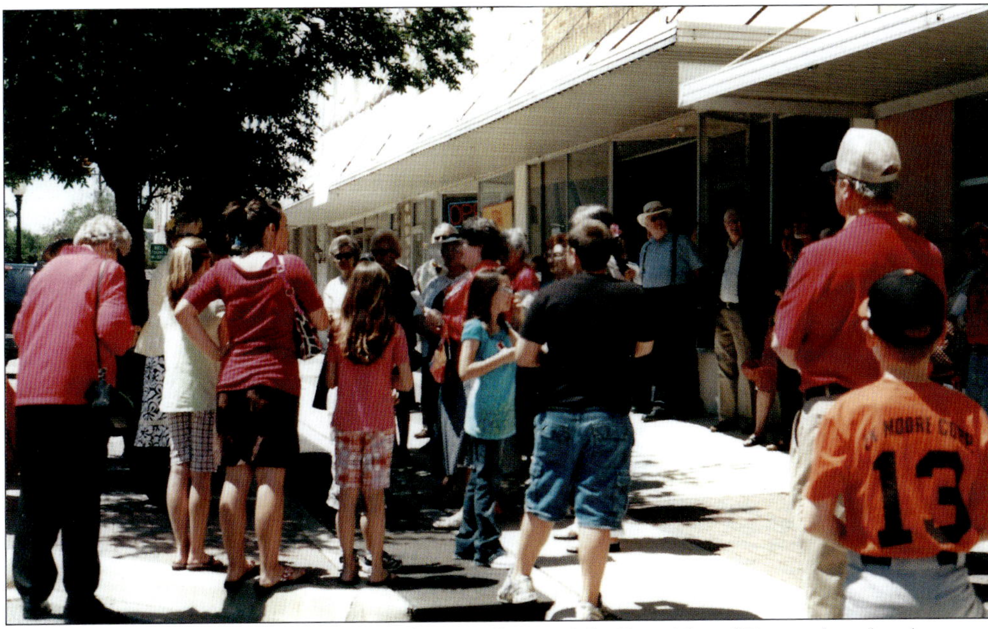

In 2008, the Sam Houston Chapter of the Daughters of the Republic of Texas placed a plaque on Main Street in Belton memorializing Sam Houston's speech against secession in 1861. A namesake of Sam Houston, prominent in the fight for independence from Mexico and first president of the Republic of Texas, the chapter strives to perpetuate the memory of those who achieved and maintained the independence of Texas. (Authors' collection.)

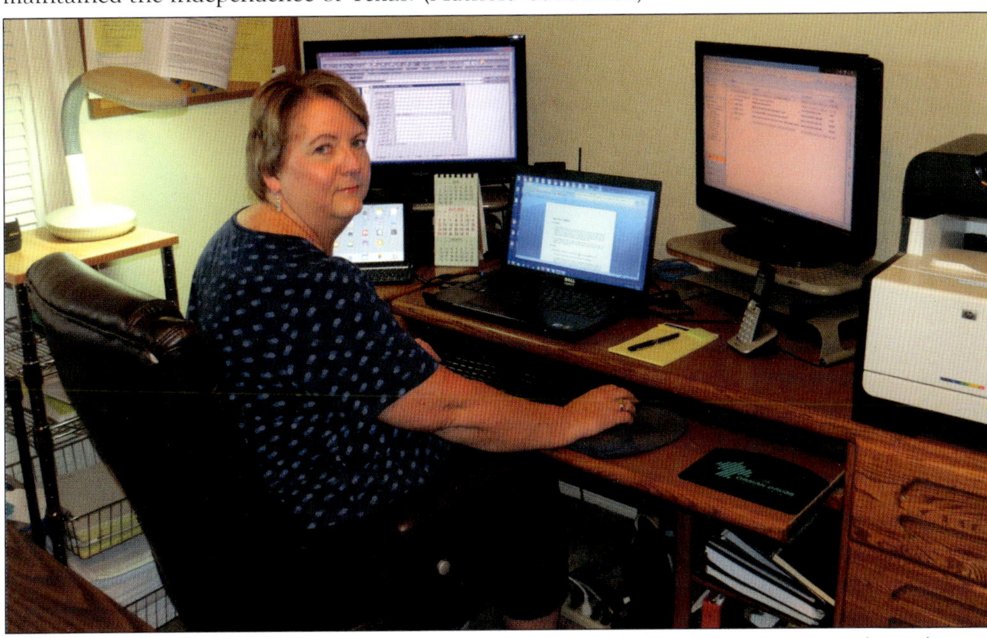

A somewhat new working arrangement, viewed as a benefit to employers and employees, telecommuting, or working from a remote location, is an arrangement made easier by portable computers, Internet, and e-mail. Kathy Taylor lives near Sparks, where she works as a paralegal for the law firm of Baird, Crews, Schiller & Whitaker. After driving to work for 27 years, she now works from her country home. (Courtesy of Jerry Taylor.)

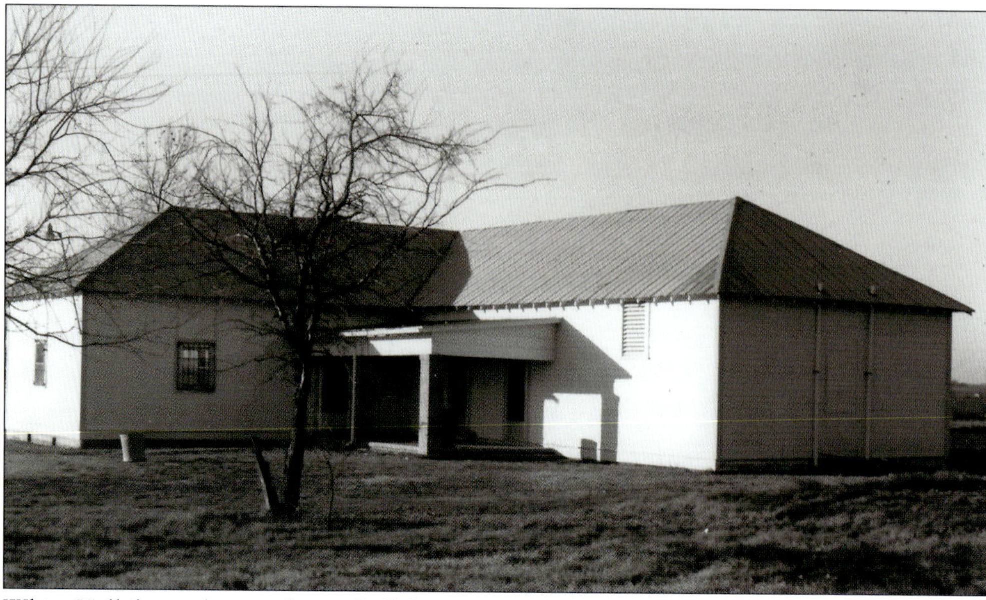

White Hall, located in northwest Bell County, is a farming community. In the early 1900s, the community had a gin, blacksmith shop, church, school, and two stores. There were 30 white students and 45 black students enrolled in White Hall School for 1923–1924. The school that served the community was struck by lightning during a thunderstorm in 1934 and burned to the ground. The black school, shown above in 1987, burned to the ground around 2000. Betty Aycock (left) and Sandra Parker Thomas (right) met again by chance in front of the old White Hall School in August 2010. Their families were from White Hall, and they knew each other when they lived there. Betty worked at the old gin in White Hall and lives in Temple, and Sandra still lives in White Hall. (Both, authors' collection.)

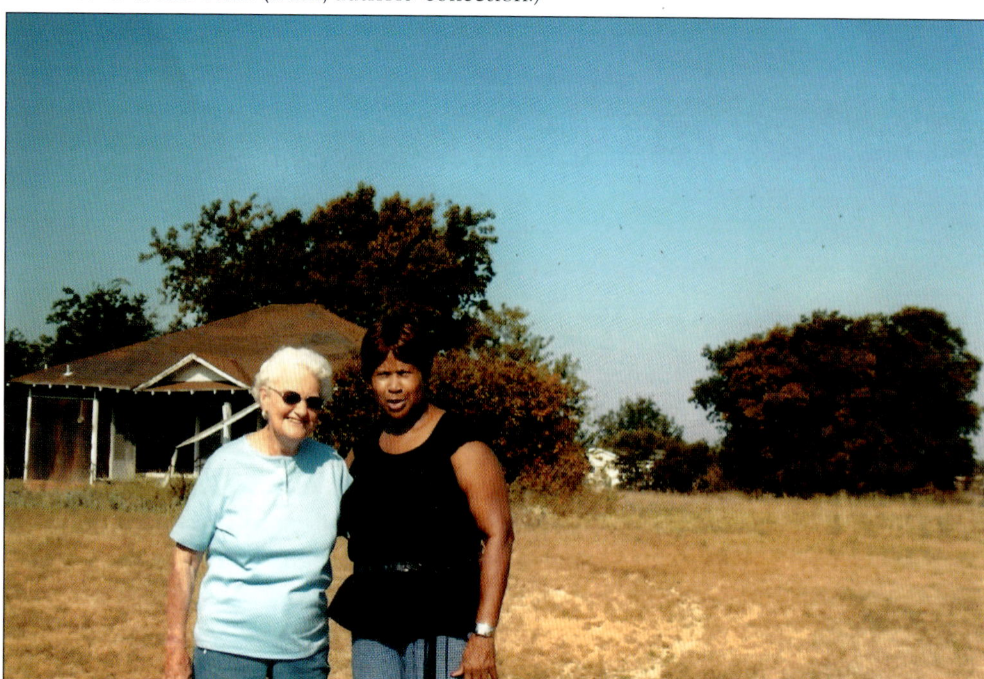

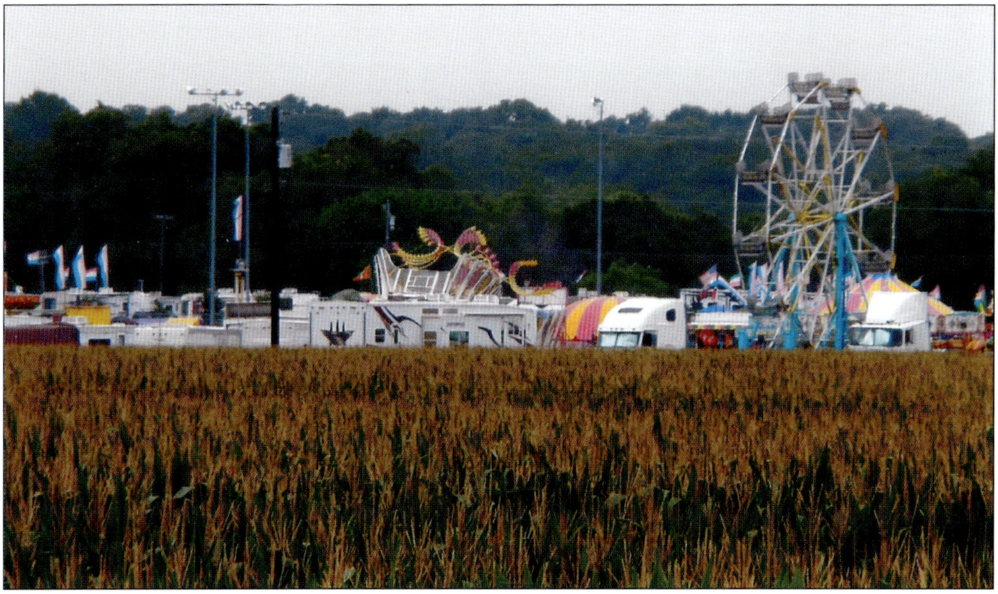

In 1881, the Missouri-Kansas-Texas Railroad bypassed the settlement of Mountain Home on Darrs Creek. When the railroad failed to reach Mountain Home, residents there moved about half a mile to the railroad and established the new town of Holland. Named in honor of early settler J. R. Holland, the town incorporated in 1882. In 1893, Holland, with a population of 500, was the third-largest town in Bell County. Monk Ivicic helped found the annual Holland Corn Festival, which celebrated its 41st year in 2015. The festival includes a parade, barbecue cook-off, arts and crafts, and a carnival. The above photograph is an aerial view of the carnival over the festival's namesake, a field of corn. Below is a photograph of the various booths of the arts and crafts vendors. (Both, authors' collection.)

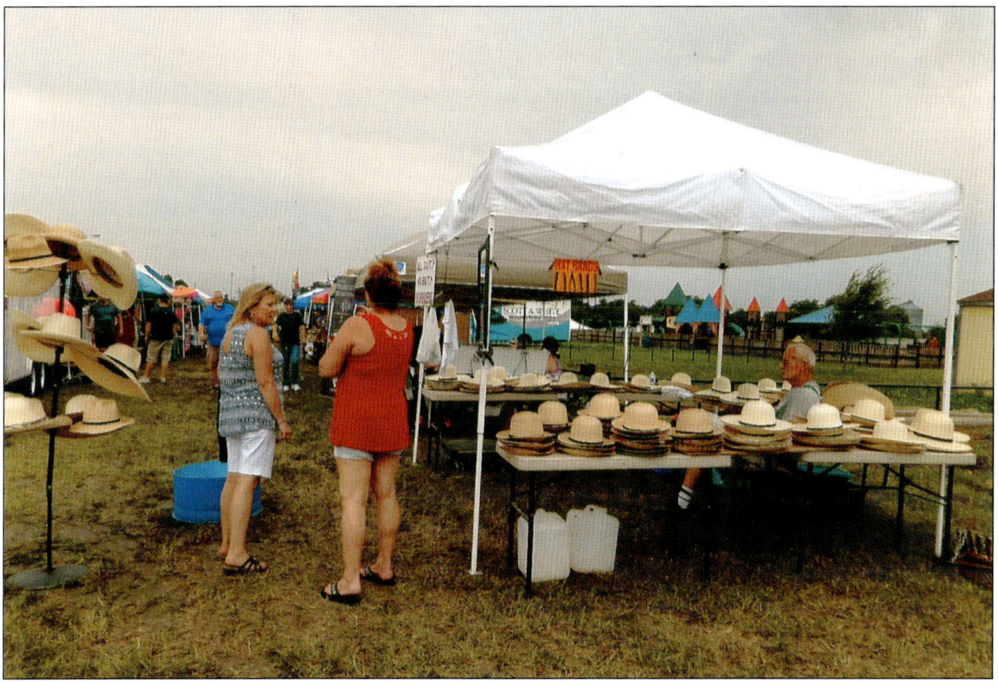

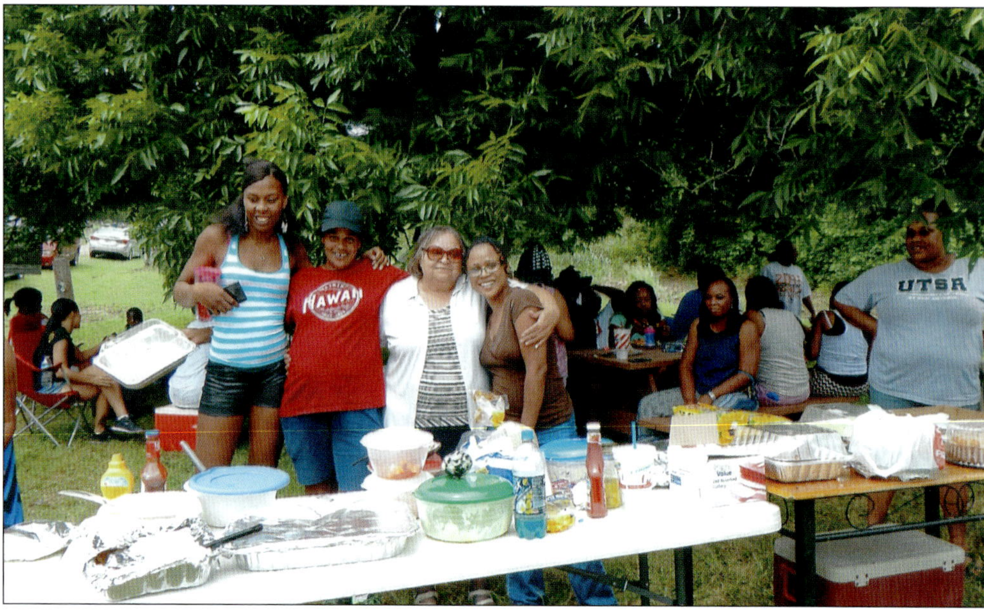

Descendants of J.C. and Mary Smith Griffin hold a family reunion each June in conjunction with the Holland Corn Festival. The Griffin family reunion started as a birthday celebration for Mary Griffin, who was born on June 17, 1918. The two people that traveled the farthest to the 2015 reunion came from Hawaii. (Authors' collection.)

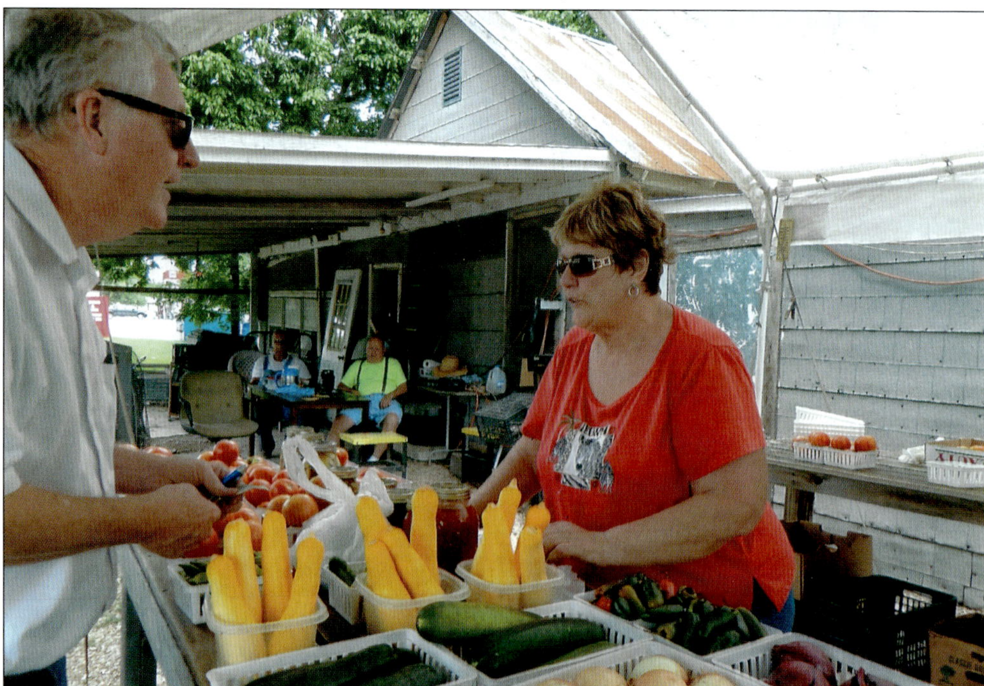

Georgia and Don Marshall have sold produce for five years on State Highway 75 in Holland. Most of the produce they offer for sale is grown locally. Residents of Holland for 30 years, the couple are retired and enjoy getting out of the house and earning a little extra money. (Authors' collection.)

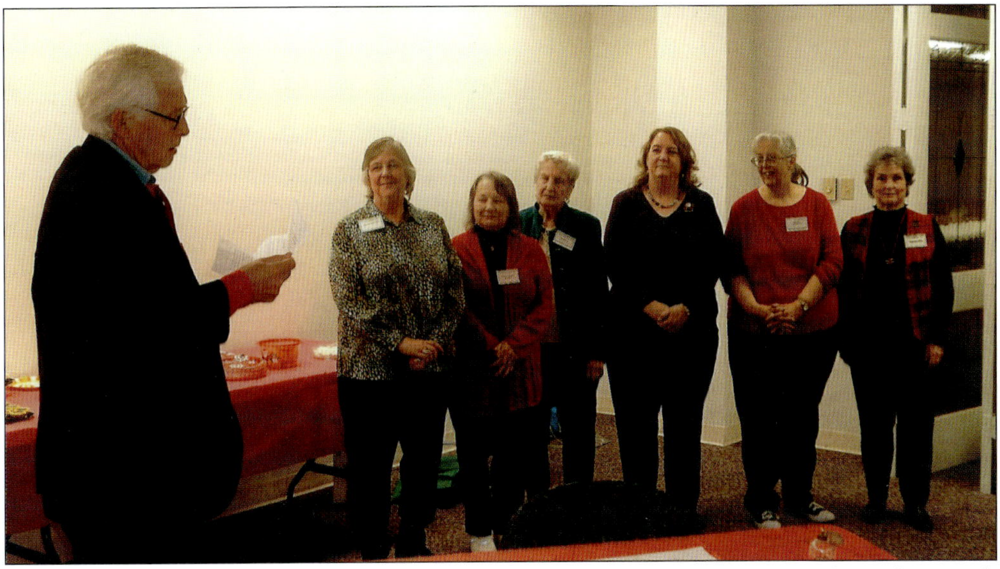

The East Bell County Genealogical Society, formed in 1991, promotes genealogical research and preservation of genealogical records. The society, now known as Bell County Genealogical Society, conducted an inventory and prepared an index of Bell County probate records on file at the county clerk's office. Richard Hooverson installed the 2014–2015 officers; from left to right are Brenda McGuire, Nancy Kelsey, Sue Hall, Kathy Taylor, Crystal Calbreath, and Jalenn Ellis. (Authors' collection.)

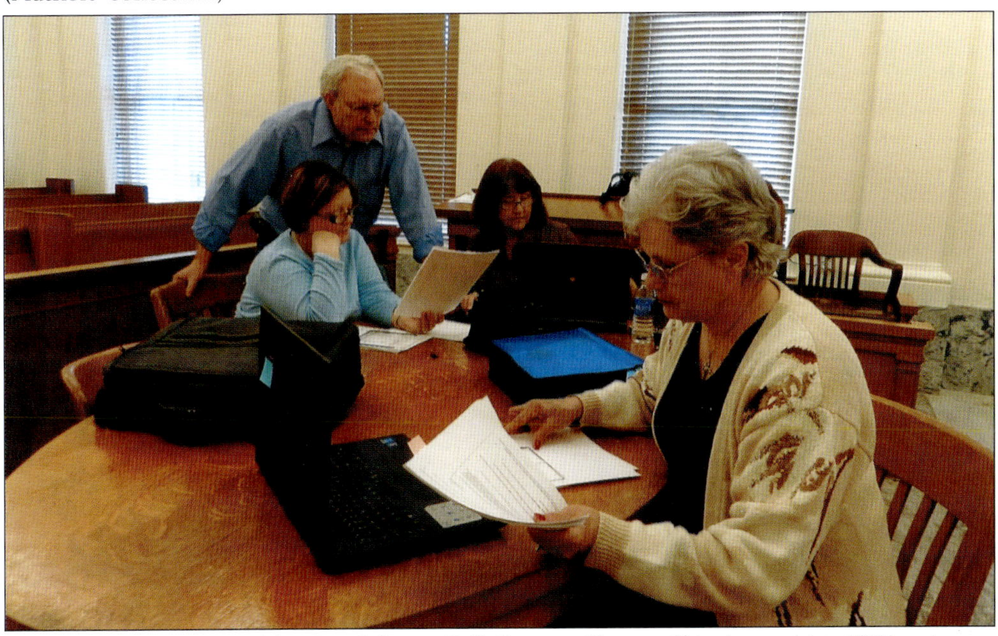

The United Daughters of the Confederacy Bell County Chapter 101, chartered in 1897, strives to meet goals supporting the society's historical, benevolent, educational, memorial, and patriotic objectives. The chapter's 2015 historical preservation project involved transcribing Civil War–era journals of E.S.C. Robertson, who served as aide-de-camp to Gen. Henry McCulloch. Pictured here transcribing the journals are, from left to right, Allen Harris (standing), Ginny Parsons, Gloria Harris, and Welba Dorsey. (Authors' collection.)

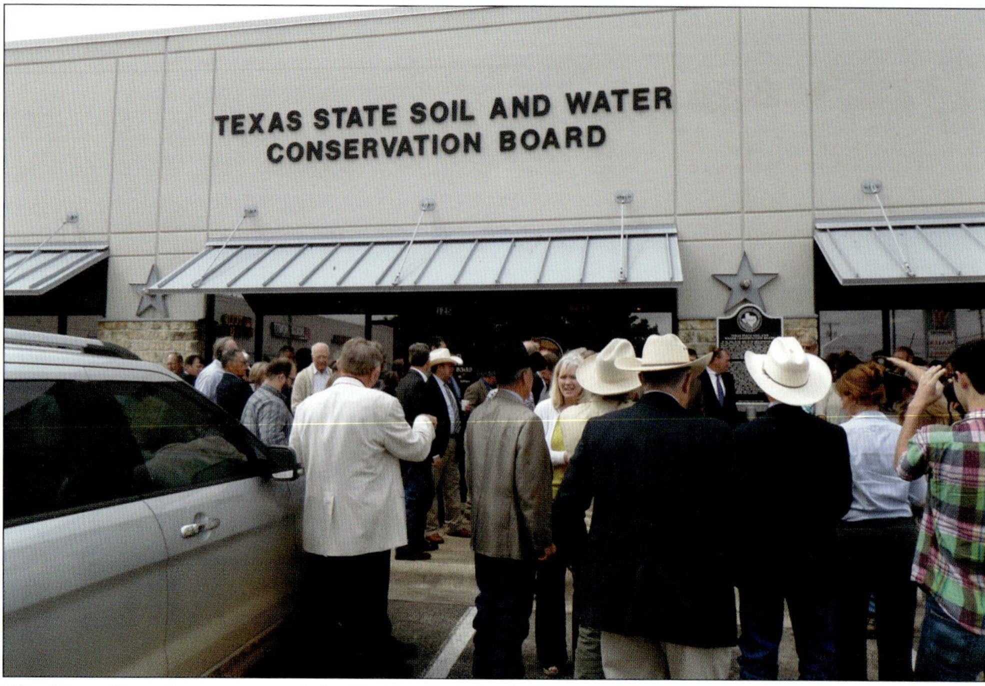

The Texas Legislature created the Texas State Soil and Water Conservation Board in 1939. From its headquarters in Temple, the board offers technical assistance to the state's 216 soil and water conservation districts. In 2015, the board celebrated 75 years of soil and water conservation in Texas with a Texas Historical Commission marker. State and local officials attended the marker dedication. (Authors' collection.)

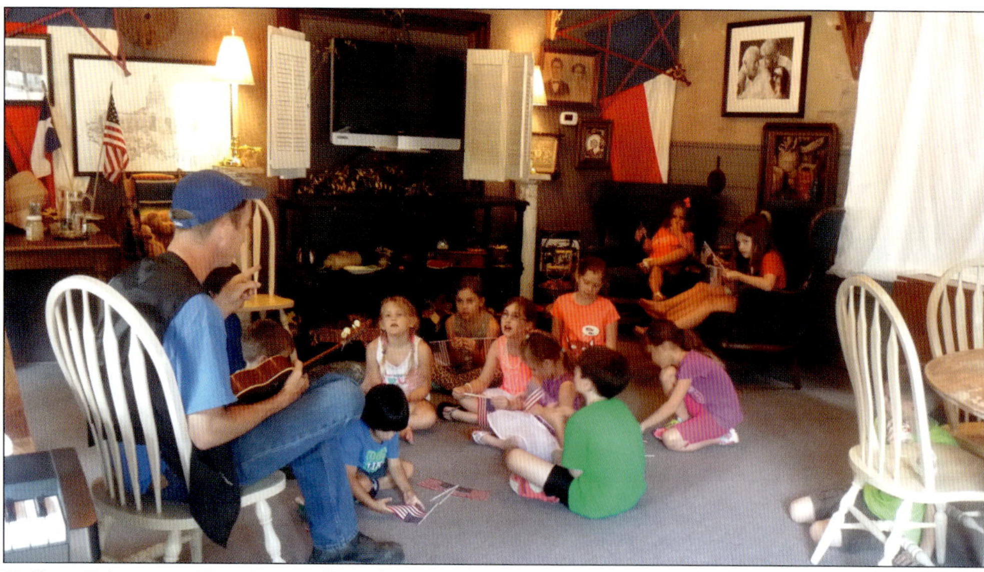

Tiffany Schreiner, Sheryl Russell, and Grainger Esch founded Salado's Silver Spur Arts Academy in 2009. The academy offers instruction in an array of arts to students ages four and up. Children attending the academy become "imagineer" students who learn to use their imagination through yoga, dance, music, and storytelling. Here, Grainger Esch leads students in the arts of improvisation, yoga, and Southern ukulele tunes. (Courtesy of Tiffany Schreiner.)

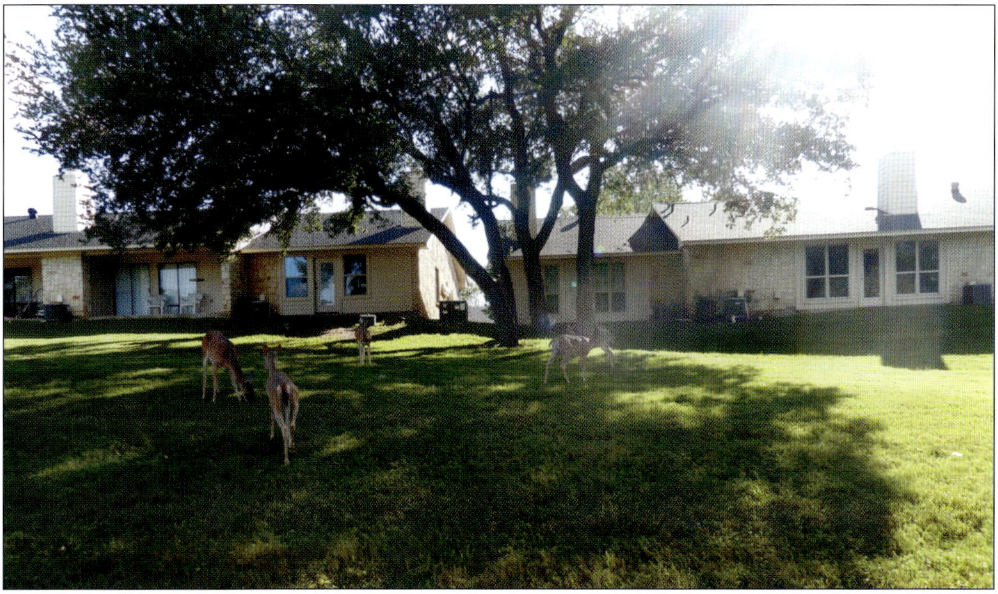

Bell County residents refer to the deer population with various levels of sentiment—some call the animals a nuisance, a threat to property and road safety, while others enjoy watching them from afar and feel they bring ambiance to the community's environment. In 2014, the deer overpopulation in and around Salado reached a critical level, and the town alderman investigated options to diminish their numbers. Pictured here are deer feeding in the backyards of houses in Mill Creek in Salado. (Authors' collection.)

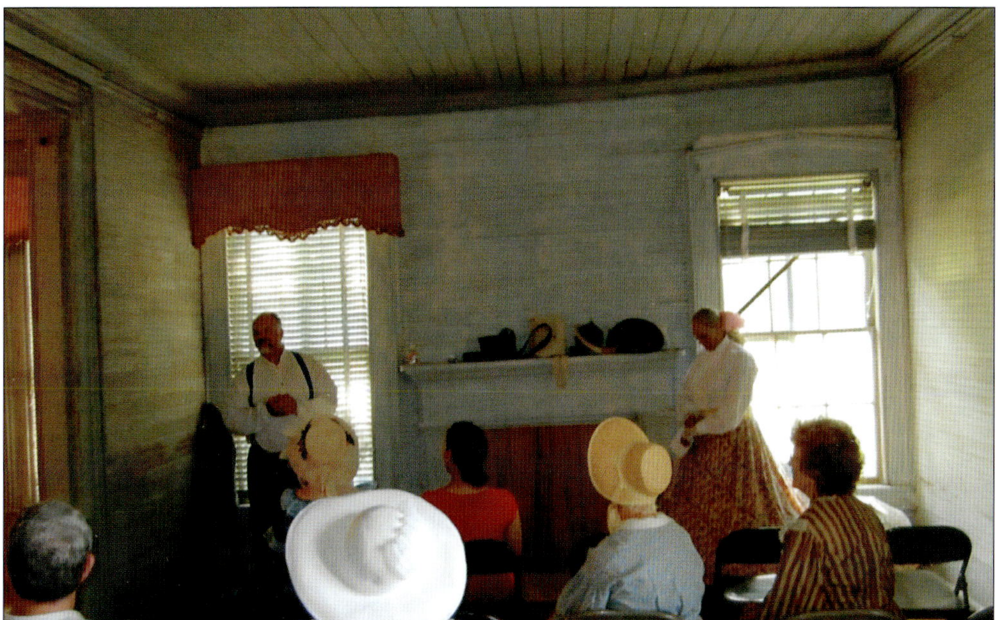

During a tour of the Robertson Plantation at Salado in 2012, Steve and Linda Wooley portrayed Col. E.S.C. and Mary Robertson. Shown here in the front parlor of the house, the couple told about the Robertson family and the town of Salado and described the family's life on Salado Creek during the Civil War. (Authors' collection.)

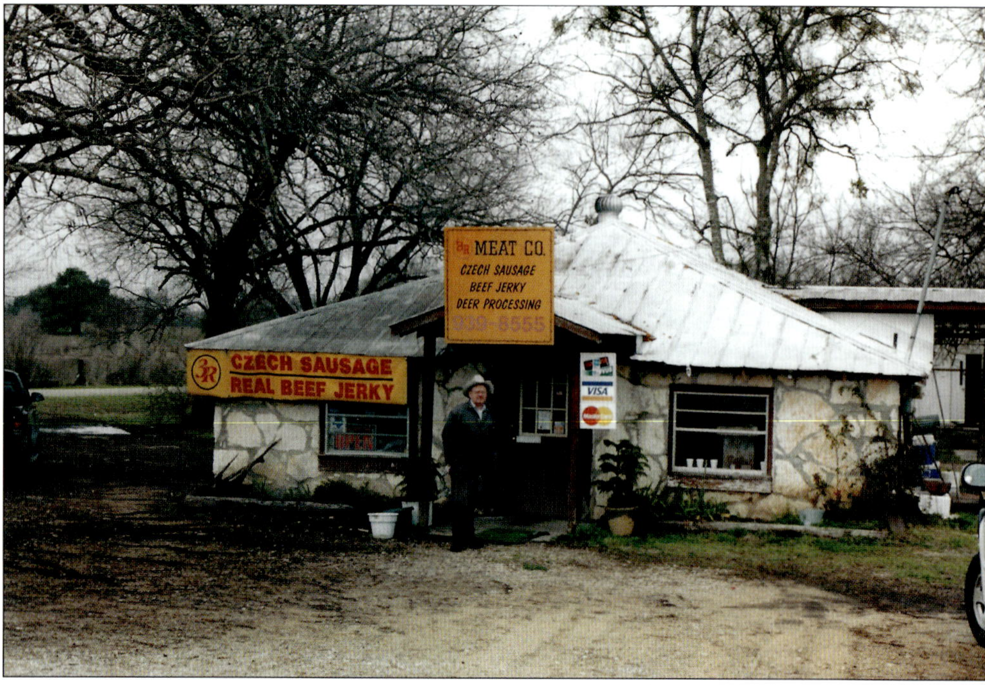

At one time, this rock building at the corner of Elm Grove Road and Elmer King Road between Belton and Salado was a Church of Christ. Shown here about 2003, Peterak's 3 R Meat Company occupied the building. The country store sold Czech sausage and beef jerky and processed deer. The building is currently vacant. (Authors' collection.)

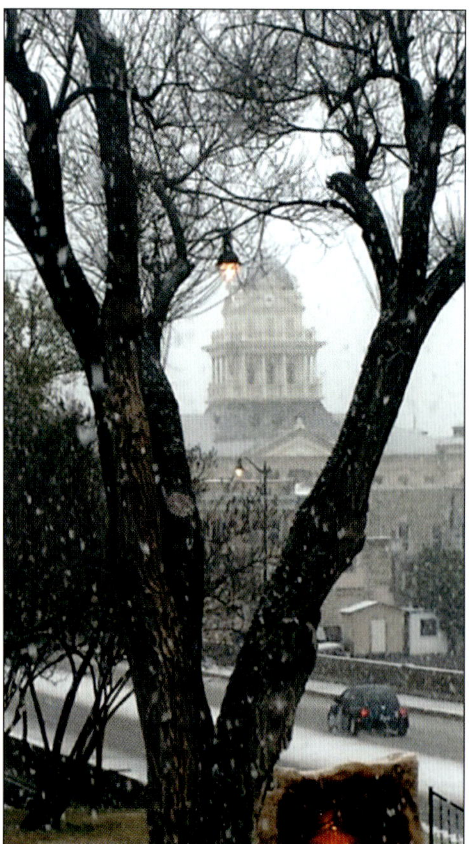

With an average annual snowfall of less than half an inch, the weather in Bell County affords little opportunity for residents to see measurable snowfall. The small amount of snow that accumulates on grassy areas melts quickly, and there is no need to shovel snow from walkways or plow it from streets. Pictured here is the Bell County Courthouse during a rare snowfall. (Authors' collection.)

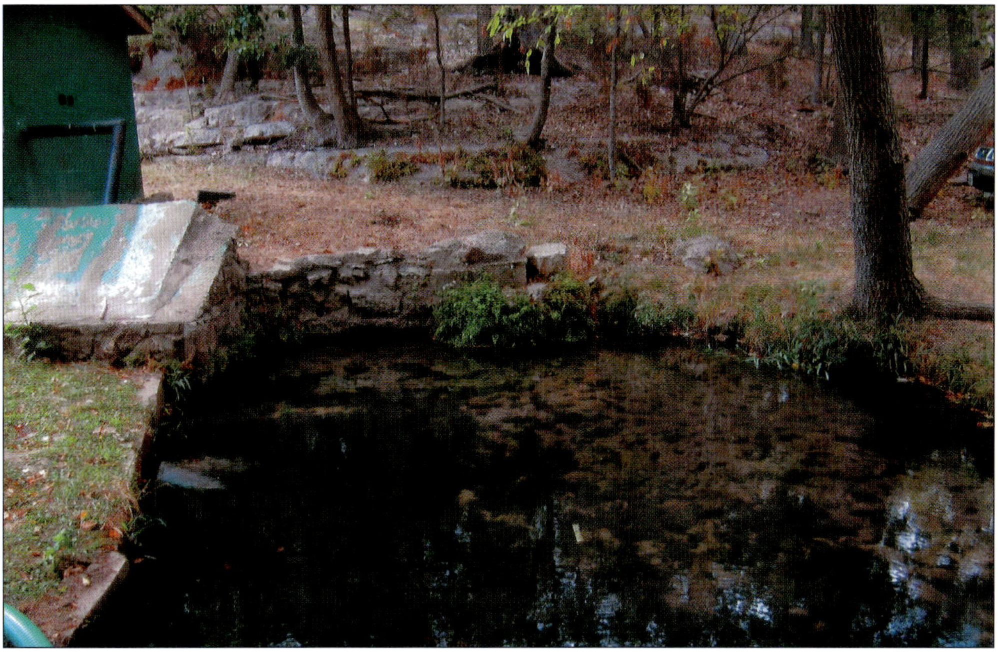

Until the early 2000s, Ozarka Natural Spring Water Company used this spring as the source for its bottled spring water. The company now sources spring water from three springs in East Texas. Some of the equipment left at the site by Ozarka is to the left of the spring. (Authors' collection.)

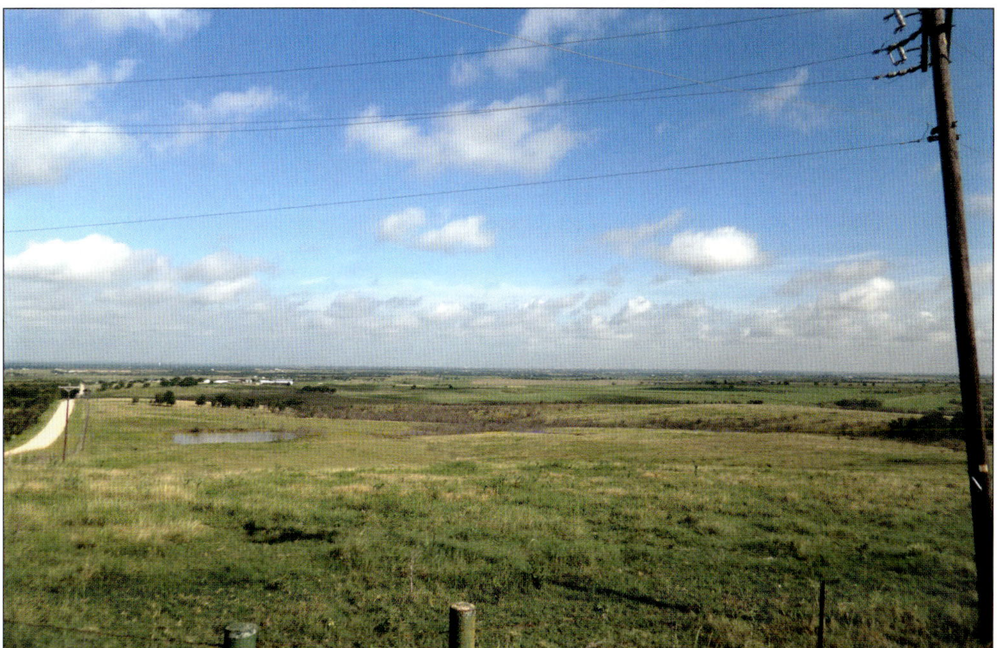

This scenic view of the open prairie from Knob Hill is near Rogers and 13 miles from Temple. Baylor Scott & White Hospital in south Temple can be observed in the distant horizon. Reeds Lake Road, on the left, winds its way through some of the earliest settlement in Bell County. In the spring, the wildflowers are abundant. (Authors' collection.)

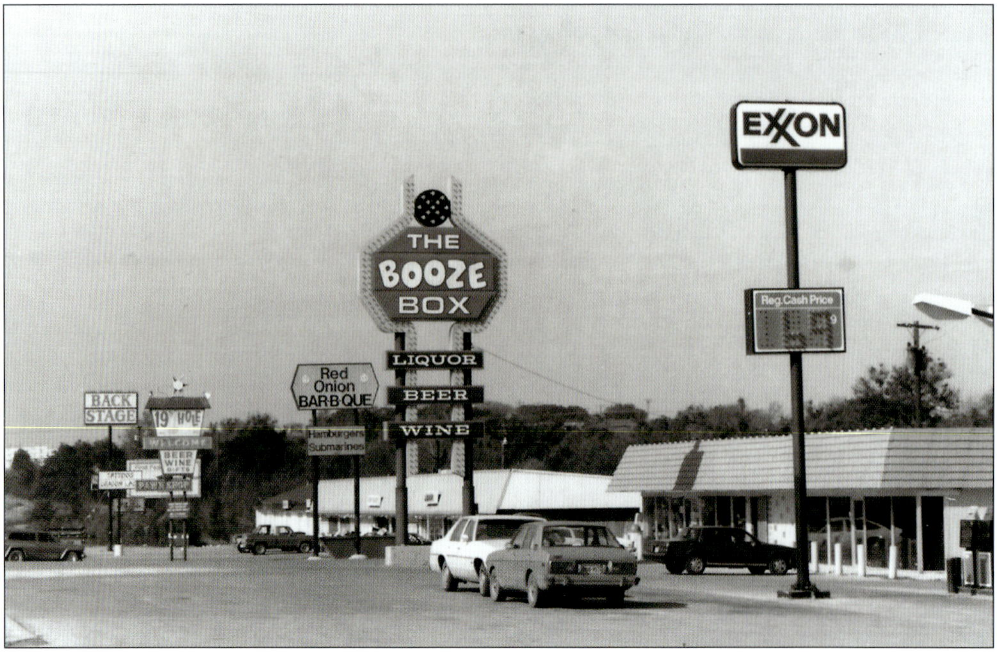

In the 1980s, on a block of Veterans Memorial Boulevard in Harker Heights were a tattoo parlor, pawnshop, the 19th Hole (a beer and wine store), a barbecue restaurant, an Exxon gas station, and the Booze Box, another spirits store. The 19th Hole and the Booze Box are still in business at the same location. (Courtesy of the Killeen Area Heritage Association.)

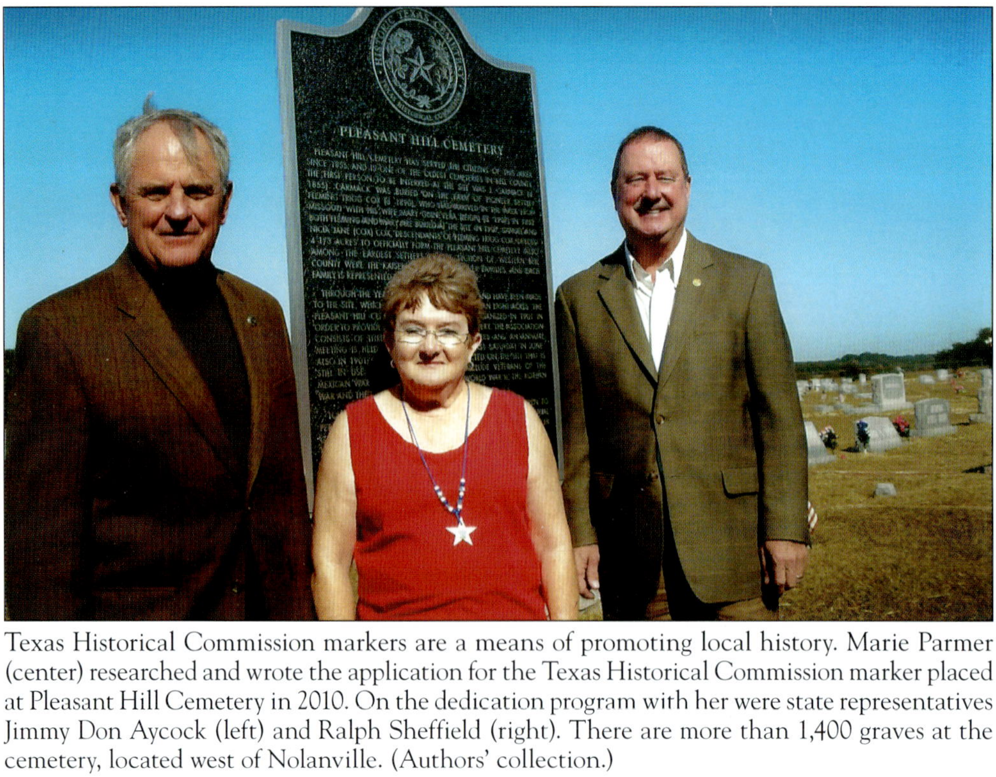

Texas Historical Commission markers are a means of promoting local history. Marie Parmer (center) researched and wrote the application for the Texas Historical Commission marker placed at Pleasant Hill Cemetery in 2010. On the dedication program with her were state representatives Jimmy Don Aycock (left) and Ralph Sheffield (right). There are more than 1,400 graves at the cemetery, located west of Nolanville. (Authors' collection.)

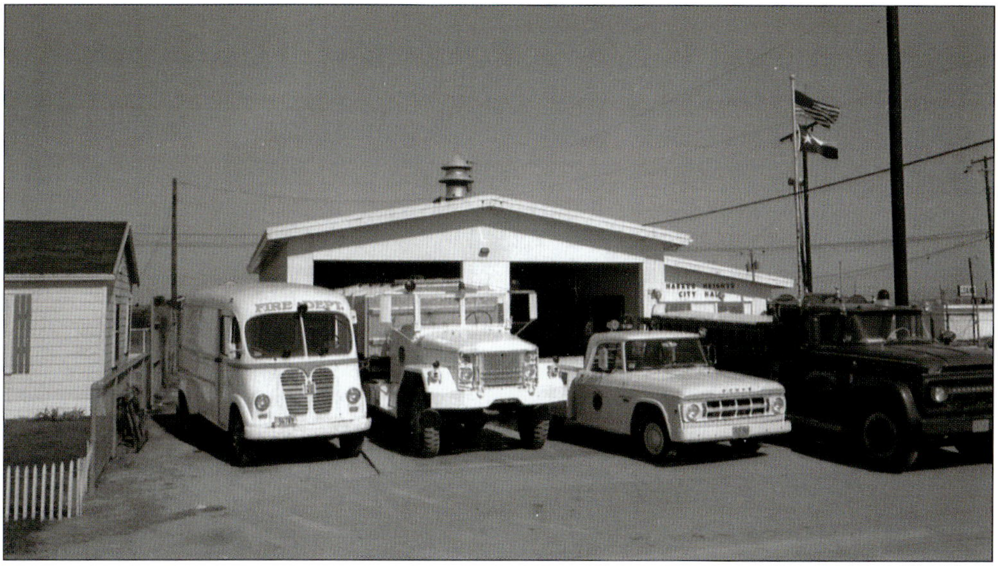

Harker Heights, one of Bell County's newest towns, has grown considerably since its incorporation in 1960. The town expanded from as estimated population of 1,000 in 1960 to more than 28,000 by 2010. Half a century of civic planning provided its residents with the public amenities of a modern city that includes parks, a library, an industrial park, a hospital, a police and fire department, and schools. Recently a 675,000-square-foot shopping center with a 16-screen movie theater was completed. Above, an infant city hall shares its facilities with the volunteer fire department. In 2011, Harker Heights Fire Department answered 632 fire calls. Below, Seton Hospital, Harker Heights' first hospital, opened in June 2012. The center includes a 60,000-square-foot medical office building. (Above, courtesy of the Temple Public Library; below, authors' collection.)

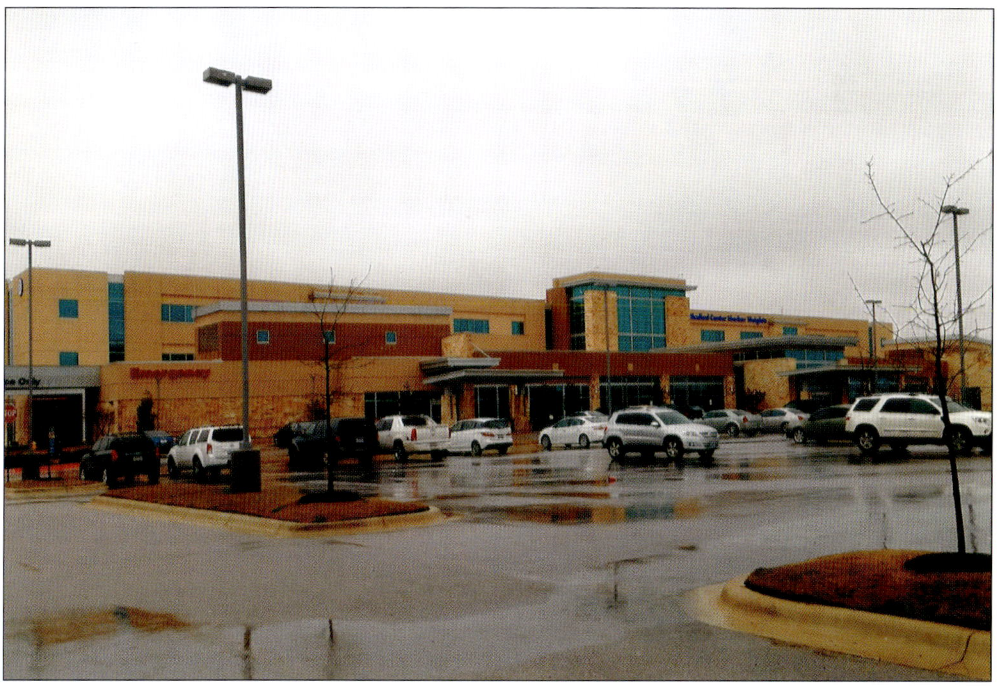

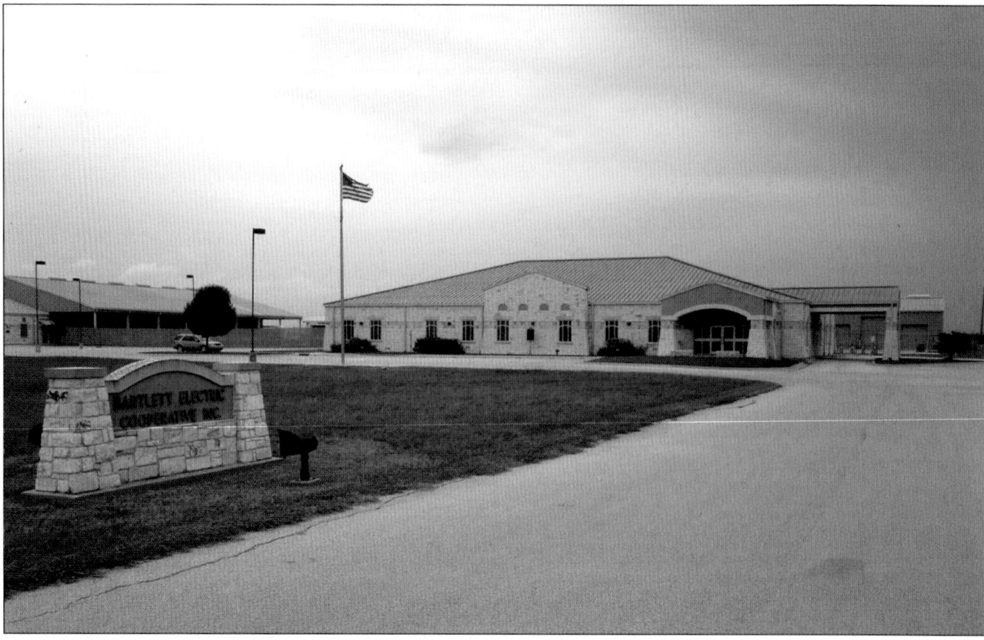

When Bartlett residents considered Texas Power & Light rates excessive, they built their own electric plant at a cost of $90,000 in 1934. The federal Rural Electrification Administration was established in 1935 to bring electricity to rural areas. Bartlett Community Light & Power Company requested assistance through this program and became the first in the country to bring electricity to a rural home. Today, Bartlett Electric Cooperative, above, serves 7,900 members across four counties from its offices. Lone Star Gas Company supplied natural gas to Temple. Customers could pay bills in person until 1995 at its office, located downtown on North Main Street. The company sold the building, below, in 1995, and within a few years, the building was in use by Temple Korean First Baptist Church. (Above, authors' collection; below, courtesy of the Temple Public Library.)

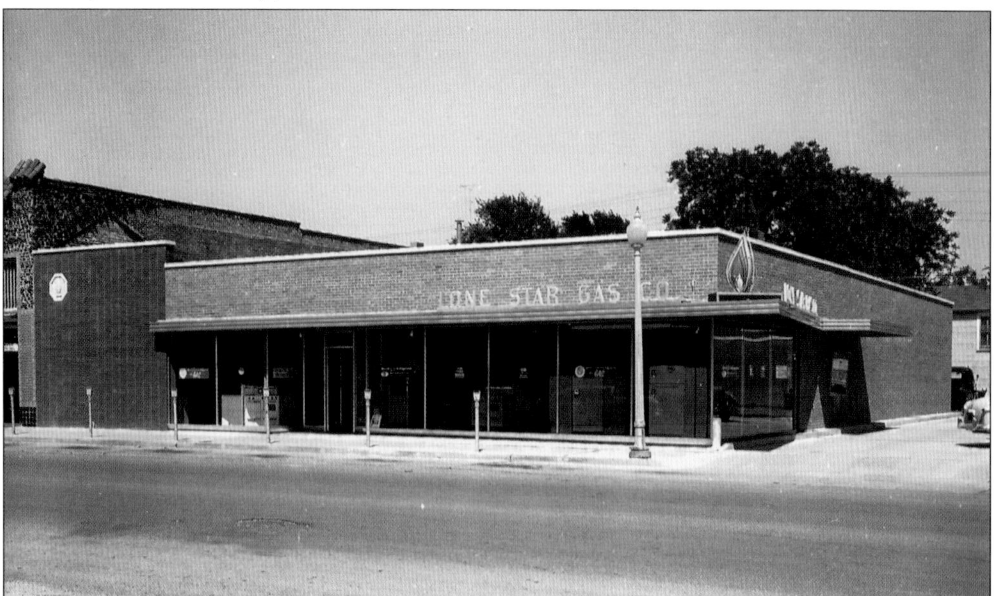

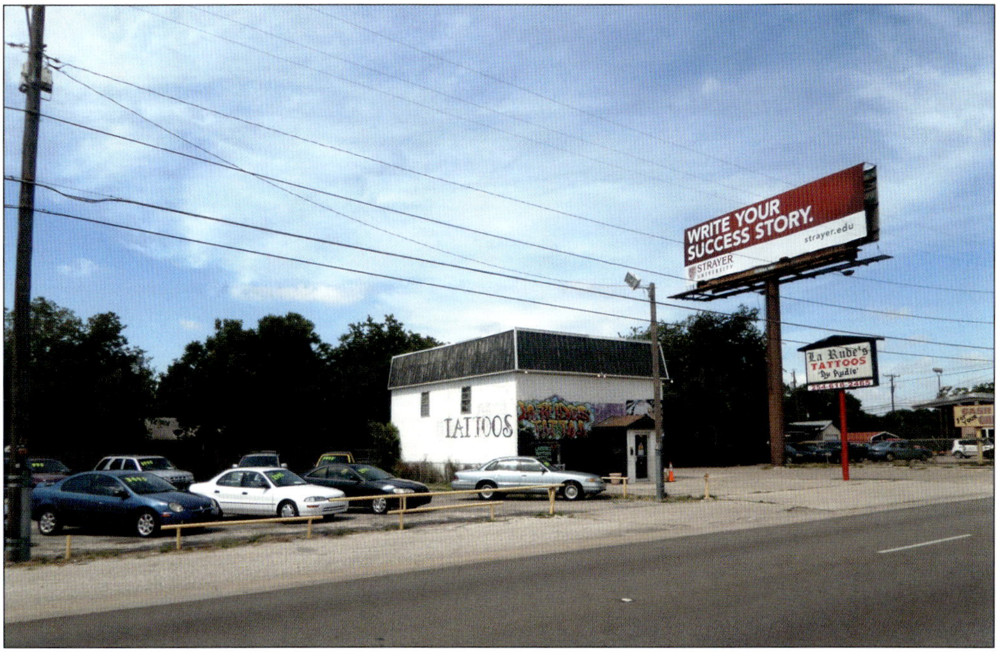

Tattooing has a long history in cultures around the world. In American culture, the practice is quite popular, though viewed by some as unacceptable. Recent surveys indicate an upward trend in the number of Americans less than 30 years of age with tattoos. In Killeen, anyone looking to get a tattoo has several shops from which to choose. This is not the case in Belton, where this type of business was not accepted until Belton's city council allowed Belton's first tattoo and body-piercing shop in 2011. Pictured below, it is visible on Interstate Highway 35 and advertised as "Belton's only tattoo shop." (Both, authors' collection.)

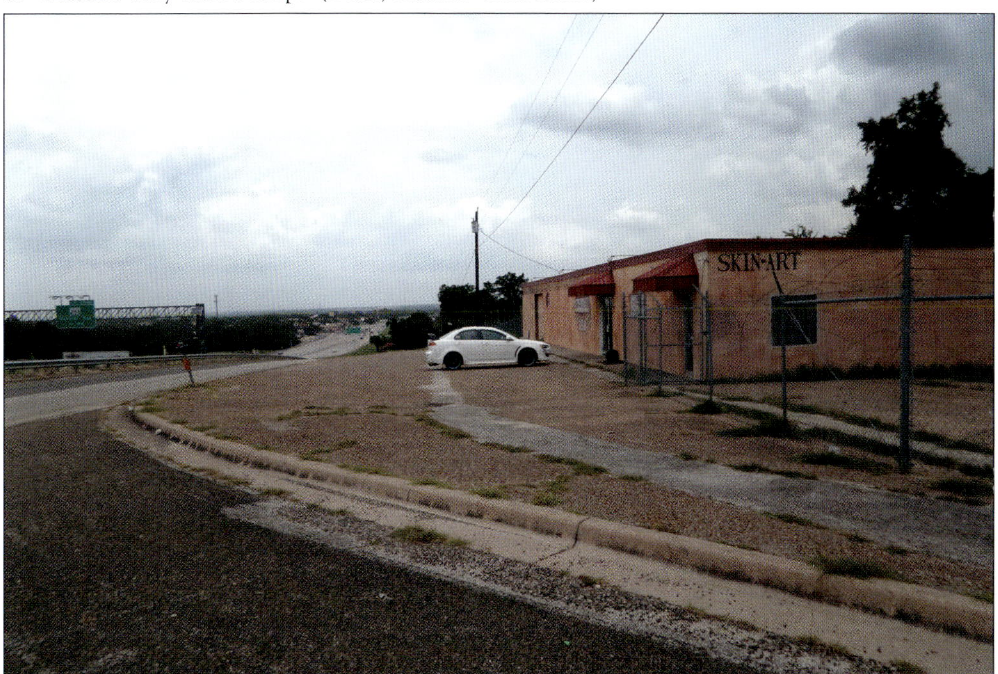

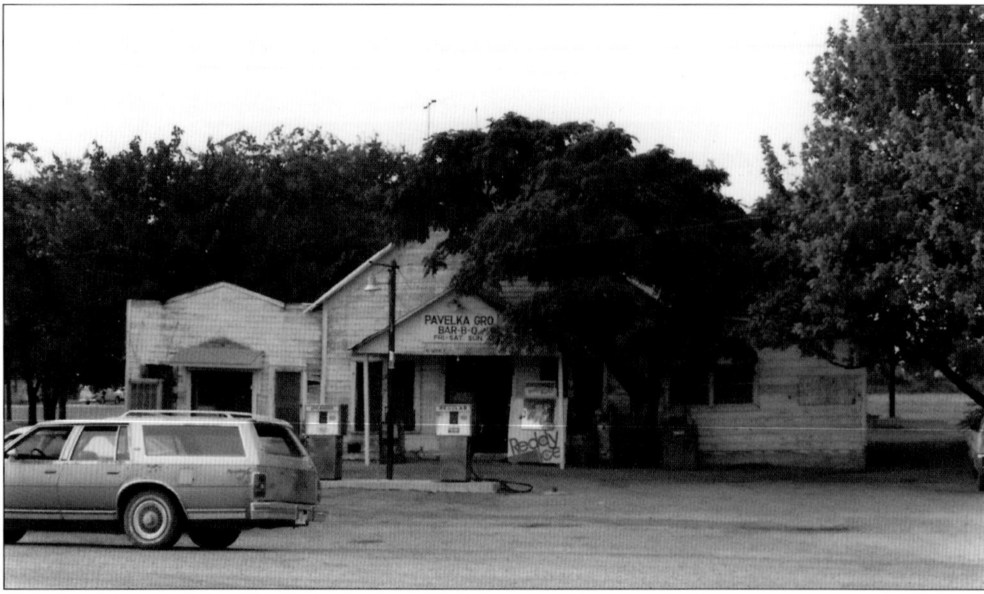

Seaton, the first Czech settlement in Bell County, is located eight miles east of Temple on State Highway 53. Seven Czech families from Rockdale, Texas, settled in the area in 1881. Frank Matejka opened the first store. The quiet community was shaken in 1923 when Tom Sefcik built a dance hall near the church and cemetery. The Czechs unsuccessfully protested the location of the dance hall. The construction of State Highway 53, one of the first concrete highways in the state, passed through Seaton in 1932. The road spawned a succession of small country stores that depended on the traveling public for their survival. Pavelka Grocery at Seaton, above in 1987, and Little Elm Grocery, below in 1987, were on State Highway 53. George Smith operated Little Elm Grocery for more than 50 years. (Both, authors' collection.)

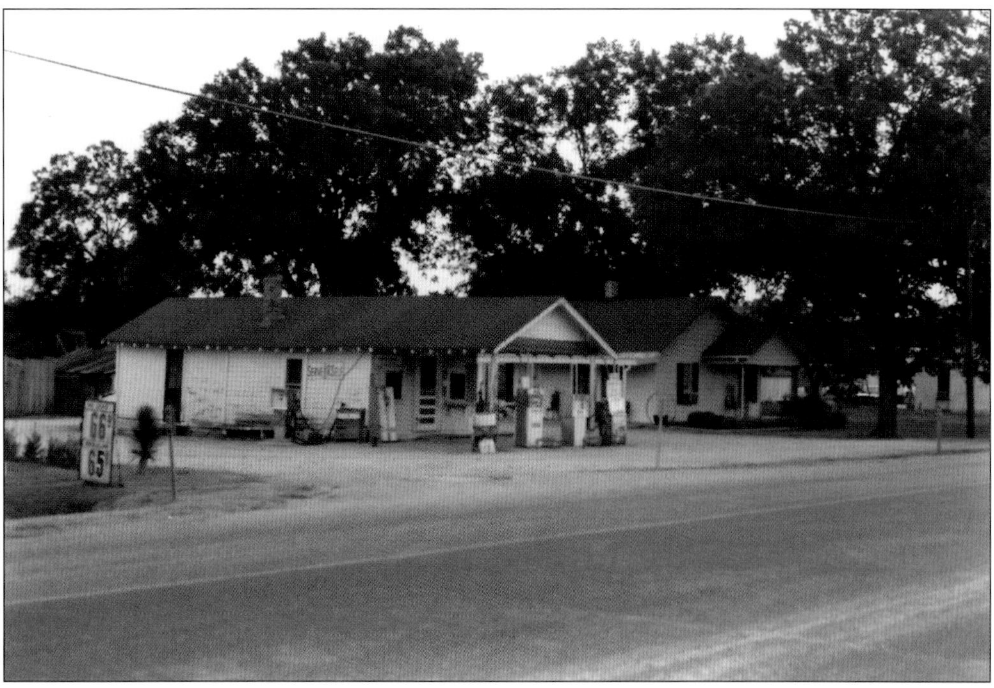

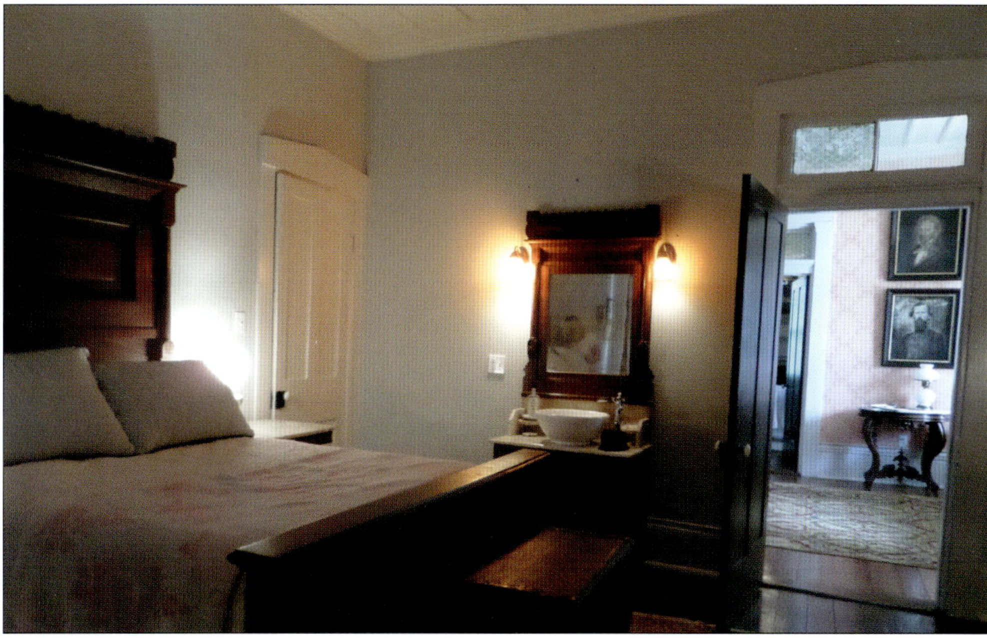

This six-bedroom house, owned and maintained by descendants of E.S.C. Robertson and Mary Robertson, was built west of the town of Salado in 1860. E.S.C. Robertson was the son of *empresario* Sterling C. Robertson, founder of Robertson Colony in the mid-1830s. He came to Texas at the age of 12 in 1832 and moved his wife, children, and in-laws to Salado in 1854, with three generations living together. Robertson was the founder of Salado and Salado College in 1859 and the town of Robertson in Hill County. He served in the Confederate army, as a delegate to the Constitutional Convention in 1875, and as postmaster general for the Republic of Texas. Shown above is a bedroom on the lower floor, and below is the front of the Robertson house. (Both, authors' collection.)

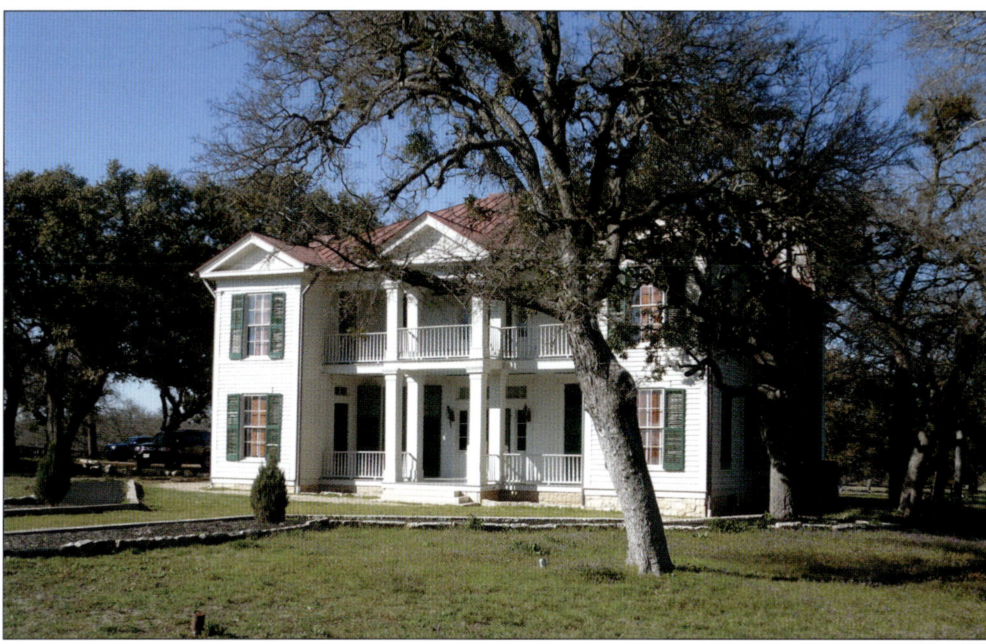

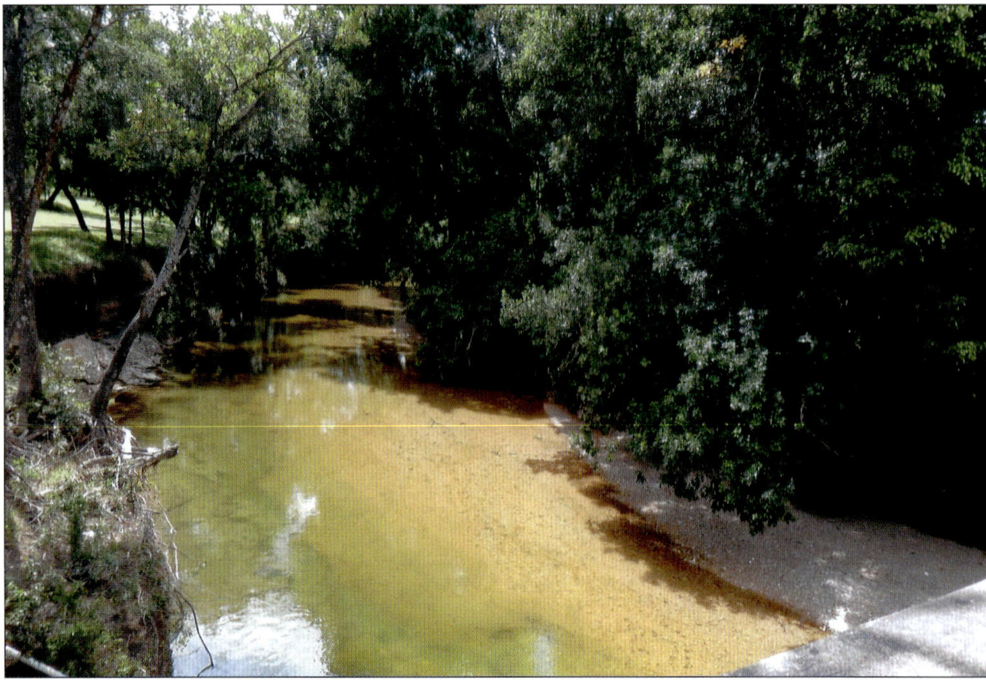

Backstrom's Crossing spans Nolan Creek in Nolan Valley. To the enjoyment of the community, Roy Sanderford, who learned to fly during World War I, would fly his apple box–like monoplane over the countryside. The area received its name from Mary Backstrom, who moved from Mississippi with her children in the late 1870s. A gravel shoal and large pecan trees provided a place for picnics and summer meetings. (Authors' collection.)

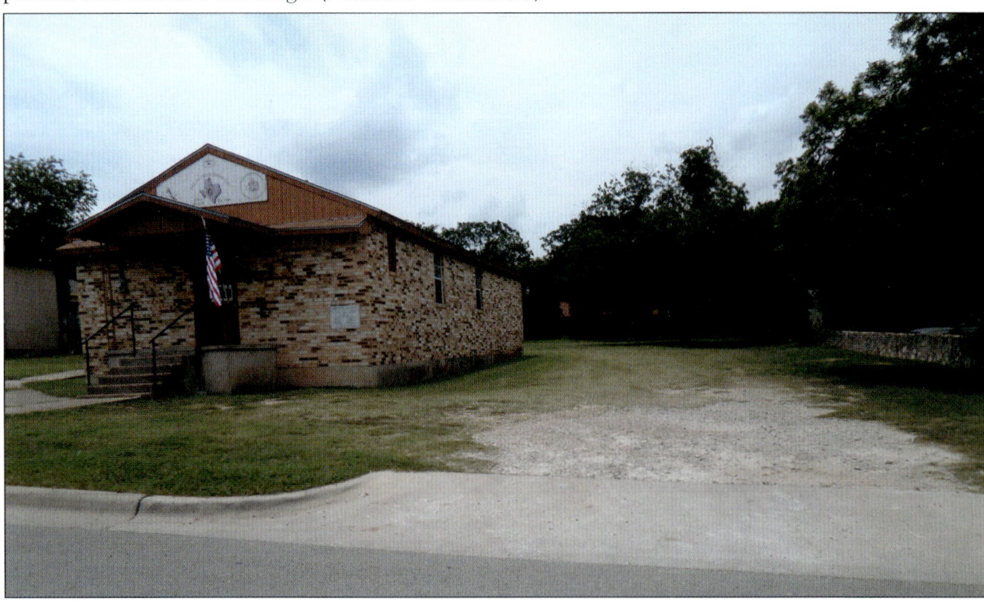

Throughout Bell County are structures that originally served as barracks at Fort Hood. Those that purchased the barracks as Army surplus transformed them for a variety of uses, such as houses, businesses, and churches. One of these barracks is in use by the Masonic lodge in Belton. (Authors' collection.)

Prior to the construction of Belton Lake Dam on the Leon River, large quantities of melons, tomatoes, onions, berries, and fruit were raised in the sandy soils of the alluvial plains of the Leon River basin. Most of the farms were small, but with hard work they were capable of supporting a family. In 1930, G.L. McDowell raised 7,000 pounds of watermelons. Below the dam lies the 260-acre Miller Springs Nature Center and Park. The park offers 11 miles of scenic trails, springs, prairie habitats, and wildflowers. The area sits in the picturesque Tennessee Valley, settled in 1851 by families from Tennessee. Caves and cliffs are noticeable along a section of the old road that led to the community of Tennessee Valley. (Both, authors' collection.)

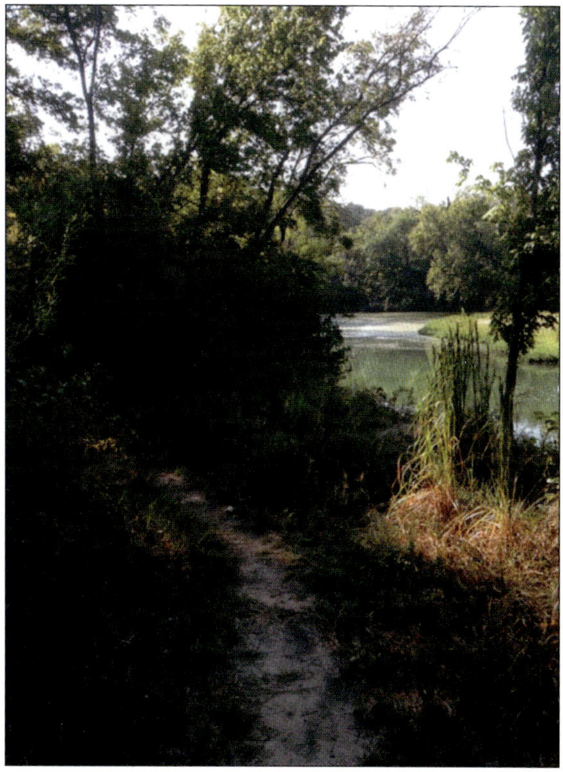

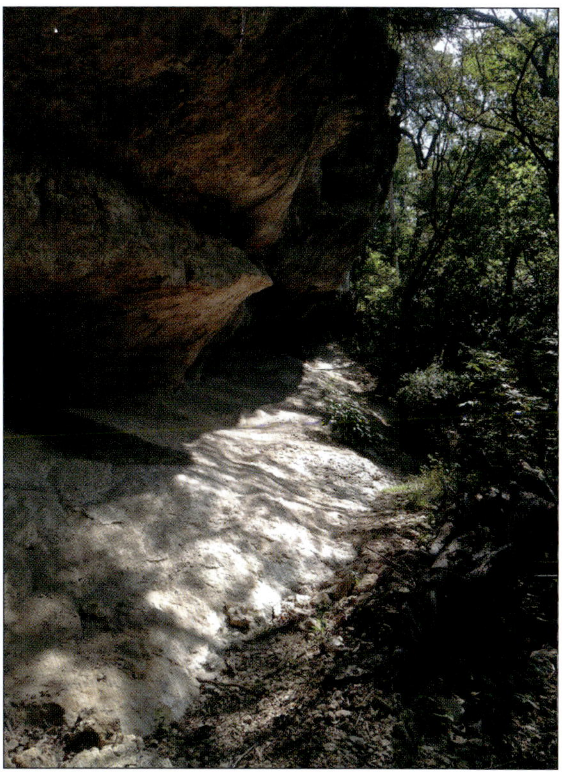